Transnational Crime, Crime Control and Security

Series editors: **Anastassia Tsoukala**, University of Paris XI, France, and **James Sheptycki**, York University, Canada

Editorial board:

Titles include:

Transnational Crime, Crime Control and Security
Series Standing Order ISBN   978–0–23028945–1 hardback
                              978–0–23028946–8 paperback
You can receive future titles in this series as they are published by placing a standing order. Please contact your bookseller or, in case of difficulty, write to us at the address below with your name and address, the title of the series and one of the ISBNs quoted above.

Customer Services Department, Macmillan Distribution Ltd, Houndmills, Basingstoke, Hampshire RG21 6XS, England

---

Globalization and Borders

Death at the Global Frontier

Leanne Weber
Monash University, Australia

Sharon Pickering
Monash University, Australia

First published 2011 by
PALGRAVE MACMILLAN

Palgrave Macmillan in the UK is an imprint of Macmillan Publishers Limited, registered in England, company number 785998, of Houndmills, Basingstoke, Hampshire RG21 6XS.

Palgrave Macmillan in the US is a division of St Martin's Press LLC, 175 Fifth Avenue, New York, NY 10010.

Palgrave Macmillan is the global academic imprint of the above companies and has companies and representatives throughout the world.

Palgrave® and Macmillan® are registered trademarks in the United States, the United Kingdom, Europe and other countries

ISBN 978-0-230-24734-5

This book is printed on paper suitable for recycling and made from fully managed and sustained forest sources. Logging, pulping and manufacturing processes are expected to conform to the environmental regulations of the country of origin.

A catalogue record for this book is available from the British Library.

A catalogue record for this book is available from the Library of Congress .

10   9   8   7   6   5   4   3   2   1
20   19   18   17   16   15   14   13   12   11

Printed and bound in the United States of America

Contents

List of Tables, Figures and Images

Tables

Figures

Images

Acknowledgements

Eva Ottavy from Migreurop, Olivier Clochard from Migreurop and the University of Poitiers, Paola and Natasha from UNITED for Intercultural Action, Liz Fekete from the Institute of Race Relations, Ernesto Kiza from the University of Freiburg, Stefanie Grant from the University of Sussex, Katje Franko Aas from the University of Oslo, Ben Hayes, formerly of Statewatch, Charandev Singh, legal practitioner, and Kanchan Dutt, ACT Chief Minister's Office, generously shared data and written material with us which was essential to the development of our analysis.

Norberto Laguía Casaus, Matt Carr and Morgana Wallace assisted with the identification of photographs. Ray Michalowski, Ray Murray, Michael Sinclair-Jones and Ryan Bavetta generously allowed the use of their photographs free of charge, which provide a powerful visual testament to the arguments presented in this book.

Elizabeth Friedman and Ludmilla Stern from the University of New South Wales facilitated French translations which were ably completed by Maud Billon, Gabriela Fearn, Mathilde Le Bolay and Natalie Spicer.

This book has benefited from feedback from colleagues following presentations of aspects of this work at the Prato Roundtables on Transnational Crime, the Criminal Justice Research Network seminar series at the University of New South Wales and the criminology group at Monash University. The insights provided by Ray Michalowski, Nancy Wonders, Marie Provine, Marjorie Zatz, Ben Bowling and Dario Melossi at the Roundtable on Border Deaths held at the American Society of Criminology Conference in San Francisco further stimulated our thinking and provided reassurance about the worth of our project.

Ka Ki Ng, Alison Gerard, Myvanwy Hudson and Tony Kiek diligently undertook a range of research tasks and contributed their diverse skills to the collection and interpretation of both qualitative and quantitative data. Christina Kirtley undertook the time-consuming task of coordinating copyright permissions. Julia Farrell provided expert copyediting and support with the finalization of the manuscript.

This research has benefited from, and contributed to, broader research programmes on the operation of borders, including a set of Australian Research Council projects including Fluid Security in the Asia Pacific (DP1093107), the Australian Deportation Project (DP110102453), Policing Migration (DP0774554) and Border Policing, Gender, Security and Human Rights (FT100100548).

We are grateful for the ongoing stimulation and support offered by our close colleagues at Monash University and the University of New South Wales: Jude McCulloch, Marie Segrave, Mike Grewcock, Claudia Tazreiter, Anna Eriksson, Bree Carlton, Dauielle Tyson, Elaine Fishwick, Jane Bolitho, Walter Forrest, Dean Wilson, Sanja Milivojevic, Alyce McGovern and Jane Maree Maher. This book benefited from the unstinting support of Leanne and Sharon's families.

The authors and publishers wish to thank the following for permission to reproduce copyright material:

Michael Sinclair-Jones for the photograph of Memorial Stones on Christmas Island.

Professor Raymond J. Michalowski Jr for the photograph of Memorial Crosses in the Arizona desert.

Ryan Bavetta for the photograph of the US–Mexico border town Nogales, Arizona (2009).

Jewel Fraser Clearwater for photographs of artworks by the Border Project Student Artists 4,18,31,33 (2007).

Migreurop for maps – Les miroirs obscurs des politiques migratoires Européennes and Evolution du nombre de morts aux portes de l'Europe from Atlas des Migrants en Europe: Géographie critique des politiques migratoires », Migreurop, édition Armand Colin, 143, p. 2009.

Springer Science+Business Media B. V. for Weber, L. (2006) 'The shifting frontiers of migration control', in S. Pickering and L. Weber (eds), *Borders, mobility and technologies of control*, Springer, Dordrecht.

The *Australian Journal of Human Rights* for Weber, L. (2010) 'Knowing-and-yet-not-knowing about European border deaths', 15(2), 35–58.

Ray Murray for the photograph of the Christmas Island cliff-top rescue.

Dianne Cook and Len Jenshel for the photograph of the Vehicle Barrier, Organ Pipe Cactus National Monument, Arizona (2006).

List of Acronyms

AAP	Australian Associated Press
ACLU	American Civil Liberties Union
ACLUNC	American Civil Liberties Union of Northern California
ACM	Australasian Correctional Management
ADF	Australian Defence Force
AFP	Australian Federal Police
AI	Amnesty International
AIC	Australian Institute of Criminology
ASIS	Australian Secret Intelligence Service
BA	British Airways
BMI	Binational Migration Institute
BORSTAR	Border Safety Initiative Search Trauma and Rescue Team
BPC	Border Patrol Command
BSI	Border Safety Initiative
CPT	European Committee for the Prevention of Torture
CCTV	Closed Circuit Television
CNDH	Comisión Nacional de los Derechos Humanos
DIAC	Department of Immigration and Citizenship
DIMIA	Department of Immigration, Multicultural and Indigenous Affairs
ECRE	European Council on Refugees and Exiles
EDM	Early Day Motion
ERA	European Race Audit
EU	European Union
GAO	Government Audit Office
HMIP	HM Inspector of Prisons
HREOC	Human Rights and Equal Opportunity Commission
ICE	Immigration and Customs Enforcement
IND	Immigration and Nationality Directorate
IRR	Institute of Race Relations
LRP	Lateral Repatriation Program
NAFTA	North American Free Trade Agreement
NAO	National Audit Office
NGO	Non-government organization
SAS	Special Air Services
SIEV	Suspected Illegal Entry Vessel

SOLAS	Safety of Life at Sea
TPV	Temporary Protection Visa
UKBA	UK Border Agency
UNHCR	United Nations High Commissioner for Refugees
UNITED	United Against Racism and Fascism

Introduction: Death at the Global Frontier

For every dead body washed up on the shores of the developed world, experts estimate there are at least two others that are never recovered. Nearly 14,000 people are known to have died between 1993 and 2010 trying to enter Europe, or while in detention or during forcible deportation. Across the three key border zones between the Global North and Global South (Europe, North America and Australia), drowning is by far the most frequent cause of death recorded by non-government organizations (NGOs) and official sources. Corpses frequently wash up on Mediterranean beaches. Other significant causes of death are suffocation, vehicle accidents and suicide. Men, women and children die from hypothermia while attempting to cross the border between Greece and Turkey, of dehydration in the Moroccan desert, or while trying to swim across rivers and bays. The hardships of unregulated modes of transport such as unseaworthy vessels, or unventilated and over-crowded lorries and containers, coupled with inadequate food and water, add to the misery and peril. Drowning is also the most frequent cause of border deaths for those trying to enter Australia, the most notable instances being the sinking of the SIEV X in 2001 and the shipwreck on Christmas Island in December 2010. On the United States (US)–Mexico border, deaths due to environmental exposure in the deserts of California and Arizona together with drownings in the Rio Grande account for a large proportion of those who die, but deaths also occur both before and after people cross borders. Illegally crossing borders has long been potentially fatal (Nevins, 2008). In this book we argue that people die because of the ways in which the borders between the Global North and the Global South are controlled. These deaths are often foreseeable and can occur by deliberate act or omission.

The explication of border deaths is not straightforward, and nor are the chains of responsibility or accountability for these deaths easily identifiable. A deeper understanding of the issues requires agility in shifting between local and international contexts and seeking to account for the various drivers for mobility and repulsion. Moreover, it necessitates consideration of the interplay between the individual and structural aspects of illegalized border crossing that create the conditions for, if not the cause of, death. While such interplays are complex, we acknowledge at the outset that conditions of security and insecurity are primarily driven by states and collective state interests subject to the demands of global capital. This is not to obfuscate the role of corporate responsibility or of powerful non-state institutions and actors, but rather to recognize that for the three key border zones we consider the state to be the primary actor, *dramatis personae*, in the performance of border control, even when that performance is devolved or contracted to corporate actors. We also recognize that the key drivers of mobility are at least shaped if not constituted by physical and economic insecurity in the relations between the Global North and Global South. Therefore, while we are indebted to rich, local empirical accounts of the border, such examinations cannot always engage with the global context of mobility or account for the international drivers aimed at achieving security for some groups by generating greater insecurities for others. Our concern with global frontiers is thus focused on drawing on the detail provided by local studies but locating them in the context of an international study of death and border control. To this extent we use the term global frontier to connote both a set of geographical sites and the politico-legal status of these sites.

On one level this book seeks to develop some of the conceptual and theoretical terrain of an interdisciplinary but primarily criminological study of border deaths. In this regard we gratefully extend the work of fellow travellers in the field who have sought to connect the traditional remit of criminology with the world of international relations, migration and international law. We pick up threads from the work on the sociology of denial by Stanley Cohen (2001) and state crime theorists such as Kauzlarich et al. (2003), and Green and Ward (2004); transnational policing scholars like Bowling (2010) and Andreas and Nadelmann (2006); border policing scholars Andreas (2001) and Nevins (2003, 2008); and most notably those who have specifically sought to explicate the criminalization–migration–security nexus, particularly Aas (2007), Pratt (2005), Michalowski (2007), Wonders (2006), Bosworth and Guild (2008) and Grewcock (2009). However, in developing this theoretical terrain we needed not only to consider, but also to contribute empirically to, what we know about border death. Methodologically we adopt Dauvergne's (2008) concept of ice core sampling to achieve the depth of under-standing required for complex analysis in a field that is infinitely broad. Dauvergne argues that, when one is confronted by the breadth of poten-tially distinct topics, the key challenge is to avoid superficiality, while still being able to speak to the broader issues. Her 'countermeasure' is to:

> adapt the ice scientist's methodology of core sampling. To under-stand the layers, the scientist extracts a narrow sample that contains a trace of each element under examination. This is the antidote to breadth. Core sampling ... means drilling into each topic under con-sideration to extract a sample that in key ways reveals something about the whole. Some sampling choices are easier than others, but they are all choices. (2008, p. 3)

In accounting for border deaths our sample choices were made because they speak to the key elements of border protection as it has come to be played out across key global frontiers between the Global North and the Global South. What is common to our choices is that they are identifiable as 'migratory fault lines' – a term that is used by the United Nations (UN) Commission on Human Rights (2004). The term 'migra-tory fault lines' is a way to describe migratory flows that are:

> triggered by economic disparities between neighbouring states. The flows take place across land and sea borders where migratory pressures are most acute because they divide states with very dif-ferent standards of living. The concept of fault lines is a useful way of thinking about individual protection needs, and also about wider asymmetries in human development, human security and human rights which drive irregular migration. (Grant, 2011a)

In studying three such fault lines, in some contexts we were over-whelmed by the volume of local material accumulated and recorded on border deaths, while in others we were stunned by its absence. In the appendix of this book we cautiously offer a count of Australian border deaths. In our research we were able to draw on data produced by NGOs in the European context, and in the United States on data produced by both government and non-government organizations. In Australia no such count has been undertaken. From available and verifiable records we have assembled what we believe to be the first such attempt at systematically recording border-related deaths in Australia. This record suffers from some of the flaws we identify in such death counts in Chapter 3, but nonetheless we consider this counting to be one of the necessary preconditions for developing a full account of border deaths. We also recognize the inevitable blind spots in the account offered, most notably in relation to those places where evidence and information on border-related deaths is either non-existent or not consistently available, or because debates around those border-crossing sites are less developed. For example, our analysis does not include places like the Caribbean and the Gulf of Aden, and many other sites where the border control policies of the Global North reverberate.

We settled on using the term 'illegalized traveller'. There are many terms available to describe transnational migrants and asylum seekers, some of which would be entirely appropriate for the purposes of this book. However, the term 'illegalized traveller' is significant for it explicitly recognizes the legal and political power of those who define who is to be included and who excluded at the border. This represents the power to determine not only entry (or its denial) but also the political and legal discourse that invariably defines representations of legal and illegal actors. We prefer the term 'traveller' for it reflects a more fluid conception of contemporary migration and mobility patterns. The North–South divide is being sharply redrawn under conditions of neoliberal globalization. Our analysis is shaped by Sassen's (1996) view of globalization as the renationalizing of politics alongside the denationalizing of economic space. This fundamental dynamic of globalization is heightening border control at the same time that the global conditions of capital and conflict are increasing the demands to cross borders. The deaths at the migratory fault lines between the North and South are emblematic of the contradictions of globalization.

Our understanding, definition and analysis of border deaths are based on the concept of 'functional borders' through which the late modern state expresses its sovereign and disciplinary power, both within and beyond its territorial limits. Moreover, we understand border control to comprise highly selective and complex performances of state power staged at multiple locations through technologies of selection, detention, deterrence, expulsion and pre-emption, involving a range of state and non-state actors.

This book contrasts militarized borders, such as the US–Mexico border, the eastern perimeter of the European Union (EU) and the northern coastline of Australia, with more bureaucratically controlled borders that are defended by means of electronic information and surveillance technologies. Although militarized borders and borderlands are most readily identifiable as zones of conflict, or at least zones of exclusion, we argue that the less visible controls that operate in the 'informated spaces' of embassies, detention centres, airports and other transit points are equally devastating in their exclusionary capacity, and are part of the chain of practices that have potentially deadly effects.

Individual borders have their own specific histories, with border control policies shaped by local and global factors. At some locations, such as the US–Mexico border, these sites of dispersed and disputed border authority are captured in the idea of 'borderlands'. Deterritorialized borders also have ramifications that are manifest through pre-emptive, non-arrival or remote control policies. In these contexts, sovereign power is expressed offshore, either directly or indirectly, through processes of immobilization and interdiction, often without due regard to the constraints and responsibilities set out in international law. These practices transcend the more terrestrial concept of borderlands and signify an emerging space of 'transnational frontierlands', where nation-states seek to defend their self-styled virtual borders.

Utilizing the concept of functional borders, which are increasingly deterritorialized, has implications for what is counted as a border-related death. Throughout this book deaths are considered to be potentially border-related if they occur at any of the functionally defined 'border sites': at the physical border, *en route*, in offshore or onshore detention, during deportation, on forced return to one's homeland, and even within the community as a result of hate crime, labour exploitation, withholding of subsistence, or the promotion of conditions of legal and social precariousness.

Border death counts have been conducted and disputed, and we consider the implications of the processes of counting and classifying adopted, or indeed of there being no count at all. We primarily consider the way knowledge is produced about border deaths and the political and legal drivers of that process. We interrogate the ways these counts promote or prevent a greater understanding of border deaths, and importantly their relation to border control processes. Counting deaths is an inherently political function that can both draw attention to the human cost of border control and be mobilized to argue for greater forms of control. The simple act of counting can reveal how border enforcement strategies vary in nature and intensity, often through different sites on the same border. Counting can implicitly or explicitly attribute cause and effect, and even reveal how different kinds of practices can result in different forms of harm or causes of death. However, our primary purpose is not to develop a more accurate means of counting border deaths (as important as some may consider this task to be). Rather, we aim to consider the extent to which the various methods of counting actually obfuscate the violence and coercion enacted at frontier territories both internal and external to the territorial nation-state.

Understanding the fatal outcomes of border control does not depend merely on the process of counting. It relies also on the interpretation of knowledge about border deaths through processes of discounting and neutralization that impact broader understanding of border controls. Drawing on Kelman and Hamilton's (1989) work on obedience to authority and Cohen's groundbreaking work on the sociology of denial, we consider how counting border deaths cannot in and of itself overcome the complex processes of distanciation, neutralization or authorization of the harmful effects of government policies.

We need to develop alternative ways of accounting for border deaths. A richer picture of death at the border is needed if we are to overcome the processes that collectively normalize the deaths that are occurring. In going beyond body counts we seek to understand the individuals who die as more than entries in a list, but as having liveable and indeed grievable lives. We explore the role played by memorializing these lives in developing this rich picture. We consider accounting for death a necessary precondition for identifying the complex chains of accountability and responsibility for the bodies that are found, never found, recorded and unrecorded in relation to border control.

Our substantive *account* of deaths at the border is examined in relation to structural violence, suspicious deaths, and suicide and self-harm. The effects of specific border control policies are not only identified in the scale of the death toll, but are also reflected in who dies, where they die and how their lives are lost. Evidence is drawn from the effects of the deterritorialized border in the form of deaths occurring *en route* to destination countries, in encounters with officials at physical borders, and at sites of enforcement within destination countries, such as detention centres, designated places of dispersal and points of arrest. Our analysis reveals how border control policies influence the age, gender and nationality of those who die, by shifting the burden of risks associated with illegalized border crossing in particular places and moments in time. In doing so, we demonstrate how border deaths, far from being random and unforeseen events, are shaped significantly by specific border policies and practices that have local inflection yet global significance. Identifying the nature and scale of the harm foregrounds our analysis of degrees of culpability and our attempts to locate the state within chains of responsibility.

By conceptualizing many border harms as arising from the structural violence of border control policies we bring a sociological perspective to complement socio-legal insights.

We are concerned with what can be identified as the most common form of border-related death – that resulting from both the intended and unintended, though foreseeable, consequences of border protection policies. We seek to trace the often hidden links between border policies and deaths occurring in a range of locations, both close to and far from physical territorial borders, but all at border protection sites. We identify that such deaths are occurring because of the heightened risks border protection policies place on illegalized travellers. Drawing on the theoretically rich work of Andreas and Nevins on the US–Mexico border, we extend ideas around the *symbiotic* relationship between border policing and border smuggling to examine the direct connections between border protection, heightened risks and death. We do so not only in relation to the US–Mexico border, where such arguments are well rehearsed in relation to funnelling migrants through the most environmentally dangerous sections of the border, but also in relation to the external borders of Europe and the maritime borders of Australia. While the realities of local landscapes shape the nature and number of the deaths, commonalities in policies are discernible among different local contexts. These commonalities reveal that deaths are not only the outcome of border protection policies but also have utility as justifications for those policies.

We also consider evidence of illegalized border crossers who are known or suspected to have died directly at the hands of state agents, border vigilantes or people smugglers while attempting illegal entry, while in detention or during deportation. While government policies and practices may be readily apparent, processes of accountability are often poorly developed. In relation to illegalized border crossers who die at their own hands, we consider how the context of their death can be traced to circumstances in which death may be regarded as the final attempt to demonstrate their need to cross borders. It is only in dying that many can be morally (if not legally) recognized as having bona fide reasons for crossing borders.

Our account of border deaths explores the ambiguities within border protection practices in the face of escalating human and economic costs. We consider how the ever-expanding matrix of deterrence and risk is constantly being built and rebuilt by the complex interplay between official policy, migrant motivation and opportunities for criminal enterprise. We begin from the position that while relatively low-level forms of border protection seek simply to prevent unauthorized border crossing, rising death tolls and political opposition have resulted in governments developing multifaceted responses also aimed at saving lives and rescuing migrants from harm. This often relies on the cooperation of non-state agents and the deployment of state agencies in roles that simultaneously require the deterrence and rescue of illegalized migrants. In considering the tension between border protection and safety or rescue objectives we contrast the experiences of US Border Patrols at the US border since the inception of the Border Safety Initiative (BSI), with the more recently initiated Frontex patrols in the Mediterranean, and Australian offshore coastal surveillance operations. We examine the available evidence on the extent of these activities and their impact on the incidence of border fatalities. These ambiguities are considered in light of the practices of border crossers that sometimes compromise their own safety as a strategy to elicit rescue. The routinization of harm is considered in relation to architectures of risk and risk avoidance, and human rights obligations. The calculus of risk comes down to whose risks are being attended to and the promotion of the security (life) of some over the security (death) of others.

In conclusion, we review a range of analytical frameworks, including those based on notions of state crime and Bowling's ideas of iatrogenesis, to consider how the control of illegalized travel as a form of crime increases rather than decreases the harms caused, and why such harmful practices persist in the face of powerful and persuasive criticism from many quarters. While a human rights approach holds the promise of a more humane framework, we identify the limitations of this approach. We look beyond the current conception of human rights to consider the potential for a reduction of border harms through the positive promotion of human security that is not wholly dependent on an individual's relationship with the nation-state.

This book is not about bodies, but about lives. Therefore, we borrow from the language of a coronial investigation to structure the three parts of this book: *border autopsy*, *border inquest*, and *from finding truth to preventing border harm*. In so doing, we are concerned with conducting an analysis of death by understanding the lives lost and preventing further deaths within the broader context of ever-escalating border controls. Therefore, the body cannot be understood without recognizing the life that was lost within the context of border crossing.

Part I
Border Autopsy: Examining Contemporary Borders

> A post-mortem examination, also known as an autopsy, is a step-by-step examination of the outside of the body and of the internal organs by a doctor known as a pathologist. The examination is carried out at the direction of a coroner and is sometimes required to establish the cause of death. (Courts Administration Authority South Australia, South Australian Coroners Court information sheet)

Although some pundits have forecast the dawning of a borderless world, the borders of nation-states are far from dead. In fact, they have been rejuvenated under conditions of globalization. Sassen (1996, p. xvi) interprets these trends as a 'denationalizing of economic space' alongside the 'renationalizing of politics', with border crossing emerging as a 'strategic site of inquiry about the limits of the new order'. As borders are revitalized, the death toll among those who seek to cross them without authorization is rising to unprecedented levels. It is estimated that the fortified border between the US and Mexico has been ten times deadlier over the nine years from 1998 to 2005 for non-citizens attempting to *enter* the US than was the Berlin Wall over its 28-year lifetime for East Germans attempting to *leave* (Cornelius, 2005).

The nature of borders is not self-evident. In this opening section of the book we subject the phenomenon of border-related deaths to a step-by-step examination. We first diagnose the general condition of contemporary borders that divide the Global North and South, finding them capable of causing death. We then dissect the processes of counting and discounting border-related deaths, revealing how these processes variously reveal, mask and obfuscate the human consequences of border control policies. Finally, we piece together an account of deaths at the global frontier that goes beyond crude 'body counts' to reveal the detailed connections between border protection policies and the deadly risks faced by illegalized travellers.

1
Charting the Global Frontier

> After crossing many physical, national borders, I found myself facing other kinds of border in Sweden, those in the minds of people. When I thought the journey had been complete and the destination reached, I still found myself standing before invisible borders, more difficult or impossible to cross … The invisible borders are as intractable as the visible ones, and the wounds they inflict no less real. (Khosravi, 2010, p. 75)

Functional borders and global frontiers

Individual borders have their own specific histories, and the policies designed to defend them are shaped by local as well as global factors. As Pratt (2005, p. 185) reminds us: 'The border is an ongoing accomplishment, yet the processes by which it is continually produced are erased by its apparent self-evidence.' Constituting borders through geographical barriers or in terms of other taken-for-granted physical referents presents them as 'primordial, timeless, as part of nature' (Khosravi, 2010, p. 1), thereby concealing their histories and their contested character. Yet in the face of globalizing pressures, borders are being reshaped in ways that reveal their dynamic and sometimes contradictory functions (Pickering & Weber, 2006). The most striking impact of globalization on the borders of the Global North, and the most relevant for our discussion, is their increasing deterritorialization.

Functional borders

National borders have become increasingly detached from sovereign territory as the late modern state expresses its power to control entry both *within* and *beyond* its territorial limits. Contemporary borders can be thought of as complex performances of state power staged at multiple locations through technologies of detection, selection, deterrence, expulsion and pre-emption, directed towards specifically targeted groups. Deterritorialized borders exist wherever border control functions are performed (Wonders, 2006), and may be enacted by a range of state and non-state actors (Weber & Bowling, 2004). Borders may be physically demarcated, or they may be invisible. They may be located precisely in space; may manifest as zones of dispersed and/or disputed authority, best captured in the idea of the 'borderlands' (Donnan & Wilson, 1999); or may be legally manipulated in both time and space, so they become elusive, ephemeral and effectively 'unknowable' to those trying to cross them. Examples of the creation of an elusive border include the 'excisions' of offshore territories by the Australian Government from a fictional 'migration zone' in which domestic immigration law is deemed to apply (Weber, 2006); and the 'long tunnel thesis' in Canada, enacted through official practice rather than legislation to deal with illegalized Chinese immigrants arriving by boat in British Columbia (Mountz, 2010). These measures are designed to create permanent conditions of non-arrival. Alternatively, for those who manage to arrive but are marked for exclusion, the deterritorialized border may be experienced as ubiquitous and perpetually present. The seemingly inescapable border constructed from networks of surveillance and information exchange, while doubtless less efficient than this characterization may suggest, pursues its project of inclusion/exclusion at a psychological level. Iranian exile Sharam Khosravi (2010) describes feeling that he had *become* the border after years of marginalization and insecurity, living without legal status or social acceptance.

Sovereign versus disciplined borders

Borders express both sovereign and disciplinary powers. The might of sovereign power is revealed most openly in *militarized* borders, as seen on the US–Mexico border, the eastern perimeter of the European Union, the Mediterranean and the northern coastline of Australia. Militarized borders are redolent with the imagery of war and of societies under siege. In Europe, exemplary here are the colonial outposts of Ceuta and Melilla on the African shores of the Straits of Gibraltar, which are encircled by prison-like fences and defended by armed border guards; and sections of the border between Greece and Turkey, which have until recently been fortified with minefields originally intended for different enemies. Before responsibility for border control shifted to Poland's eastern neighbours, its border with Belarus and Ukraine was described as the 'new iron curtain', boasting 156 watchtowers and an 18,000-strong border patrol (Webber, 2004). At the time of writing, a cash-strapped Greece, now the entry point for the majority of illegalized travellers to Europe, is peti-tioning the EU for funds to build a similar barricade along its eastern perimeter. In the past, Europe relied on the natural barrier provided by the sea for the defence of its southern borders. However, national mari-time patrols are now supplemented by armed patrols coordinated by the European Agency for the Management of Operational Cooperation at the External Borders of the Member States of the European Union (Frontex).

The project for a 'militarized Mediterranean' (Fekete, 2003) was mod-elled on Australia's longstanding naval blockade codenamed Operation Relex, which was established to 'deter and deny' the entry of Suspected Illegal Entry Vessels (SIEVs) (Howard, 2003). Australia's resort to mil-itary protection of its northern sea border gained international notor-iety in 2001 following the government's refusal to allow the *MV Tampa* to land 430 rescued asylum seekers at an Australian port (Grewcock, 2009; Marr & Wilkinson, 2003; Mares, 2002; Magner, 2004; Weber, 2007). However, the original blueprint for military interdiction came from the US blockades of the Caribbean in the 1980s, when thousands of Haitians fled the violence of the Papa Doc regime. In contrast to the ready acceptance of Cuban exiles, Haitians who took to the high seas in small boats were intercepted by armed coastguard vessels, subjected to truncated refugee determination procedures (or none at all), and faced detention in Guantanamo Bay (Motomura, 1993; Mitchell, 1994). Although the US Government has historically relied on invisible 'remote control' policies operated through visa regimes to exercise border control, these strategies have proven inadequate in recent decades with respect to the US–Mexico border (Zolberg, 2006). Marked along some of its length by a menacing razor-wire fence, and buffered along other sections by the seeming impenetrability of the Arizonan deserts and the fast-flowing Rio Grande, this borderland is protected by a combination of armed border patrols and vigilantes (Michalowski, 2007; Nevins, 2002). This southern border, defended by 9000 or so border patrol agents at 115 official entry points, contrasts markedly with the Canadian border which is twice as long but guarded by a mere 334 agents posted at 41 checkpoints (Zolberg, 2006).

Borders signify territorial security through powerful displays of technological mastery. Disciplined borders operate at airports, seaports and other regulated places of arrival. The bureaucratic technologies of disciplined borders are designed to process high-volume traffic; they include electronic travel authorities, passenger databases, international alert systems, sanctions for airlines carrying 'inadequately documented' passengers, scanning devices and biometric identification systems. 'Risk-smart borders' (Pratt, 2005) exhibit their disciplinary power through information, scanning and surveillance technologies. In Europe, advanced technologies such as the Schengen Information System, the Eurodac fingerprint database, and a variety of systems designed to register movements both into EU territory and at the external border apply varying regimes of surveillance to travellers distinguished according to risk categories (Aas, 2011). Only 'responsibilized' passengers who can establish their identity and authority to travel may cross these switch points and thereby 'access the benefits of liberty' (Rose, 2000, p. 326).

Pratt (2005) has argued that the *internal* border, perhaps most clearly manifest in programmes of detention and deportation, lies at the intersection of sovereignty and governmentality. Its sovereign power to exclude is expressed through modalities of risk management and 'moralizing categorization' concerning responsibility and desert. In relation to detention, Pratt (2005, p. 22) notes: 'The forcible confinement of these individuals does not aim to "correct", "reform", or "transform" souls, habits, or risks. It has no official purpose other than to confine and ultimately expel the actual bodies and undesired noncitizens.'

Frontier zones

Contemporary border enforcement practices are taking relations between states and non-citizens into uncharted legal terrain. Where sovereign power is exerted through complex networks involving state and non-state actors, often offshore or in dispersed locations away from sight, these practices operate in the shadow of the law. This signifies an emerging transnational (and sometimes sub-national) 'frontier land', where powerful nation-states may seek to defend their virtual borders without observing either the due process rights accorded to citizens or the requirements of international human rights law. Frontiers may be offshore (at sea or on prison islands) or onshore (in detention centres located in sparsely inhabited deserts or other remote regions). They are distinguished by what Butler (2004, p. xv) characterizes as 'a lawless and unaccountable operation of power', exerted where the rule of law is either suspended, or deployed tactically or partially to suit the requirements of the state, in particular to monitor and constrain specific populations. In Butler's formulation, this amounts to the 'resurgence of sovereignty within the field of governmentality' (Butler, 2004, p. 16), creating a new constellation of potentially illegitimate power, whereby the law is selectively activated or erased.

Interdiction policies in particular have demonstrated the 'lacuna between the physical spaces in which states exercise jurisdictional control and the spaces in which they will assume juridical responsibility' (Morris, J., 2003, p. 2). Australian interdiction policies have been described as efforts to 'draw a line in the sea', not merely against asylum seekers, but also against the incursions of international law (Perera, 2002, p. 3). In fact, a common feature of interdiction policies across many jurisdictions is their legal immunity from judicial review, which is reinforced by the geographical remoteness of the interdiction arena. High Court Judge Mary Gaudron likened the creation of offshore detention centres in the Pacific for asylum seekers interdicted by Australian naval patrols to the creation of a 'legal no man's land' by the US Government at Guantanamo Bay (Banham, 2004). Irregular migrants who are intercepted at the external borders of the Global North are thereby caught in a rights-free, unprotected zone from where 'they are chased away, kept from our borders lest they engage the law in responsibility' (Douzinas, 2002, p. 32). The withdrawal of legal rights for irregular travellers coincides with the granting of extra-legal powers for agents of the state. Operation Relex required that defence personnel be granted 'special authority' to board vessels outside Australian territorial waters in the area of diluted sovereignty known as the 'contiguous zone' (Howard, 2003).

As with the external border, internal border controls also seek to place irregular migrants beyond legal protections. This is achieved not so much through the creation of rights-free spaces, but through the constitution of the individuals themselves as 'illegals', who are liable to detention and ineligible for many of the entitlements of legal residents. It is important to acknowledge that developments in liberal governance, such as observance of due process, human rights and the rule of law, have to some extent been successful in 'democratizing sovereignty', so that even non-citizens in liberal democracies are rights-bearing subjects to varying degrees (Pratt, 2005, p. 16). Nevertheless, Khosravi (2010) – informed by his own experience as an illegalized traveller – describes the condition of illegality in terms of being cut off from most sources of social and legal protection. Drawing on the philosophy of Giorgio Agamben, he argues that, '[i]n their capacity as *hominis sacri*, irregular migrants are left vulnerable not only to state violence (through regulations, political arrangements, laws, priorities, and police) but also to the violence of ordinary citizens, without being able to protect or defend themselves' (Khosravi, 2010, p. 3). A similar state of vulnerability is articulated by Butler through the concept of 'precarity': 'Precarity designates that politically induced condition in which certain populations suffer from failing social and economic networks of support and become differentially exposed to injury, violence, and death' (2010, p. 25). However, Butler distinguishes her conception from Agamben's idea of 'bare life' in that precarity is not so much passively constituted through the withdrawal of law and legal protections, but is actively produced through the coercive exercise of state power freed from the constraints of law.

Border sites and border technologies

Recognizing the multiple sites at which the power of the global frontier is exerted, and identifying the particular technologies employed, is crucial to understanding the risks faced by illegalized border crossers. Where and how borders are defended influences who dies, and where and how they perish. Under conditions of globalization, physical borders are transforming into 'risk-smart borders', where new technologies are employed to sort desirable from undesirable passengers with maximum efficiency (Pratt, 2005). At the same time, the coercive border function is both transnationalized and internally dispersed, and targeted towards groups that are prevented from crossing borders through regulated entry points at airports and seaports, or whose continued presence is considered a threat. For island nations such as Britain and Australia, checks at the border have long been the preferred method of immigration control, and Continental-style population surveillance involving identity cards and police checks has been strongly resisted. Constitutional protections, federalism and a strong suspicion of centralized state power have produced a similar preference within the US towards the defence of the periphery. However, under pressure to control spontaneous migration and respond to international terrorist threats, preventative and enforcement activity has increased across the Global North, and shifted both inwards and outwards. The arsenal of exclusionary devices involves, in varying combinations: pre-emptive measures to prevent and deter unauthorized arrival (the external border); punitive responses, such as administrative detention, exclusion from essential services and forcible deportation (the internal border); and technologies that facilitate the efficient sorting of desirable and undesirable passengers at the physical border.

The external border

Border externalization strategies are a logical consequence of the hege-monic mentalities of risk that shape governance in late modernity. Shearing and Johnston (2005) have argued that, in pursuit of pre-ventative governance, pre-emptive thinking may merge with punitive paradigms, so that the infliction of pain, expressed through punish-ment or exclusion, becomes one of many techniques available to limit perceived threats, and is best applied *before* any harm arises. This aligns with Butler's conception of a resurgence of sovereignty expressed through governmentality (2004), and with Pratt's observations on the intersection of these historically distinct modalities. In relation to border control, mentalities of early intervention have geographical implications, leading governments to extend their regulatory networks beyond their physical borders. In the Australian context this desire to selectively prevent arrival has led to policies of 'punitive pre-emption' (Weber, 2007) and the creation of 'offshore exclusion zones' (Grew-cock, 2009). The American equivalent has been dubbed 'remote control policies', indicating their invisibility (Zolberg, 2006); while in Europe commentators have discussed the externalization of the border in terms of 'non-arrival' policies (Rodier, 2006), a terminology that alludes to their often tragic consequences. Preventing unwanted arrivals has the legal advantage of limiting claims to refugee status or other entitlements (Morris, J., 2003), and avoids the political risks associated with spectacles of forced deportation which 'make dramatic television and are likely to trigger a public outcry and tarnish the inter-national credentials of the perpetrators' (Bauman, 2002, p. 111).

The external border is located not only in the immediate vicinity of the physical borders of the Global North, but also in overseas embassies within the Global South, and in non-geographical 'informated spaces' (Sheptycki, 1998), where the selective granting or refusal of visas is per-formed. This seemingly routine administrative procedure, supported by enforcement measures aimed at interdicting and returning 'inade-quately documented' passengers at major international checkpoints, effectively immobilizes illegalized travellers in countries of origin or transit. Huge stockpiles of sovereign power are therefore invested in the discretionary act, delegated to low-level officials, of issuing or with-holding visas. Of course, the exercise of discretion is not unfettered. In Australia, which operates a universal visa system, access to visitor visas is mediated by nationality-based risk profiles. Travellers from 'low-risk countries' (largely from the Global North) who are deemed unlikely to seek asylum or to overstay based on aggregate statistical profiles are channelled into an online application process that issues electronic travel documents with minimal checking. Individuals from countries largely from the Global South, considered 'high-risk', are individually scrutinized and must submit photographs and other personal information for retention on file (Weber, 2007).

Beneath the benign, administrative veneer, the power of visas as sorting mechanisms is easily revealed. Visa regimes are enforced through networks of overseas-posted liaison officers trained in the identification of falsified documents; through carriers' liability legislation (enacted in parallel by governments of the Global North), which penalizes airlines for carrying 'inadequately documented' passengers and effectively redeploys airline staff into the role of border guards; and through electronic information systems that monitor licit and illicit journeys, and issue alerts on suspect travellers. Pre-emptive measures adopted in Britain have included the introduction of explicit, publicly announced targets for blanket reductions in asylum applications; 'juxtaposed' border controls operated on behalf of the British Government in France, Belgium and the Netherlands; and the posting of overseas liaison officers to prevent the embarkation of targeted ethnic or national groups from points of transit or origin, largely in continental Europe. Australia also supports its visa regime with a network of liaison officers posted across major transit points in South-East Asia, with 'capacity building' exercises in countries of origin and transit to increase the likelihood of interdiction, and an Advanced Passenger Processing System which requires the transmission of information about all passengers and crew members and imposes fines on airlines for failing to comply. Official reports describe the Australian border strategy as follows: 'Australia manages the movement of non-citizens across its border by, in effect, pushing the border offshore. This means that checking and screening starts well before a person reaches our physical border' (Department of Immigration, Multicultural and Indigenous Affairs [DIMIA], 2004, p. 3). The US now demands a higher level of checking even of travellers from visa waiver nations. They now must have their travel details entered and approved via the Electronic System for Travel Authorization. Without this approval airlines will not check-in a traveller attempting to depart their country of origin or transit.

Military interdiction strategies at maritime boundaries are also premised on the cooperation of governments from the Global South. To the south of Europe, Spain and Italy have long been seen as the weak links in the European fortress, open as they are to irregular entry via sea routes from Albania and Montenegro to Italy, from Libya via Malta to the

Italian island of Lampedusa, and across the narrow straits of Gibraltar, as well as by land from Morocco into the Spanish enclaves of Ceuta and Melilla. The militarization of the Mediterranean as part of an EU-wide strategy of 'non-arrival' (Fekete, 2003) has necessitated a series of bilateral agreements among a 'circle of friends', including Morocco (Carling, 2007), Senegal (Spijkerboer, 2007) and Libya (Green, 2006),[1] aimed at facilitating the summary return of intercepted migrants and disrupting onward journeys. Similarly, Australia's 'war on the border' (Grewcock, 2009) has required the intervention of its northern neighbours, particularly Indonesia and Malaysia, in operations aimed at identifying organized people-smuggling groups and disrupting onward travel (Weber & Grewcock, 2011; Pickering, 2004). The Australian Government has supported the construction and use of offshore detention centres in both of these countries to warehouse interdicted passengers, and offered Nauru and New Guinea considerable financial incentives to hold asylum seekers intercepted by Australian naval vessels on their behalf as part of the so-called Pacific Solution (Grewcock, 2009). The interdiction of Haitian asylum seekers in the 1980s by the US Coast Guard relied on the availability of the now notorious military base at Guantanamo Bay, located on Cuban territory leased by the US Government from Cuba since 1906. Under the administrations of George Bush and Vicente Fox, in negotiations said to be inspired by regional deals between the EU and aspiring member states, the Mexican Government undertook to 'discourage illegal immigration and tighten Mexico's southern border against Central Americans' in return for improved rights for Mexican workers already in the US (Zolberg, 2006, p. 440). Accordingly, at the time of writing, Mexico is considering building a fence along its Guatemalan border. These strategies of government-at-a-distance (Garland, 1997) all require processes of negotiation, coercion and the provision of incentives to broker cooperation. It is possible that the future promise of freer movement of Mexican workers within the North American Free Trade Agreement (NAFTA) zone may encourage the further reinforcement of that economically defined boundary, just as internal mobility within the EU has been defended through fortification of the periphery.

The internal border

Some commentators have argued that globalization, perhaps via the slowly growing influence of human rights thinking or the dismantling of the welfare state, is eroding distinctions between citizens and non-citizens with respect to domestic entitlements (Morris, J., 2003; Jacobsen,

1996 cited in Dauvergne, 2008). However, Dauvergne observes that individuals with illegal immigration status have benefited little from what are primarily formal developments in international human rights protections, and are therefore still largely dependent on states for their legal status. While noting that some developments (for example, in EU citizenship) are reinforcing the benefits enjoyed by citizens relative to those of other legal residents, she agrees with Sassen that 'the gulf between those with some kind of migration status and those without it is vitally important' (Dauvergne, 2008, p. 21). The implications of the internal border enforcement practices described in this section extend beyond the criminalization of asylum seekers and irregular migrants. They also serve to reinforce the identity and perceived security of the nation-state and its legitimate members through what Bosworth and Guild (2008) have called 'governing through migration control'.

The internal border seeks to redraw a sharp divide between citizens and non-citizens, both legal and illegal. According to Khosravi (2010) these demarcation processes amount to 'technologies of anti-citizenship'. Indeed, Aas (2011) has argued that the liberal language of citizenship is proving inadequate to capture emerging systems of entitlement and belonging which produce 'novel categories of globally included and excluded populations', such as 'third country nationals' (lawfully resident non-citizens) and 'violent troublemakers' (generally citizens), thus highlighting new external and internal modes of 'otherness'. However this is determined, access to the entitlements of citizenship directly influences an individual's 'conditions of life' (Butler, 2010). As Butler asserts, human life is neither self-evident nor self-sustaining. Rather, social and political institutions situate individuals within lives that are more or less precarious. The universal potential for precarity is one way of understanding the underpinning for human rights.

Although Butler does not address border control policies in her discussion of precarious lives, aspects of the internal border fit her description of 'legalized violence by which populations are differentially deprived of the basic resources needed to minimize precariousness' (2010, p. 32). Policies of immiseration are a case in point. These policies have been systematically pursued in countries of the Global North, most obviously in European countries that have a residual commitment to social welfarism. In Britain, following the progressive withdrawal of *both* access to social security benefits *and* work rights for asylum seekers, additional enforcement strategies were announced in 2007 that were openly designed to create difficult living conditions for those without the legal status to remain (Home Office, 2007).

Arguably, no practice expresses unfettered sovereign power as directly as indefinite detention, which does not conform to the instrumental rationality generally associated with governmental concerns (Butler, 2004). The use of administrative detention to contain asylum seekers and illegalized migrants has proliferated throughout Europe and North America, where the expansion of privately run detention facilities is fuelling a rapidly growing industry (Bloch & Schuster, 2005; Welch & Schuster, 2005). However, among the governments of the Global North, it is the Australian Government that has arguably made the most uncompromising claim of absolute sovereignty over its borders, through its mandatory detention policies and the deliberate placement of detention centres in remote and hostile environments. These politically charged policies of deterrence and containment apply only to undocumented asylum seekers arriving by sea, who comprise a small but visible proportion of the population of asylum seekers, and are the group most likely to be legally recognized as refugees (Grewcock, 2009). Why else, apart from its powerful nationalist symbolism and supposed deterrent effect, would asylum seekers be detained in remote deserts and distant islands, at enormous cost to Australian taxpayers, against all the neoliberal dictates of fiscal responsibility?

Deportation is another border control strategy widely adopted by governments of the Global North. The forced repatriation of non-US citizens has risen exponentially in recent years (Brotherton, 2008), and, like the British Government before it, there is speculation that the Obama administration could introduce targets for expulsions, particularly of 'criminal aliens', under the Development, Relief and Education for Alien Minors (DREAM) Act (Napolitano, 2010). Resistance to highly publicized deportations of 'failed asylum seekers' and 'immigration offenders' on commercial airlines, from both deportees and other passengers, has forced the British Government into partnerships with other EU countries to conduct coerced expulsions through expensive and secretive, jointly administered charter flights (European Race Audit [ERA], 2010). As with detention, private security companies have been engaged to escort deportees on international flights. In fact, in Australia's biggest state New South Wales, accompanying deportees is reportedly the most popular extra-curricular employment undertaken by off-duty police officers (Weber, 2012). Nicholls (2007, p. 167) identifies Australia as 'one of the world's leading deporting countries', with a historical readiness to use deportation as an immigration control and problem-solving device. A notable trend in Australian deportation is the prioritization of lawfully resident non-citizens convicted of criminal offences for visa cancellation and deportation under broad 'character' grounds contained in section 501 of the *Migration Act 1958* (Cwlth). These practices exemplify the emergence across the Global North of an 'enemy penology' which uses deportation to exclude dangerous or unworthy individuals and groups from the social body (Krasmann, 2007).

The detection of individuals within the community who are candidates for detention and deportation is increasingly effected through surveillance networks that draw a wide range of state and non-state actors into a migration policing role. Despite its historical opposition to internal controls and reliance on 'remote control' policies (Zolberg, 2006), immigration enforcement has become the fastest-growing sector of federal law enforcement in the US (Kretsedemas & Brotherton, 2008). The ramping-up of the federal effort, including state–federal partnerships, has still fallen short in the eyes of many members of the public, particularly residents of border states. Arizona became the first state to pass a controversial law (Senate Bill 1070) providing municipal police with unprecedented powers and responsibilities to check immigration status (Provine & Sanchez, 2011). Critics of this legislation argue that it encourages racial profiling (American Civil Liberties Union of Northern California, 2011). Nevertheless, governors in a number of other states, reportedly some with very low populations of undocumented residents, have seized upon the provision as a template for introducing their own similar measures.

In Australia, police have a longstanding role in the detection of unlawfully present non-citizens (Weber, 2011). As in the US, immigration enforcement is a federal responsibility; however, state police are 'designated officers' under the Migration Act and, in law if not in practice, possess all the powers of immigration officers. Recent legislation has widened the network of agencies involved in the detection of 'unlawful non-citizens' to include the Australian Taxation Office and Centrelink agencies, which exchange information on taxpayers and social security recipients with the Department of Immigration and Citizenship (DIAC); private employers, who face sanctions for employing staff who have no legal authority to work; universities, which are required to report regularly on the attendance and academic progress of international students, as this impacts the validity of their student visas; and members of the public who are encouraged to use the so-called Dob-in Line to inform immigration authorities about suspect workmates, neighbours or family members.

The most recent expansion of the internal border in the UK began with increased search and arrest powers for immigration officers and the formation of joint 'snatch squads' of police and immigration officials in the 1990s, who were charged with achieving publicly announced targets for the removal of 'failed asylum seekers' and 'immigration offenders' (Weber & Bowling, 2004). This followed the formation of a specialist enforcement section in the United Kingdom Immigration Service to concentrate on after-entry controls rather than visa checking at ports of arrival. These developments have since been subsumed within the UK Border Agency (UKBA), a uniformed agency with an unambiguous focus on enforcement. The UKBA website makes it clear that its first priority is border security: 'The UK Border Agency is responsible for securing the UK border and controlling migration in the UK. We manage border control for the UK, enforcing immigration and customs regulations. We also consider applications for permission to enter or stay in the UK, and for citizenship and asylum' (UKBA, 2011a). Policing of the internal border has been even more deeply embedded in continental Europe, notably in Italy, where the Berlusconi government has introduced requirements on service providers to report illegalized migrants to authorities and has criminalized various acts of assistance to illegalized migrants (Fekete, 2009a).

The geographical border

Despite the increasing deterritorialization of the border, the physical border retains enormous symbolic, political and practical importance, and may be evoked as an indicator of national security and stability. In their different guises, geographical borders play out what Agamben describes as the 'fiction of sovereignty' (cited in Khosravi, 2010). Some borders, like the eastern perimeters of the EU, the European enclaves of Ceuta–Melilla, sections of the US–Mexico border and, potentially, the border between Mexico and Guatemala, convey the myth of total security through the solidity of a wall, drawing on theatrical representations of sovereignty that portray 'fantasies' of containment, security and innocence (Brown cited in Aas, 2011).

In contrast to this myth of solidity and permanence, contemporary European borders present a complex and evolving picture, shaped by the continuing expansion of the EU, with its relaxed (although still selective) internal borders and fortified external border. Collective responsibility for external border controls shifted to the EU with the Treaty of Amsterdam in 1999, while migration and asylum policies continue to be exercised by individual states (Dauvergne, 2008). Green and Grewcock (2002) have linked the building of so-called Fortress Europe to the forging of a new pan-European identity, with responsibility for blocking entry from the east passing to successive waves of aspiring member states, and operating as a precondition for EU membership. Thus, when Poland entered the EU in 2004, the job of maintaining the 'fantasy' of peripheral security shifted to Ukraine and Belarus, which were then expected to act as buffers not only against the illegalized entry of citizens of former Soviet states, but also those who journey from Asia and Africa through the Middle East. With the accession of Bulgaria and Romania to the EU in 2007, Turkey remains the only 'buffer' to irregular land crossings in the south-east.

The border between the US and Mexico carries the historical legacy of the 1848 war between the two countries, which resulted in the loss of land rights for Mexican and Native American peoples. Nevins (2008) argues that the present-day 'violence of conservation' stems from this original 'violence of foundation'. Despite attempts to sharply delineate US and Mexican national territory along the walled sections, the border has historically functioned as a dynamic borderland. Various economic and trade agreements with Mexico have seen the development of complex arrangements resulting in semi-permeable borders and ongoing relationships between US and Mexican towns and cities dotted along the border (Wonders, 2006). In the Border Project (see photographs), high school students living in the borderlands between Arizona and Mexico depict contemporary manifestations of the border from their diverse perspectives, reflecting recurring themes of economic inequality, division and danger.

The consequences of illegalization

Despite all their border control efforts, governments of the Global North have failed to eradicate illegalized border crossing. Put simply, '[w]here there is a border there is also border crossing, legal as well as illegal' (Khosravi, 2010, p. 4). Instead, selective illegalization has created people-smuggling markets and fuelled a cycle of deviancy amplification with increasingly deadly results (Weber & Grewcock, 2011). Illegalized border crossing, Dauvergne (2008, p. 169) argues, is the key to understanding how globalization is transforming sovereignty 'because it contributes to the objective of excluding even when physical borders fail to do so'. Illegalized travellers may have little choice but to embark on circuitous, expensive and hazardous journeys. If they manage to arrive at their destination, they must live with the consequences of illegality. Where the ontology of the border is naturalized, unauthorized border crossing may be apprehended as pathological (Khosravi, 2010, citing Malkki). Where

High school students taking part in the Border Project in the US–Mexico borderlands express what the border means to them
© 2007 Jewel Fraser Clearwater

the politico-juridical authority of the border is taken for granted, border transgressors can be readily portrayed as criminal (Pickering, 2005; Grewcock, 2009). Further, where borders are seen as sites for the production of security for existing populations, uncontrolled crossing is often equated with racialized conceptions of disease, social decay and threats to the very fabric of the nation-state (Pickering, 2005). It is precisely to counter these hegemonic readings of border transgression that we have chosen to use the unwieldy term 'illegalized' throughout this book, as it expresses the active role of the state in the attribution of this politico-juridical status to those marked for exclusion.

The selectivity of borders

Insofar as travellers are categorized as either 'legal' or 'illegal', the border acts like a sieve (Wonders, 2006), separating legitimate from suspect mobilities (Weber & Bowling, 2008). This filtering produces transnational systems of social stratification based on mobility entitlements (Bauman,

1998). Perhaps it is more accurate to conceive of the border as a series of sieves or filters, sorting travellers according to a range of legal entitlements reflected in different visa types. However, because this book is concerned with the implications of *illegalized* status, the demarcation between legal and illegal remains pivotal. Thus, a narrow focus by US authorities on illegalized Mexican border crossers as 'illegal workers' prevents any recognition of their possible humanitarian protection needs in a context of escalating borderlands violence (Boehm, 2011). Similarly, the construction of unauthorized boat arrivals by the Australian Government as a problem of people smuggling (Pickering, 2004; Grewcock, 2009) rhetorically erases their identity as refugees. Oelgemöller (2010) argues that governments even make premature attributions of 'illegality' while travellers are still in countries of so-called transit, justifying the construction of 'transit zones' to contain them. These justifications are based on routine assumptions, made without evidence, about the intended destinations of illegalized travellers, many of whom, Oelgemöller argues, see 'transit' countries as potential sources of work and relative safety. These assumptions reduce the complexity of individual motivations to cross borders to a single label, closing off other understandings of mobility and the factors that drive it.

The selectivity of borders is highly racialized, gendered and classed. De Giorgi (2010, p. 151) notes that, while virtually non-existent for capital and global elites, borders have 'resumed all their symbolic and material violence against specific categories of people' who are identified by the 'marginal position they occupy in transnational circuits of production'. Khosravi recounts being singled out and detained at Bristol Airport on the basis of his ethnicity – ironically on his way to convene a seminar on irregular migration – and being cast into a 'petrifying immobility': 'I could move neither in nor out. I was indistinguishable from the border' (2010, p. 98). This embodiment of the exclusionary force of the border by targeted individuals and groups parallels the idea of a non-geographical, 'personalized border' facilitating the relatively unfettered movement of favoured travellers (Weber, 2006). The politico-juridical sorting mechanisms enacted through the border have profound implications for the demographics of illicit border crossing and therefore for the interface between human vulnerability and objective risk. The predominant image of the immigrant, particularly the illegalized immigrant, may be of young, single, seemingly risk-resilient males; but illicit border crossing is increasingly attempted by whole families, by single and accompanied women, and – most problematically of all – by unaccompanied children. The hardships of arduous voyages, indefinite detention, unregulated work in the illicit economy or exposure to the animosity of host populations in places of transit or destination are experienced by many illegalized travellers. Yet they are likely to impact differentially according to age, gender and ethnicity. Overall, the systems of 'defensive geography' erected across the Global North (Perera, 2002) create a shifting matrix of risk associated both with illegalized border crossing and illegalized residence. This matrix of risk plays a significant role in determining *who* dies a border-related death, *how* they die, and *where*.

Risky journeys

Risky journeys can begin when illegalized travellers step onto an overcrowded and barely seaworthy boat; conceal themselves, alone or with others, inside an airless lorry or shipping container, or in the undercarriage of a train or plane; or when they set out ill-equipped to cross a scorching desert, swim a fast-flowing river or scale a high mountain range. These hazards form part of the everyday matrix of risk experienced by illegalized travellers *because* of their illegalized status, and lead to deaths by drowning, environmental exposure and asphyxiation. Government strategies of non-arrival, supported by sophisticated technologies of detection, force illegalized travellers into ever more clandestine modes of travel and ever more convoluted routes, which increase the duration and dangers of their ordeals (Maccanico, 2006). In Europe, the increasing fortification of land borders, and the externalization of the border through bilateral agreements with countries in North Africa and the Middle East, has diverted routes for illegalized travel to Europe to longer and more hazardous sea voyages up the west coast of Africa to the Canary Islands, and more recently into overland routes via the Sinai and Turkey towards Greece. Geographical displacement has also been a consistent outcome of border fortification at other locations in the Global North. The intensification of efforts by Australian-funded taskforce teams to apprehend and prosecute people smugglers in Indonesia is reported to have pushed departure sites further and further north as facilitators seek to evade detection (Brown, 2010). Similarly, the construction of a border wall between California and Mexico in the 1990s shut off traditional crossing points into the US and channelled unauthorized crossings into the more treacherous terrain of the Arizonan and Texan deserts.

Moreover, imposing penalties for people smuggling and increasing the risk of detection turns illegalized travellers into incriminating evidence, at risk of being disposed of at the sight of approaching patrols (Carling, 2007). Ramping up the risks and consequences of organized illicit travel also creates an environment that favours the most organized, well-resourced and unscrupulous facilitators. According to Interpol, people smuggling has emerged as the third-largest money maker for organized crime syndicates after drug and gun trafficking (Australian Federal Police [AFP], 2001). While it is important not to overlook the continuing survival of small-scale operators whose intentions are either humanitarian or fall within the boundaries of acceptable commercial practice, there are also indications of the increased involvement of criminal groups in facilitating illicit travel. According to a former Australian intelligence officer, Andrew Wilkie, Australia's anti-people-smuggling measures had precisely this effect: 'Initially the smugglers were relatively amateurish. They operated openly, with little concern for the Indonesian authorities, and in the belief they were out of reach of Australian agencies. They did eventually become more professional, but only after Australian and regional countermeasures started to bite' (Wilkie, 2003, no page). The US–Mexico border has seen the growth of criminal people-smuggling enterprises to an even greater extent, complicated by the cross-border trade in illicit drugs. Those crossing the US–Mexico border illegally once relied on small-scale opportunism by locals. Following measures to tighten border control, the cost increased exponentially so that many small, relatively low-risk operations were forced out by larger criminal networks that use labour bondage and violence (Nevins, 2002). More than 70 per cent of those who cross the US–Mexico border in recent years are said to have used the services of human smugglers (Cabrera, 2010).

Risky journeys do not only occur when illegalized travellers make individual choices, however free or constrained they may be, to leave their country of origin. Risky journeys may also be instigated by the decisions of governments and border officials to expel unlawful residents against their will, repel illegalized travellers at the border, or interdict them in transit. The phenomenon of 'stranded migrants' affected by border externalization projects has been described as a 'structural change in migration systems' which poses threats to migrant safety (Collyer, 2006, 2010). The summary return of asylum seekers to transit countries that are either not signatories to the *UN Convention on the Status of Refugees* or do not operate credible refugee status determination procedures risks breaching international humanitarian obligations of *non-refoulement* insofar as refugees are being returned to possible danger. Furthermore, immobilizing illegalized travellers in ever more distant places of origin or transit puts them at risk of hostility and violence at the hands of local populations, confinement in overcrowded detention centres, or even formal punishment due to their illegal status. Amnesty International (AI) has called on Malaysia – a country that is host to many thousands of illegal-ized travellers interdicted at the behest of the Australian Government – to end its practice of punishing them by caning (AAP, 2011). AI reported that 30,000 migrants had been caned over a five-year period, including asylum seekers on their way to Australia. Reports are also emerging about overcrowding, trauma and mistreatment of interdicted asylum seekers detained in Indonesian detention camps (Brown, 2010), suggesting the displacement of harms related to Australian border protection policies to unaccountable locations offshore.

For many illegalized travellers who have managed to breach the bar-riers placed in their way and remain in countries of the Global North for days, months or even years, forcible expulsion marks the beginning of another risky journey. The trend towards setting removal targets in many jurisdictions has been linked to the increasing use of force during expulsions. Although certainly not the highest category of border-related deaths in numerical terms, it has been observed that deaths during depor-tation are the fastest-growing category of border-related death in Europe (Fekete, 2009b). Individuals who refuse to leave voluntarily, or are not offered opportunities for so-called voluntary return on the basis of risk assessments, face potential dangers from the inappropriate use of restraints and excessive force by the private security guards or other law enforcement officers charged with 'escorting' them.

Risky residence

Illegalized travellers are also increasingly confronted with life-threatening risks posed by the operation of the internal border. Dauvergne (2004, p. 601) argues that labelling certain people as 'illegal' shifts the bound-aries of exclusion, allowing them to be 'erased from within'. The spread of migration policing networks is intended to increase the risk that illegal-ized migrants will be detected in the community through reports from neighbours, employer checks, data matching of government records and *ad hoc* encounters with an expanding range of law enforcement officials. Laws being introduced across Europe that criminalize those who assist undocumented migrants could reasonably be expected to deter affected people from seeking essential services such as healthcare, and many exam-ples of this are recorded in the NGO data (Fekete, 2009b). Ethnic com-munity liaison officers working for an Australian police service reported that residents with unlawful or uncertain immigration status feared con-tacting police because of their role in enforcing immigration law (Weber, 2012). McDowell and Wonders (2009/10) conducted focus groups with immigrant women living without legal status in Arizona, and found that fear of being detected by police or reported by members of the public led them to self-regulate their use of public space. The risks for those living in the community with insecure immigration status can be more immediate. The instigation of so-called snatch squads in Britain in the 1990s swiftly led to a spate of 'balcony deaths' as individuals earmarked for forced deportation attempted to flee from official custody (Weber & Bowling, 2004). Immigration detention, described by Khosravi (2010, p. 101) as 'exposing undesirable non-citizens to abandonment or even death', has claimed lives through acts of protest, third-party violence and suicide. Policies of destitution designed to encourage 'voluntary departures' have sometimes led to protracted suffering, or even death. Solyman Rashed is said to have been 'so ground down by his experiences in the UK' that he accepted 'voluntary' return to Iraq, where he survived just two weeks before being killed by a car bomb (Fekete, 2009b, p. 5).

Illegalized travellers may also experience various forms of legal, social and civil 'death' arising from extreme experiences of exclusion and social isolation. Various forms of living death have been articulated in the literature, including the ideas of 'wasted lives' (Bauman, 2004), 'unlivable lives' (Butler, 2010), 'barely life' (Michalowski, personal communication), 'bare life' (Agamben, 1998) and exclusion from the 'right to have rights' (Arendt, 1968). Khosravi (2010, p. 3), citing Schütz, argues that the mismatch between illegalized travellers and established politico-juridical categories situates them as 'a politically unidentifiable "leftover"', a 'no-longer human being'. Oelgemöller (2010, p. 419) has argued that the 'suspension' of illegalized travellers in transit constitutes them as the 'invisible living dead'. Discriminatory welfare regimes that stigmatize and isolate asylum seekers within the community are also capable of exercising this level of exclusionary power. Indefinite detention without due process can be equated to juridical death, and is arguably so distanced from the normal experience of personhood as to approach a form of social death. The consigning of illegalized travellers into domains of social and legal death may have repercussions beyond individual deprivation and suffering. In order to qualify as 'grievable', Butler (2010, p. 23) argues, lives must first display the conditions needed for a fully 'livable' life. We will argue later that policies of immiseration and exclusion dehumanize illegalized travellers, thereby creating the conditions in which systematic practices that lead to their deaths are not recognized as human rights abuses.

Sites of resistance

The project of defending the borders of the Global North from illegalized crossings does not proceed as smoothly as might be inferred from the discussion so far. Despite the risks they face, many illegalized travellers reach their destinations relatively unscathed, and may eventually obtain legal resident status and/or manage to establish livable lives and send remittances home to their families and communities. Stories of resistance and resilience abound, and the intentions of border control policies are often undermined. For example, the increased risks associated with illegalized travel appear to have had the effect of encouraging *longer* stays by undocumented migrants in the southern US – a situation which, while problematic for the migrants themselves, hardly represents a victory for US border protection policies. Moreover, despite broad agreement that states of the Global North are seeking to increase their levels of deportation, there is some doubt about their actual ability to deport, and detainee populations are expanding beyond the capacity of governments to build more detention centres to hold them.

At virtually all the borders of the Global North, processes of opposition spring up to protest and undermine them. Community groups such as Humane Borders, No More Deaths and Samaritans travel deep into the Arizonan deserts to provide water and other assistance to border crossers (Cabrera, 2010; Michalowski, 2007; Walsh, 2008, 2010). Members of the Sanctuary Movement openly defied the law in the 1990s to assist Salvadoran and Guatemalan refugees to cross the US–Mexico border (Coutin, 2005). Direct action groups such as the National Coalition of Anti-Deportation Campaigns in Britain (www.ncadc.org.uk) assist migrants facing deportation to wage political campaigns to garner local support for them to stay. An online memorial and campaigning site (www.sievx.com) has been established by concerned Australians to focus attention on the catastrophic sinking of the ship known as the SIEV X in 2001 and demand official enquiries into the 353 deaths of those on board. Across the Global North, airline passengers object to forcible deportations, health professionals provide services to undocumented migrants despite threats of legal sanctions, school teachers and pupils rally to help fellow pupils and their families remain in the community, campaigning groups lobby for the closure of detention centres, and local churches provide practical and pastoral support to asylum seekers made destitute by deliberate policies of immiseration.

Resistance to the exclusionary policies of the Global North is also manifest in the legal domain, through appeals against decisions in individual cases, to Constitutional challenges concerning the legality of state practices. Coutin (2005) identified a range of 'legalization strategies' pursued by Salvadoran immigrants to the US, and Schuster (2005) found that migrants in Italy often move back and forth between periods of legality and illegality. Successive Australian governments have been repeatedly criticized by the Human Rights Committee of the United Nations, which monitors compliance with the *International Convention on Civil and Political Rights*, for their extreme policies of mandatory detention of those arriving without visas by sea. Interdiction policies present one of the most formidable barriers to mounting legal challenges as they are played out in transnational spaces. Nevertheless, avenues of redress under international law that might be called upon to challenge the pre-emptive practices of states include the fundamental principle of *non-refoulement* to danger, the right to seek asylum contained in both the *Universal Declaration of Human Rights* and the *International Covenant on Civil and Political Rights*, and provisions within the *UN Convention on the Status of Refugees* that prohibit punishment for illegal entry. Moreover, legal precedent has already been established within US jurisprudence to conceptualize the border as 'not a fixed location but rather wherever the government performs border functions', which creates the capacity in law to hold states accountable for harm arising from acts perpetrated by their agents in zones of disputed legal authority (Motomura, 1993, p. 712).

Historical examples of resistance to border control policies are often lauded today as acts of heroism in pursuit of social justice, although their perpetrators were often subjected to censure and/or serious sanction at the time. The British intelligence agent Frank Foley is credited with saving thousands of lives before the Second World War by issuing visas to Jewish applicants in direct contravention of his orders (Smith, 1999; Weber, 2005). The groups and individuals, both black and white, who operated the legendary 'underground railroad' that assisted fugitive American slaves to cross internal borders and escape into Canada are now feted as opponents of an unconscionable injustice (Cabrera, 2010). In the present moment in history, we need to ask ourselves why those assisting escapees from unlivable lives in the Global South are threatened with criminal sanctions, while deaths and avoidable harms arising from border control practices are not recognized as large-scale human rights abuses.

Conclusion

In this chapter we have outlined the nature of contemporary borders and mapped the risks arising from illegalized border crossing. Consideration of illegalized border crossing in previous eras highlights the injustice of the present-day treatment of those who seek to cross the borders of the Global North without permission, sometimes with fatal consequences. Perhaps these practices persist because some deaths remain invisible, or simply do not count. In the next chapter we turn our attention to the ways in which border-related deaths are counted and discounted. We consider the *purposes* of counting from a range of perspectives, discuss technical disputes about the *process* of counting, and identify various strategies used to legitimize border control policies by discounting their deadly impacts. In considering these processes of counting and discounting we apply the broad conception of the non-geographical border set out in this chapter to make links between border functions and border-related deaths wherever they occur.

2
Counting and Discounting Border Deaths

> When the authority of authority is secure, when authoritative judgements carry inherent authority, when the legitimacy of their authority is not subject to sceptical scrutiny and challenge, experts have little need of numbers. But where mistrust of authorities flourishes, where experts are the target of suspicion and their claims are greeted with scepticism by politicians, disputed by professional rivals, distrusted by public opinion, where decisions are contested and discretion is criticized, the allure of numbers increases. (Rose, 1999, p. 208)

> [S]keptical treatments of statistics tend to receive significantly less media attention. This is due in part to the fact that many people are relatively innumerate. (Andreas & Greenhill, 2010, p. 3)

Counting deaths

Counting as statecraft

Nikolas Rose has argued that numbers make late modern modes of governance both possible and judgeable (Rose, 1999). According to Andreas and Greenhill (2010) we live in a 'hyper-numeric' world in which something counts because it can be counted. On the one hand, quantification can transform the political domain into a docile arena where the 'apparent facticity' of numbers can silence debate. On the other hand, in contemporary democracies, numbers not only serve as a mechanism of control used by ruling elites, but are also subject to competing claims and can provide a foundation for debate and accountability. What counts, in the end, is how numbers are embedded within mentalities of rule.

When the ship *MV Tampa* was turned away from the Australian territory of Christmas Island in 2001, with its decks overcrowded with asylum seekers rescued from a stricken Indonesian vessel, the conservative Prime Minister John Howard staked his capacity to govern on his ability to control the numbers of asylum seekers arriving on Australian shores. As the numbers of unauthorized boat arrivals dwindled, the Prime Minister lauded the success of his government's Pacific Solution (see Figure 2.1). Reducing the complexity of worldwide refugee movements to a single number that appeared amenable to control marked the Howard government as a government that could achieve 'the taming of chance' (Rose, 1999, p. 203). The renewed arrival of asylum seeker boats in 2009 sparked another frenzy of counting. Drawing on imagery familiar to a sports-obsessed public, the media heralded each new sighting as a step towards, and then beyond, the iconic 'century' mark, as boats were tracked with apparent military precision on their journeys towards outlying Australian territories. The count enabled the conservatives, who were by that time in opposition, to sheet home responsibility for the mounting numbers to the partial dismantling of the Pacific Solution by the incoming Labor government. Opposition claims of having 'turned back the boats' provided them with huge political capital, which almost carried them back into power in the close-fought 2010 election. The rising numbers of detainees held in overcrowded detention centres on Christmas Island and the Australian mainland have proven to be equally 'bad numbers' for the Labor government.

Figure 2.1   Number of unauthorized boats arriving in Australia 1990–2010

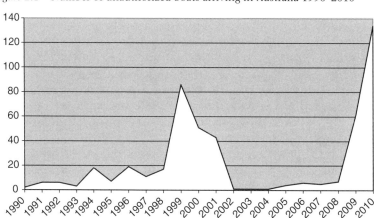

Data source: Phillips & Spinks (2011), Appendix 1

Contestation over numbers relates not only to the numbers them-selves. As Rose observes, '"political" judgements are implicit in the choice of what to measure, how to measure it, how often to measure it and how to present and interpret the results' (Rose, 1999, p. 198). In an attempt to counter the political rhetoric around unauthorized boat arrivals, Australian refugee advocates have tried to contextualize and reinterpret the figures: first, by arguing that it is 'push factors', not border control – and particularly not deterrence-based policies – that constitute the prime determinant of boat arrivals; and, second, by pointing out the miniscule share of the world's 'refugee burden' that is borne by the wealthy Australian nation.[1] NGOs have also tried to shift the agenda away from the obsession of governments with counting – as evidenced in pledges to minimize boat arrivals and/or asylum applications, or in the establishment of quantitative targets for deport-ation and removal – toward measurements that reflect the harm and suffering experienced by these targeted groups. These efforts seek to reverse the perception of refugees and undocumented migrants 'as a problem', and recast them as people with very serious problems of their own. A press release from the Institute of Race Relations (IRR) in London (2003) reads: 'Governments count the numbers coming in. But who counts the numbers who don't make it ... In spite of the vast human tragedy taking place on Europe's periphery, the total number of people dying is not known, as no EU body takes responsibility for monitoring these deaths.' In the remainder of this chapter we examine the processes through which governmental and non-governmental groups in the Global North have sought to enumerate and problema-tize border-related deaths.

Providing a quantitative count of border-crossing deaths has also become an important function of both academic research and the advocacy work carried out by NGOs. Being able to measure deaths at the border implies a need for action (Andreas & Greenhill, 2010). It is also increasingly used by government agencies in crafting and recraft-ing migration and security policies. While the enforcement of any border creates conditions conducive to border-related deaths (Nevins, 2003), not all states quantify or classify deaths at the border.

How deaths at the global frontier have been counted has overwhelm-ingly been shaped by who does the counting and the political purpose of the count. As noted by Rose (1999, p. 208): 'The apparent facticity of the figure obscures the complex technical work that is required to pro-duce objectivity.' A range of methodologies have been used by govern-ment and non-government agencies to count the deaths of illegalized border crossers. Some counts depend on bodies found; some on reports of departures that have no corresponding arrival information; some on bodies found and the conclusions reached about the cause of death, and whether or not such causes may reasonably be attributed to the border; while others use complicated estimates of apprehensions, entries and the extrapolated estimates of border-related deaths (Cornelius, 2001).

Regardless of the methodology used, the primary function of counting has been the demarcation of death, the production of a tally of bodies, and the identification of where and when the deaths have become known to those doing the counting. International boundaries are inherently shared (Gavrilis, 2008), not only by the two states separated by a border, but also by the borderland communities that develop in and around a border. These communities include civil society, organizations and individuals who have come to attach a high level of importance to counting deaths. The counting of bodies is important because the border is seen, in one way or another, to be instrumental in those deaths. Yet the reasons why and how the death is attributable to the border are keenly disputed. There is an implicit assumption in the majority of the academic literature that the numbers and basic details of the death will allow responsibility to be correctly attributed to the state, the migrant or the smuggler (Fekete, 2003).

In Europe, the NGO UNITED Against Racism and Fascism publishes an online 'List of deaths' arising from border controls which is regularly updated and openly available on its website.[2] The organization adopts an expansive view of border control that aligns closely with the notion of the 'functional border' described in the previous chapter. Drowning and other causes of loss of life at sea dominate the list. However, deaths arising from the internal border, such as suicides in detention, loss of life through lack of access to medical care, suffocations during clandestine crossing of land borders, deaths arising from dangerous work conditions directly associated with illegal status, and violent deaths during deportation or in other circumstances involving border control officials, are also included (see Figure 2.2). No death count across these disparate contexts can ever hope to be complete. The UNITED list is compiled primarily from media reports and information exchanged across a network of 550 NGOs in Europe and North Africa. Although the reports are cross-corroborated where possible, it would seem that coronial reports or the findings of other official inquiries are rarely available.

The motivation to collect this data is clearly related to UNITED's campaigning function, and is directed towards public education and the promotion of the accountability of European governments. UNITED receives

Figure 2.2   The indistinct mirrors of European migration policies

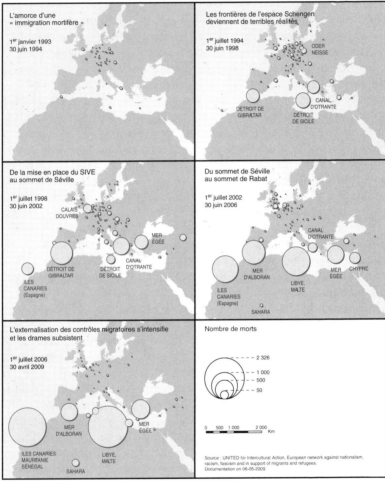

Évolution du nombre de morts aux portes de l'Europe

Source: Atlas des Migrants en Europe, p. 117 © Migreurop 2009

funding from the European Commission and is a member of the
Advisory Council of Europe. The organization is known and respected
for its work against racism and fascism. UNITED's collection of information about border-related deaths is independently funded, and sits
within a campaign entitled the Fatal Realities of Fortress Europe, which
aims to use the documentation on border deaths to 'wake up Europe's

conscience'. These objectives have shaped the way in which the list of deaths is collected. Care is taken to document the sources of all reports, but the emphasis is on collecting the widest possible range of information. The organization makes no claim to 'scientific objectivity' and recognizes that the data is probably not suitable to quantitative analysis. Other commentators have pointed out that this vital function of 'counting the dead' is inevitably affected by biases in both directions: on the one hand, by the increased attention to border deaths by NGOs, which may have contributed to what they call the 'explosion of the figures'; and on the other, by the significant number of fatalities that remain undetected (Blanchard et al., 2008). Blanchard, Clochard and Rodier claim that one immigration official from the Canary Islands speculated that the number of people who perish at sea could be up to ten times the number of bodies that are washed up on their shores – an estimate that is used by Red Cross representatives. Reluctance to go to the aid of those in peril also contributes to the undercounting of deaths at sea, not to mention the likelihood that drownings will occur in the first place. Blanchard et al. (2008, p. 30) therefore ask:

> In this scientifically unreliable context, why attempt to count migration deaths? ... Counting the total number of lives sacrificed to the altar of 'migratory risk' is a way of giving these nameless deaths an existence. Even if the estimates lack precision, they make it possible to understand a situation that is too often considered fate or trivial. Therefore, the war on migrants goes from a metaphorical level to a context where consequences must be documented. In order to understand the situation, it is then necessary to undertake an impossible census. It is also a kind of moral requirement, and a tribute to be paid to the victims. (*Translated from the French*)

Blanchard et al. conclude that activists and researchers have no choice but to brandish these imperfect figures in the hope of being heard. To capture attention, large headlines on the home page of the UNITED campaign website showing the latest total of known border deaths convey the sheer size of a slowly and relentlessly unfolding tragedy. Further instructions on the site inform individuals and groups of how they can campaign and raise awareness of border deaths by focusing on one specific death or fatal event. As of 20 January 2011, the death count on the UNITED list stood at 14,037 since the collection began in 1993. Blanchard et al. (2008) claim that the total number of victims of this 'ignored massacre' may be two or three times that number. While there are few markers of the location of these deaths, there are some exceptions. The 'no man's land of Tinzaouatine' that lies on the border between Mali and Algeria has a cemetery that houses the 'tombs of migration's anonymous victims' (Blanchard et al., 2008, p. 31). Calais, Toulon, the Canary Islands and Lampedusa Island are all sites with 'discrete gravestones [that] remind us of the huge cemetery that the borders of the European Union are today' (Blanchard et al., 2008, p. 30).

An independent source of data on European border deaths has been collected by academic researcher Ernesto Kiza (2008), with a view to providing 'scientifically sound data on a phenomenon that is mostly taking place in the dark and outside the eyes of the public' (Kiza, 2009, p. 12). Kiza also uses media reports as his data source, and includes reports of missing persons whose bodies are not recovered. Yet he adopts a narrower definition of border-related death than that used by UNITED, recording only deaths that occur during the travel phase of migration. Kiza was able to demonstrate a steady rise in the number of deaths from 1999 until 2004, and the increasing proportions of sub-Saharan Africans within the mounting death toll (Kiza, 2009). He estimated the proportion of known deaths *en route* to Europe that occurred at sea to be 80 per cent due to the increasing dangerousness of sea crossing

Table 2.1   Causes of death related to European borders for all recorded deaths 1993–2010

Drowned	9870	70.1%
Not known	1632	11.7%
Starved	864	6.2%
Suicide	334	2.4%
Suffocated	292	2.1%
Vehicle crash	277	2.0%
Homicide	254	1.8%
Frozen	214	1.5%
Exploding mines	73	0.5%
Lack of medical aid	62	0.4%
Fear / terror	49	0.4%
Arson	36	0.3%
Poisoned	23	0.2%

Source: UNITED List of deaths www.unitedagainstracism.org/pdfs/listofdeaths.pdf
downloaded 20 January 2011

during this time. (For comparison, see Table 2.1 for the causes of all deaths recorded by UNITED.) While acknowledging the significant 'dark figure' of unreported deaths, Kiza sees the power of statistics in their ability to capture the attention of governments and publics with their sheer scale, as a first step towards the attribution of responsibility: 'But with numbers comes responsibility. While we might say that even one death is too much, history clearly shows us that only problems of scale attract the attention of the public and their leaders' (2009, p. 2).

In Australia, only one source of information on border-related deaths was available when the writing of this book commenced. This data was collected by a group of concerned individuals, who came together largely in response to the single greatest tragedy in the recent history of Australian border control – the sinking of the SIEV X on 19 October 2001. It is believed that 146 children, 142 women and 65 men died on that day, although many bodies have never been recovered. The boat foundered before reaching Australian waters and no official inquiry into the sinking has ever been conducted. In the absence of official recognition of these deaths, the group that came together undertook to support the survivors and relatives of those who died, and protest the lack of any official response to the tragedy by establishing an online record of the names, nationalities, genders and ages of all known passengers, whether survivors or victims. The website also carries testimonies from the survivors (available at sievx.com). One survivor spoke of seeing 'dead children like birds floating on the water' during a 22-hour ordeal while awaiting rescue. He says: 'At the end, a boat came to rescue us, the ones who died have found comfort, as for us; our lives have been destroyed.'[3] The testimony of this young man reminds us that even the most carefully prepared death count cannot enumerate the impact on the living, or discern clearly where the distinction lies between death and a life still felt to be worth living. Foremost in the minds of the SIEV X campaign group members has been the importance of naming the dead, and memorializing the many families who were impacted by the tragedy on the SIEV X website through a gallery of family portraits. The group directs particular criticism at the AFP for failing to release the names of some of the passengers, apparently because of ongoing investigations into people-smuggling charges.

The desire to establish a more comprehensive list of Australian border deaths across all the 'border sites' identified in Chapter 1 led the authors initially to contact DIAC. The answer to our emailed request about statistics on deaths arising from immigration enforcement on the Australian mainland returned the answer '1'. In contrast to the efforts of the SIEV X group to identify and name the dead, and to place them within the context of their families, no name was provided, no date of death, and no details of how the death occurred. Following further research, it transpired that this person had a name – Seong Ho Kang – and that he died in July of 2004 after being struck by a taxi in Strathfield, Sydney. The death occurred while Seong Ho Kang was trying to evade capture in one of the 'raids' that frequently take place in workplaces in this area. In relation to deaths at the external border, the authors were referred by the Department of Immigration to the Customs and Border Protection Service, which operates the offshore surveillance and interdiction programme. Identifying workplace deaths of illegalized workers proved particularly elusive, with enquiries to regulatory bodies resulting in a spiral of cross-referrals. Inquiries to state coroner's offices were frustrated by the lack of recording of visa status among the records of reported deaths. 'Border-related deaths' was clearly neither an easily definable statistical category for the authorities, nor a legally relevant one. A combination of media searching and networking with NGOs and lawyers resulted in the list presented in Appendix 1, which unfortunately is destined to remain a work in progress.

Most of the deaths that have occurred on the Australian mainland have resulted in a coronial report. Deaths occurring beyond Australian waters, yet within the surveillance zone patrolled by Australian naval and coastguard vessels, are unlikely to result in any official documentation. It seems that the location of the death is crucial in determining responsibility for documenting and enumerating deaths associated with the operation of Australian border controls. This lack of official data is all the more perplexing given that, in a debate between Labor and Liberal spokespersons held at the prestigious National Press Club in Canberra just prior to the 2010 election (Media Monitors, 2010), the Shadow Immigration Minister Scott Morrison cited a figure of 170 known deaths off the northern coast of Australia in the previous two years which he attributed to people-smuggling activities (rather than border controls). Inquiries to the Shadow Minister's office and other authorities failed to identify a source for this number. Since the matter of offshore deaths was constructed in terms of people smuggling, it is possible that the data sources that do exist are produced within a law enforcement framework and are considered highly sensitive. The lack of openly accessible data on border-related deaths occurring within and *en route* to Australia is a severe impediment to a full understanding of the human costs of border controls.

In the US, official Border Patrol statistics record a total of 4375 deaths along the US–Mexico border from 1998 to 2009 (Anderson, S., 2010). The figures reflect a general upward trend from 263 in 1998 to 417 in 2009 – a death toll of more than one person each day. A 'unique and scientifically rigorous study' by the Binational Migration Institute (BMI) of all deaths of illegalized border crossers in Pima County, Arizona, sought to produce a 'fine grained portrayal' of such deaths by studying autopsy reports in Pima County (Rubio-Goldsmith et al., 2007). Noting the serious undercounting of deaths by the US Border Patrol, and the fact that possibly two-thirds of the deaths in Arizona are detected on the tribal lands of the Tohono O'odham nation which lie outside the designated Border Safety Initiative (BSI) zone in which the Border Patrol collects death statistics, they conclude that the 'actual number of migrant deaths is, at present, unknowable' (Rubio-Goldsmith et al., 2007, p. 4). The BMI study focused on the personal attributes of those who died, in deciding whether or not they were illegalized migrants – relying on the presence or absence of a social security number, place of residence or lawful US immigration status; their nationality; the travel route taken; and even personal possessions found with the body to determine their status.

The counting of border deaths has become a significant part of wresting back control of the US–Mexico border. The counting and classification of deaths – where and how and of whom – can be regarded as a method of imposing order on what has been viewed as a situation out of control. Official *government* counts (albeit incomplete and partial) from US Government agencies and the Mexican Government reinforce the geographical absoluteness of the border and assume that vast spaces can be systematically known and controlled. On this view, once this data is available, increased fortification of the border is considered a reasonable and indeed desirable response. The counting of border-related deaths assists broader government efforts to rationalize and demonstrate the purpose, and efficacy, of border protection. For example, the US Border Control consistently refers to the numbers of deaths and rescues in terms that support its activities along the border. For NGOs in the US, Latin America and Europe, counting border deaths is a mechanism for attributing responsibility for these deaths, as well as contesting the absoluteness of sovereign claims over the ways and means of protecting national borders. As Jimenez has argued in her report for the American Civil Liberties Union and Mexican National Commission for Human Rights:

> In enacting border and immigration policies, nations have the sovereign prerogative to protect their territorial integrity and defend their citizenry. That power, however, is restricted and constrained

by international obligations to respect fundamental human rights. Unfortunately, these restraints have not precluded the U.S. government from deploying deadly border enforcement policies and practices that, by design and by default, lead to at least one death every day of a migrant crossing the border. (2009, p. 7)

Disparities in the numbers of deaths have primarily been linked to the variability and reliability of sources utilized. Official government counts of border deaths along the US–Mexico border are kept by both the US Government and the Mexican Government. The US Government has attempted to count border deaths since 2000 through the BSI tracking system. This data compiles numbers and locations of deaths and rescues, as well as identifying trends and high-risk areas. It is used to allocate resources for BSI projects and as a measure of their effectiveness (US Government Audit Office [GAO], 2006). The tracking system relies on data being collected and collated by the Border Patrol through either its direct identification of bodies or deaths, or consultation with other local officials. The counting of deaths by US agencies therefore serves a number of state objectives: to act as a deterrent to would-be migrants and to verify the harm-minimization approach adopted, but also (largely by the border patrol agencies) to determine their allocation of resources.

For media outlets, such as the *Arizona Daily Star*, the focus has often been on recording the local costs of border control and migration for local communities and responding to the fear generated by border deaths. The newspaper's website compiles data drawn from a range of sources, including county medical examiner offices, and publishes the annual number of deaths counted along with a searchable database, with a translation into Spanish. The *Arizona Daily Star* describes its attempt to count border-related deaths as follows:

With no official record-keeping system, the exact number of illegal border crossers who died along Arizona's stretch of U.S.–Mexican border has never been known ... We hope this database provides a service to the loved ones of those who have disappeared. We also hope it helps the general public gain perspective on the number of lives lost. (2010, website)

Similar data is collected and published by Coalición de Derechos Humanos as part of its Recovered Bodies Project, which is also restricted to identifying deaths that occur in Arizona. The naming of the Coalición initiative highlights its primary motivation to assist in identifying and publicly proclaiming the dead, with a view to informing wider social and political change. These intentions are clear from the introductory information on its website:

> in order to alert our government and the public as to the true extent of these casualties, accurate numbers of deaths must be recorded. Currently, conflicting numbers are constantly being released, mostly because of the complicated nature of recovering and identifying individuals who often carry little or no identification with them, and the many agencies this information is passed to … In an effort to honor every life that has been lost on our borders, Coalición de Derechos Humanos records the number of bodies that are recovered on our border. With the cooperation of Arizona county officials, as well as the Consular offices of México, Guatemala, El Salvador, Honduras, and Brazil, and the Binational Migration Institute, we are attempting to put names to our migrant sisters and brothers, and bear witness to the deaths of those unknown, of whom there are hundreds buried in our communities. As we attempt to comfort their families who mourn, let us also promise to seek justice, peace, and an end to the walls that separate and divide our communities. May we honor the spirits of those who have died with the commitment to peace and dignity on our borders. (Coalición de Derechos Humanos, 2007)

In total, 2104 deaths have been recorded by Coalición de Derechos Humanos since 2000. In contrast to the pan-European data collected by UNITED, and the plurality of circumstances of death arising from its wide-ranging definition of the border, the deaths that are counted by these local agencies on the US–Mexico border are defined almost exclusively by the location in which bodies are found (see Table 2.2). The relative uniformity of the nature of the unidentified remains, found at a location so removed from everyday life that it can only be identified with a Global Positioning System coordinate, evokes the desolation of the desert itself. The frequency with which cause of death cannot be determined due to the skeletal condition of the 'remains' (a word that is notably distanced from human life) underscores the isolation of the bodies that lie undiscovered for weeks, months or even years. Where known, the cause of death is most often exposure, but is also frequently violence, drownings and motor vehicle accidents.

46

Table 2.2 Extract from Coalición de Derechos Humanos list of recovered remains

1 October 2010–31 December 2010

	Name	Sex	Age	Country	Discovery date	Location Discovered	Cause of death
18	Teresa del Carmen Reyes Vasquez	F	26	Unknown	11/5/2010	N 31 44.448 W 112 10.074	Undetermined
19	Unknown	M	Unk	Unknown	11/5/2010	N 32 29.275 W 111 47.720	Undetermined
20	Unknown		Unk	Unknown	11/7/2010	N 31 52.355 W 111 57.477	Probable hyperthermia
21	Unknown	M	Unk	Unknown	11/7/2010	N 32 46.258 W 111.57.568	Undetermined (skeletal remains)
22	Unknown		Unk	Unknown	11/9/2010	N 31 32.856 W 111 43.240	Undetermined (skeletal remains)
23	Unknown	M	Unk	Unknown	11/10/2010	N 32 43.440 W 112 05.320	Undetermined (skeletal remains)
24	Unknown	M	Unk	Unknown	11/13/2010	N 31 52.837 W 111 21.633	Undetermined
25	Unknown		Unk	Unknown	11/13/2010	N 31 47.010 W 111 59.633	Undetermined (skeletal remains)
26	Julio Cesar Urquilla-Reyes	M	31	Unknown	11/15/2010	5000 West Caterpillar Trail	Probable dehydration and hypothermia
27	Unknown		Unk	Unknown	11/18/2010	N 31 41.625 W 112 12.758	Undetermined
28	Hipolito Luis Lorenzo-Lopez	M	42	Unknown	11/22/2010	N 31 55.525 W 112 05.916	Undetermined (skeletal remains)

Disputed/disparate counts

Counting deaths at the border reveals that border enforcement strategies vary in nature and intensity (Gavrilis, 2008), often across different segments of the same border. For example, it has been demonstrated that government policies of securing the US–Mexico border have pushed migrants to cross the border via the most inhospitable terrain, including lengthy desert crossings where temperature extremes result in more deaths and the need to seek out assisted crossings using the services of human smugglers (Jimenez, 2009; Guerette & Clarke, 2005). In this regard, efforts to count deaths at borders invariably describe how different numbers of deaths are found in different sections of borders, suggesting the direct relationship between how many people die and the specific local attempts to secure the border. The processes adopted to count border deaths have to varying degrees sought to include micro and macro factors in attributing cause and effect. Examining these processes grants us insight into how different border enforcement practices result in different types and degrees of harm. Yet the primary concern of this chapter is not how a more accurate counting of death may reveal a *new and improved* way to enforce borders, but rather the extent to which the various methods of counting obfuscate the violence and coercion enacted on frontier territories, whether land or maritime. As Nevins (2003) has cogently argued, research on deaths at the border reveals problematic foundational assumptions regarding the nature of the border, the recognition of the structural violence enacted at the border, and impoverished interpretations and applications of human rights. Some of these assumptions become apparent when the methods of counting are considered.

Invariably, counts of border-related deaths are disputed by the different parties to the border. The most notable counting disparity has been between the US and Mexican governments, specifically between the numbers of deaths tallied by US Government (and allied) agencies, and the counts made by the Mexican Government and various NGOs and media sources. Moreover, counts of border-related deaths by the US Border Patrol differ from those of other key US agencies such as counts found in medical examiner records. Official agency counts, such as that compiled by the US Border Patrol, are considered notoriously imprecise for they only include bodies that the Border Patrol recovers and not bodies found by other agencies. As Michalowski asserts:

> According to the GAO (2006), the Border Patrol's Tucson Sector under-counted migrant deaths by 32% in 2002, 43% in 2003, and 35% in

2004 ... In an attempt to compile more accurate death counts, the Mexican Ministry of Foreign Relations began recording all Mexicans *reported missing* on a journey into the United States. According to these calculations, the Border Patrol figures may underestimate actual migrant deaths by as much as 300%. (2007, p. 64)

Medical examiner records have limitations for they can only include bodies recovered and cannot and do not include the bodies of migrants who die after entry into the US, those who drown and are not recovered, and a range of other scenarios which result in bodies not being processed by the county medical examiner office.

The distinction between the various ways different agencies count deaths predominantly emanates from how they define the circumstances and causes of death (Cornelius, 2001). There is no standardized or generally accepted definition of border-related death, and hence no standard criteria for determining which deaths are to be counted on the US–Mexico border, or for that matter any other contested border-crossing zone internationally. For example, the US Government has utilized the following definition:

The BSI methodology defines border-crossing deaths as those occurring in the furtherance of an illegal entry and includes guidelines for recording those deaths occurring within its target zone – an area consisting of 45 counties on or near the southwest border with Mexico. (GAO, 2006, p. 1)

If we look across global frontiers, it appears that definitions of deaths at the border consistently rely on bodies being visible, temporal and calculable.

According to Michalowski, differences in counts arise because the US Border Patrol only counts deaths as 'migration-related' if found *in situ* in the vicinity of the border. This adheres the count to a strict geographic definition of borderlands and a functional definition. The US Border Patrol excludes suspected people smugglers, and skeletal remains from unknown years – so the definition is temporally as well as geographically limited. The reality of desert-based death also presents significant difficulties when counting deaths based on skeletal remains – often bones are so bleached and/or disturbed by animals that it is not even possible to count how many people they represent. Overall, the approach of the GAO is to concentrate on auditing bodies and producing accurate numbers (an almost impossible task), while NGOs aim to identify individuals and work with families on building knowledge about the deaths. As Michalowski's ethnographic work with NGOs on the border found:

> Nearly every week that I was in Tucson, the migration rights organization I worked with received calls, e-mails, or faxes from Mexico seeking information about loved ones who attempted a desert crossing and were never heard from again. Equally poignant were the homemade signs I would see taped to bus stops in the heavily Latino city-within-a-city of South Tucson. Sometimes computer-generated, but more often handwritten, they contained the name, description, and sometimes a photo of a missing migrant whose destination had been Tucson, along with a telephone number to call should someone have any information regarding the person's whereabouts. (2007, p. 65)

There are also ongoing disputes between both US and Mexican government counts and those collected and published by civil society. For example, the *Arizona Daily Star* collects and tallies evidence from a range of sources; however, there are often disparities between the data from different years. Some years include evidence from all Arizona medical examiner offices, while information from other years is only available from some offices. These counts, because of a state focus, are difficult to compare to counts undertaken by NGOs such as Coalición de Derechos Humanos simply because the *Arizona Daily Star* counts per calendar year, whereas Coalición de Derechos Humanos counts from 1 October to 30 September.

US Government interest in counting deaths peaked when it launched a 'harm minimization' approach (often considered the launch of the BSI in 2004), which entails sending patrols to find migrants in distress, and a greater emphasis on 'search and rescue' functions. The recording and classification of deaths by US agencies at this time was a means of validating this 'humanitarian' mission to reduce the harm of their own border enforcement practices – practices that were explicitly designed to deter migrants by making it more dangerous to cross the border. An important case study was presented in a recent report of the GAO. The GAO Report was critical of the US Border Patrol's attempts to prevent deaths under the BSI. However, its dissatisfaction was not with poor or conflicted policy, but rather with a failure to comprehensively pursue the statistical verifiability of deaths:

> Comprehensive evaluations of the BSI and other efforts by the Border Patrol to prevent border-crossing deaths are challenged by data and measurement limitations. However, the Border Patrol has not

addressed these limitations to sufficiently support its assertions about the effectiveness of some of its efforts to reduce border-crossing deaths. For instance, it has not used multivariate statistical methods to control for the influences of measurable variables that could affect deaths, such as changes in the number of migrants attempting to cross the border. (GAO, 2006, Preface)

The GAO Report is notable for highlighting the collapse of the apparently bifurcated function of the Border Patrol under the BSI (the enforcement of the border, on the one hand, and the prevention of death, on the other). However, with a focus on the quantifiability of death data, the issue becomes one of producing verifiable statistical evidence to determine resource allocation, rather than the production of knowledge about deaths at the border:

> As the Border Patrol is primarily an enforcement agency, search and rescue activities often occur simultaneously with enforcement activities, thus making it difficult to separate the resources dedicated to each type of activity ... In the absence of using multivariate statistical methods that control for the influence of other measurable factors, the effectiveness of these programs' impact on border-crossing deaths cannot be demonstrated. (GAO, 2006)

Unsurprisingly, the requisite response to flawed counting methodologies is the enhancement of the elaborate bureaucratic effort that underpins border enforcement. This approach necessitates better and more consistent protocols for the collation and recording of information on border-related deaths:

> the Border Patrol needs to continue to improve its methods for collecting data in order to accurately record deaths as changes occur in the locations where migrants attempt to cross the border – and consequently where migrants die. Improved data collection would allow the Border Patrol to continue to use the data for making accurate planning and resource allocation decisions. (GAO, 2006, Preface)

The drive to count border deaths among state agencies is heavily influenced by more efficacious border enforcement objectives. Harm-minimization strategies dependent on the production of quantitative counts of deaths at the border are absorbed into the greater effort of total enforcement.

The Mexican Government uses a range of sources to count border-related deaths, including newspaper reports, border agencies, hospital records and autopsy reports. Academic disciplines have similarly drawn from a range of sources in constructing counts (Cornelius, 2001, 2005; Reyes et al., 2002; Meneses, 2003; Carling, 2007; Spijkerboer, 2007). Increasingly there has been a trend to use medical examiner reports as the most reliable source of records of deaths at the border (see, for example, Eschbach et al., 1999; Rubio-Goldsmith et al., 2006). The key issue regarding sources has been whether they undercount or over-count the number of deaths and the appropriateness of their sample parameters. Government and non-government agencies have deployed diverse methodologies in counting deaths at the border. Some argue that, while this results in divergent numbers, the data produced by different organizations generally demonstrates similar trends in the levels of death (GAO, 2006). In fact, significant effort has been made to draw disparate figures together into a generalizable whole such that discrepancies are erased. As Rose notes, the numbers rather than the practices and outcomes become the ongoing focus of official concern:

> When such numbers are used as 'automatic pilots' in decision-making they transform the thing being measured – segregation, hunger, poverty – into its statistical indicator and displace political disputes into technical disputes about methods. (1999, p. 205)

The methodologies often differ, however, in how agencies define border-related deaths, the ways they identify a death and quantify known and unknown deaths, the documentation sources used, the spatial location of the counting, the temporal parameters of the count, and the models developed and applied to the calculation of numbers of deaths. These issues will form our focus in detailing the current practices of counting deaths at the border.

Traces of life and visible death

Counting deaths is ultimately about finding a trace of life that can be recorded. However, counting relies on what Butler (2010) has referred to as the visual and narrative dimensions that also work to delimit public discourse: while traces of life may work to make deaths knowable, they may also work to make deaths unknowable. What is counted is, as in Butler's example of grievable life in war, haunted by those deaths that are not counted. We cannot passively receive the knowledge held within the various death counts, for it is possible that the act of counting, and indeed of receiving the count, conditions and regulates our understanding of border-related deaths and violence. In short, counting deaths contains within it acts of violence when the counts remain unchallenged, unexamined and largely unexplained. Examining some of the definitional, visible, temporal and spatial dimensions of the death counts evidences how difficult it is to get a fix on knowable deaths at the border.

It is common for criminologists to remark on, if not spend significant effort theorizing, the implications of visibility for the understanding (or indeed misunderstanding) of crime (Young, 1996). Central to such analysis is how in late modern society the visibility of criminal acts, often seen through Closed Circuit Television (CCTV) or fictional depictions in high-rating television crime drama, becomes knowable to the broad population to the extent that the ensuing fascination with violent crime itself requires significant explanation and investigation.

By contrast, border-related deaths are often invisible. Despite unprecedented activity at and around the border, deaths often go unnoticed or unrecorded. Often this is attributed to inhospitable terrain, even for government patrol efforts, or to the clandestine nature of the lives border crossers must lead. Moreover, bodies are often the byproduct of unsuccessful smuggling operations – operations precisely designed to remain hidden. People smuggling as an illicit enterprise is designed to be undetected without the usual array of self-published quantification of cash flow, business volumes, customer testimonials and growth projections of legal enterprises (see Andreas, 2010). Bodies can be rendered visible by either passive or active discovery, by both government and non-government agencies. If no body is found then the count becomes reliant on any data evidencing a departure and/or the absence of communication with migrants post-arrival.

The visibility of death is an important consideration because the vast majority of counts only include those bodies that are found. Despite significant discrepancies in counts of border-crossing deaths, the magnitude of underreporting has undoubtedly increased as enforcement has driven crossers into less patrolled sections of the border, whether land or maritime borders.

Reports from the US–Mexico border indicate changing trends over the past few years in relation to border crossing and border-related deaths. Over the past 12 months organizations have recorded a significant increase in the number of bodies recovered of 'unknown gender'. This euphemism refers to the insufficient quantity of the skeleton recovered to enable identification of the gender of the deceased person

(Coalición de Derechos Humanos, 2007). It also indicates that such bodies have remained invisible for longer periods, possibly due to their location in increasingly inhospitable terrain. Crossing the border in more isolated areas may decrease the likelihood of detection by the authorities but it also greatly increases the associated risks.

For maritime borders where death is often the result of drowning, counting is reliant on the estimates provided by survivors. As was noted in the Jimenez report, drownings occurring near or across the US–Mexico border often do not appear in counts because they do not include those 'who may have drowned in a river, canal, or ocean but whose corpses were deposited by currents on the Mexican side or who are classified as locals by Mexican authorities' (2009, p. 15).

Passengers on boats that are known to have left port but do not reach their destinations are not routinely recorded as deaths. As noted earlier, the SIEV X sank between Indonesia and Australia in 2001 and 146 children, 142 women and 65 men drowned. This incident became a focal point of media concern for a number of reasons. Notably, it occurred during an election year when the issue of asylum became intermeshed with post-September 11 anxieties around national security and racial 'otherness'.

A locatable body is used to produce documentation not only about death but also about the person. The documentation of death – varying uses of death certificates, and other documentation regarding place of birth, residence and cause of death (GAO, 2006) – produces a counted death. As Butler has noted, invariably a death is only recognized if death documents are produced. The lack of documentation for a migrant not only works to prevent their arrival but also to prevent their death being known. NGOs have attempted to record invisible bodies by measuring the discrepancy between the numbers of those known to have departed with the numbers of arrivals. While organizations on the US–Mexico border like Coalición de Derechos Humanos only count bodies, the European organization No Fortress Europe records a range of maritime incidents as well as departures that have no corresponding arrivals.

In February 2009 a delegation of Salvadorans belonging to the Committee of Relatives of Dead and Disappeared Migrants visited southern Mexico to press the Mexican Government to investigate and document the deaths, or presumed deaths, of their missing family members (AI, 2010). Amnesty International has noted the disparity between the vigour with which Mexico pursues its argument with the US over the death counts of its own citizens, and its failure to take seriously the deaths of hundreds of migrants each year on Mexican territory, many the result of homicide. AI concludes that 'failure to investigate effectively and fully all migrant deaths and record evidence that a crime has been committed can amount to concealment of a crime' (AI, 2010, no page).

Ironically, estimates of departures with no corresponding arrivals have been used to justify increased levels of border enforcement. In arguing for an expansion of the total enforcement effort, Australian political parties have asserted that it is the dangerousness of the sea journey from Indonesia to Australia and the risk of drowning that informs attempts to either prevent departure altogether or to turn intercepted boats around. They have used deaths at sea to argue their case. In April 2009, an explosion occurred on a vessel carrying asylum seekers from Indonesia to Australia, resulting in the death of three, and a period of time passed during which it was unclear whether there had been any other unknown fatalities from the explosion. The Opposition Immigration Spokesperson claimed the Labor government indirectly caused the deaths because it had rolled back some of the most repressive policies of the previous government:

> You can't slash funds, you can't take your eye off the ball, you can't announce a softer policy and then expect people not to lose their lives through people-smuggling ... Which, of course, is all about cash, nothing to do with getting an individual, a young person, a family safely to Australia. (Maley, 2009)

Visibility of border deaths is primarily about where bodies are counted. Visibility is dependent on local border contexts – in terms of both geographical terrain and social and legal landscapes. For example, most European populations are geographically buffered from witnessing bodies washing up on southern European beaches. In contexts away from physical borders, deaths in detention or during deportation force visibility even when they occur within secure facilities or within the custody of the state or its agents. This is, however, determined by a state's approach to the operations of the border and its willingness to make information known. This means that in order to measure the harms that occur at borders we need to understand the increasing spatial mobility of borders. If we accept that borders are enforced in a range of locations, and not only at the geographical border, then the manner in which we count the deaths of undocumented migrants at these functional borders comes into question. We are compelled to ask: where do we draw the line in counting? The US Government only includes deaths that occur at the geographical border, or in the spaces between the border and large towns or cities. Most non-government agencies (UNITED being a notable exception) take this approach. In relation to the mobile border frontier, the *Arizona Daily Star* produces lists of those who have died on the US–Mexico border, along with maps denoting where undocumented migrants have died. European NGOs have similarly produced maps (see Figure 2.2) that indicate the locations of deaths, and show that they radiate out from border frontiers to include internal locations not ordinarily associated with border crossing.

An examination of the deaths that occur at these various internal borders – in custody, in hospital, by roadsides, in workplaces – high-lights the dangerousness of everyday life for a migrant with extra-legal status. However, the inclusion of these deaths in counting border-related deaths invariably raises concerns about where the border can be considered to finish – once a migration occurs, do borders ever cease being crossed? Is it a fair and reasonable exercise to count border deaths at the various pre-emptive and enforcement border locations maintained by governments, such as those that occur in airports or *en route* to embarkation? As these sites seem to be in a constant state of flux such measurement may be even more unreliable than attempts to count deaths along a geographically fixed border.

If we agree that the difficulties of counting deaths at the spatially mobile border compound the shortcomings of attempted counts at the geographically fixed border, then attempting to count deaths at the *temporally* mobile border is even more difficult and perplexing. Temporally mobile borders have been used as quick political fixes to the 'problem' of arrivals of extra-legal border crossers, who bring governments particularly bad press by raising the spectre of 'borders out of control'. This approach has been used as a way to delimit access to legal redress, both in the immediate and the intermediate term.

However, in order to thoroughly interpret border death counts we also need to acknowledge that the different times at which bodies are found may determine whether or not they are included in a count. There is also a question about the time duration up to the point of dis-covery of a body. In relation to the US–Mexico border there has been debate as to whether human remains found in a border zone years after the death should be included in a count. For example, forensic experts question the level of certainty that can be attributed to the location of death after a certain period of time has elapsed.

Calculating the count: The inevitability of death

The counting of border-related deaths has given rise to estimates of future deaths. Based on numbers of apprehensions and estimates of numbers of unauthorized crossings, these future estimates mean that death becomes not only knowable and quantifiable but also predictable. In this regard, arguments for the alleged inevitability of deaths in illegalized border crossing can be seen to have parallels with arguments surrounding the inevitability of collateral deaths during wartime. For example, Carling (2007) has used trends in migrant interceptions and fatalities to develop a migrant mortality rate that is an expression of the risk of dying linked to attempts at unauthorized border crossing. The key components of the calculation include the number of fatalities, the number of departures, the relevant time period, the number of arrivals, the number of apprehensions and a multiplier for undetected fatalities. Carling (2007) recognizes the importance of understanding the specific dynamics of migration and control along borders, in relation to the broader context of migration, regularization and return, and the somewhat symbiotic relationship between border enforcement and people smuggling. The end point of enhanced measurement is a ramping-up of deterrence measures alongside more efficient management. Such calculation of numbers of deaths, and even calculating the predictable levels of death at a given border or in relation to a particular policy, has predominantly focused on the exactness of numbers, their inclusion and exclusion criteria, and the extent to which the process of counting lends itself to the actuarial logic of risk. However, Carling's argument relies on including a whole range of unknown variables within complicated models which must all be assumed for they are simply unmeasurable.

Discounting death

When counting does not count

Despite all the effort undertaken to quantify and measure, the counting of border-related deaths is too easily discounted. While the intellectual and political wrestle of the acts and omissions of counting border-related deaths is important for the sociological insights it yields and to inform platforms for social, legal and political action, both government and non-government sponsored counts of border-related deaths often end up counting for little. This is not an argument against undertaking such counting, but rather a call to carefully consider why *even when we do manage to count border-related deaths a series of processes discounts them.*

Research on moral exclusion and obedience to authority arising from post-Holocaust scholarship has identified the linked processes of *neutralization* and *dehumanization* (where the humanity of targeted groups is devalued or denied), *authorization* (whereby official pronouncements are accepted uncritically as guides to legitimate action), and *distanciation* (which separates actions from their consequences and meanings) as key elements in the 'normalization' of systematic harm against specified groups (Kelman & Hamilton, 1989). Each of these plays a role in keeping the counting of border-related deaths outside the realm of moral concern.

Distanciation in the case of counting border-related deaths can be both literal (that is, mediated by geographical separation between the sites at which border deaths occur and any potentially concerned observers) and conceptual (due to the obfuscation of chains of responsibility). In relation to literal distanciation, it should be evident from the discussion in Chapter 1 that the deadly effects of border control policies often fail to be recognized because they can be significantly displaced in both space and time, where they are 'hidden even further from the European gaze' (Fekete, 2003, p. 4). Furthermore, the outsourcing of European border control functions to the governments of Morocco, Senegal and Libya, or to private security companies operating immigration detention centres or escort services for deportees, helps to foster conceptual distanciation and hinders accurate counting. Conceptual distanciation may even prevent observers from connecting the tangible reality of counting the bodies lying on the beach with the various policy decisions and human interventions that produced them. This effect is illustrated by the following eyewitness account from the writer Garcia Benito, who is a resident of southern Spain:

> Dead people appear, who haven't been killed by anybody. Who truly kills them? The dinghy-captain, another wretched person who undertakes the journey as well? The law? Rather, it seems like a horror story in which the culprit fails to appear. They say the local people are showing solidarity, when what they are doing is cleaning up the beaches of dead people. The complaints that are voiced never receive any answer. (Benito, 2003)

These consequences are much less visible to Europeans living away from the Mediterranean coast, whose governments point to reduced numbers of asylum applications as proof of the 'success' of their non-arrival policies. The events at Christmas Island just prior to Christmas 2010 briefly became the focus of outrage and grief by leaders and ordinary

Australians alike, since the deaths of at least 48 Afghan and Iraqi asylum seekers, many of them women and children, were witnessed in horrific detail as their vessel broke up in rough seas on the island's rocky shore. The normally hidden processes of border control became visible in the most shocking way as television cameras captured images of terror-stricken passengers and local people desperately trying to mount a make-shift rescue. Still, the complex chain of policies that contributed to the risks and dangers faced by these people was not so visible, and voices calling for deeper explanations were soon drowned out by the Opposition's demands for the government to return to Opposition policies in order to 'stop the boats'.

Onshore deaths that occur in detention or directly at the hands of border officials also have some potential to elicit public outrage, but never result in the serious examination of border control objectives or the systemic chains of cause and effect that produce fatalities. Those emblematic cases of border-related deaths that become individually visible and 'counted' above the mass of counting (or not counting) often foster managerialist rather than transformative outcomes. For example, the inquiry into Joy Gardner's death in 1993 at the hands of UK police and immigration officials, after her hands and mouth were bound with metres of tape, led to recommendations to improve training and tighten controls on the restraint techniques used, rather than a fundamental questioning of the policy of forced removals. Similarly, repeated spectacles of bound and struggling deportees escorted onto commercial flights, which have elicited both sympathetic and self-interested reactions from other passengers, have led to the increased use of private charter flights to hide the violent practices from view, rather than an abandonment of forced removal policies.

Whose death is being counted also qualitatively alters the meaning of the numbers of border-related deaths. The acceptance of overt or structural violence, even where counts occur, may be more likely if there is a psychological distance between subject and observer, which results in the *neutralization* of the victims. Opotow (1990, p. 2) observes that moral exclusion arises where social actors 'perceive others as psychologically distant, lack constructive moral obligations toward others, view others as expendable and undeserving, and deny others' rights, dignity and autonomy'. In compiling its data on border-related deaths, the IRR relied primarily on press reports, which have the potential to bring border fatalities to the notice of wider populations. However, Athwal & Bourne noted that 'these deaths of un-named, un-British, un-white men are not news' (Athwal & Bourne, 2007, p. 107). It is as if asylum seekers are invisible, or exist somehow in a perpetual state of 'unknowability' (Malloch & Stanley, 2005). The setting of removal targets is an example of a border control policy that has the capacity to neutralize the humanity of those it targets.

Whereas *neutralization* can be equated to the presence of a count but the psychological absence of a victim, whereby those who are the object of harm are simply beneath notice, *dehumanization* represents a more active process of exclusion, effected through persistent derogatory labelling. Kelman and Hamilton (1989) note that dehumanization produces exclusion, not only from a particular moral community, but also from all bonds of human empathy and protection. Stripped of their humanity, excluded groups do not necessarily disappear from view but may become unrecognizable as bearers of human rights. This effect in relation to asylum seekers is suggested in the following passage from Malloch and Stanley (2005, p. 54):

> In the UK, public concerns have been heightened by media coverage that portrays those seeking asylum as a problematic, homogenous group. Media coverage of the numbers of foreign nationals entering the country illegally is juxtaposed with suppositions of the burden 'they' will undoubtedly incur on 'our' health and welfare services. Such representations, meted out to the public on a daily basis, suggest that few of those seeking asylum are 'genuine', while the broader influx of 'claimants' have the potential to pose a very real risk to liberal democratic states.

In Australia, asylum seekers have been subject to demonizing representations in the media that are prefaced on the representation of those who arrive without visas by boat as 'illegal' (Pickering, 2001, 2005). Through a systematic discourse analysis, Pickering (2005) has identified a 'mundane process of criminalisation', effected primarily through media reporting and sometimes supported by legal processes, which portrays asylum seekers as racialized and/or diseased deviants who pose a threat to the Australian state. These dehumanizing processes have at times been reinforced by strategies designed to prevent media reporting which might *rehumanize* asylum seekers, such as the enforcement of exclusion zones around unauthorized boat arrivals (Watson, 2009). According to Khosravi, the vulnerability of illegalized travellers is best demonstrated by their 'animalization':

> The terminology in this field is full of names of animals designating human smugglers and their clients; coyote for the human smugglers and *pollos* (chickens) for Mexican border crossers (Donnan & Wilson

1999: 135); *shetou* (snakehead) for Chinese human smugglers and *renshe* (human snakes) for smuggled Chinese (Chin 1999: 187). Iranians usually use the term *gosfand* (sheep) or *dar poste gosfand* (in the skin of sheep) to refer to 'illegal' border crossers. Dehumanised and represented in terms of chicken and sheep – two animals traditionally sacrificed in rituals – the border transgressors are sacrificial creatures for the border ritual. (2010, p. 27)

Use of the terms 'hunting' and 'dog wagons' by Minutemen vigilantes on the US–Mexican border also demonstrates this form of dehumanization (Michalowski, 2007, p. 69). The very act of labelling migrants and asylum seekers as 'illegal' has proven to be a powerful form of dehumanization in itself, and has militated against the purpose of counting their deaths. Fan (2008, p. 727) describes the 'illegal' or 'sacrificial' migrant as 'literally banned from the symbolic order of law's promise of benefits, security and succor, rights and entitlements'. The Transatlantic Trends survey published in 2008 also reveals a sharp bifurcation in European opinions about legal and illegal immigration. While 60–70 per cent of respondents approved of more open immigration policies, around 80 per cent said they supported tough measures against illegal immigration (Transatlantic Trends, 2008). It would seem that 'illegal immigrants', or simply 'illegals', are easily relegated to a category wholly defined by their unlawful status, where they are liable to be designated as threatening and undeserving. This is equally so in the case of counting – the figures are not necessarily convincing or compelling, for they can 'inaccurately' count people who have no right to be counted. To return to Butler's terminology discussed in Chapter 1, their lives may become 'ungrievable' (2010).

The processes of moral exclusion described above often operate as a precondition for the *authorization* of officially sanctioned harm. Even where counts of border-related deaths are undertaken, the explanatory frameworks that define collateral damage or unintended consequences undermine the aim of recording the harm of death. Opotow (1990, p. 4) notes that 'adverse social circumstances create the conditions necessary for ordinary people to dehumanize, harm, and act with incredible cruelty toward others'. The destabilizing conditions of globalization and the concomitant preoccupation with uncertainty and risk could therefore be seen to create suitably adverse conditions for the authorization of harm against border crossers. Moreover, systemic harm is often perpetrated under the guise of a 'transcendent mission, which supersedes the usual moral standards and automatically justifies whatever human costs it may necessarily or inadvertently entail' (Kelman & Hamilton, 1989, p. 336). In the context of border control, Dauvergne (2008, p. 99) has described how post-September 11 conditions have shifted border security towards the 'unquestionable plane of exceptional security measures' to such an extent that she finds her Canadian audiences 'fact resistant' to messages that are at odds with the official discourse of unmitigated threat. Fan (2008) attributes a readiness to accept extreme forms of legally sanctioned exclusion to 'fetishism' about law, in which law is interpreted as an unassailable force for justice, regardless of its content. Extreme nationalist ideologies are particularly likely to elevate border control to the level of a transcendent mission. An extraordinary readiness to ignore the human costs in pursuit of border control is clearly evident in the following statement made by Northern League politician Umberto Bossi when he was a minister in the former Berlusconi government:

> Either our ships will tackle the illegal immigrants' vessels and take onboard only women and children, or else we write down in black and white that force will be used, and that is the way I want it. After the second or third warning, boom … the cannon roars. The cannon that blows everyone out of the water. Otherwise the business will never end. (cited in Fekete, 2003, p. 5)

On other occasions, the authoritative messages may be more measured, but their apparent reasonableness within the context of the generally accepted right to protect borders further justifies their exclusionary rhetoric. Announcing yet another ratcheting up of internal border controls in the UK in 2007, the British Home Secretary John Reid cast illegal workers as an unmitigated threat to social harmony, and the government as therefore compelled to act in response to serious public concern:

> the fact that many immigrants, at the end of their journey, end up in shadowy jobs in the grey economy undermines the terms and working conditions of British workers. That's not fair. It chips away at the social fabric of our country. Resentment of it breeds discontent and racism … The public want people to play by the rules, and they don't like people who don't. (Home Office, 2007)

Increasing the salience of victims, both as human beings and as targets of authorized harm, has often been suggested as an antidote to these exclusionary processes. This has led NGOs to engage in strategies of 'rehumanizing' those who die at Europe's borders. An item on the

UNITED website that explains the organization's campaign against border deaths asserts: 'These deaths are not isolated incidents … We must make sure that all these deaths are known and mourned' (UNITED, 2007). Mexico's National Commission of Human Rights issued a report in 2007 entitled *Todos Saben, Nadie Sabe* ('All Know, No-One Knows') which was intended not so much to report the extent of border-related deaths, but to highlight the widespread indifference to this knowledge (Jimenez, 2009). In the mainstream media, multiple fatalities do have the potential to attract shocked, sometimes sympathetic media coverage. Webber (2004, p. 134) notes that the asphyxiation of 58 Chinese asylum seekers during a clandestine crossing of the English Channel, and the drowning of 18 Chinese cockle pickers, attracted 'blanket coverage' in the British press. Yet she also observes that these media stories 'focused on the distress of those who had found the bodies and on the criminality of those who had brought them, rather than attempting to understand the issues thrown up by the deaths' (Webber, 2004, p. 134). A very similar pattern of reporting was apparent in relation to the Christmas Island shipwreck tragedy. The initial shock and sympathy at the events were quickly replaced by report after concerned report describing the trauma visited on the Christmas Island community. Moreover, while some reportage continued of the suffering of the bereaved relatives, some of them already themselves detained on Christmas Island, uninjured survivors of the wreckage quietly languished in the detention centre with no allowances made to the strict policy of mandatory detention.

The distinction between grievable and ungrievable deaths was brought into sharp relief when human body parts were washed ashore in Dubrovnik in 2008, raising fears that they belonged to missing Australian backpacker Britt Lapthorne. Early reports in the Australian press quoted Croatian police as saying the remains were unlikely to be those of the young traveller, and explaining that it was 'not unusual' to find the bodies of asylum seekers along that part of the coast (Alberici, 2008). Sadly for Britt Lapthorne's family, the remains were later confirmed to be those of the missing woman. Yet the contrast between the reactions to the named (and therefore grievable) and the anonymous (and seemingly ungrievable) deaths is striking.

Denying border deaths

The work of Stanley Cohen (2001) on the 'sociology of denial' provides further insight into how it can be possible for governments and populations to know, and yet at the same time *not* to know, about border-related deaths. Cohen observes that governments, faced with reports of atrocities or suffering, and allegations of state responsibility for them, often resort to some form of denial. Strategies of denial include: *literal* denial – claiming that the reported events simply did not happen; *inter-pretive* denial – acknowledging the events but seeking an interpretation that absolves authorities of blame; and/or *implicatory* denial – down-playing the significance of the reported events or subordinating them to higher imperatives. Elements of each of these strategies are likely to coexist, even when they are seemingly contradictory. Collectively they constitute what Cohen calls a 'deep structure' that is 'ideological' rather than 'logical'. The subversion of logic by belief makes it possible, he argues, to simultaneously 'know-and-yet-not-know' about atrocities and human suffering. This phenomenon represents a significant challenge to the project of counting border-related deaths.

According to Cohen, *literal* denial in authoritarian regimes is effected through open suppression of information. Democratic regimes with an interest in appearing to adhere to human rights norms may use less direct methods, such as attacking the credibility of the observer. Blanchard et al. (2008) report that Italian authorities refused to believe the accounts of survivors of a shipwreck that claimed the lives of nearly 300 people in 1996 off the southern-most tip of Sicily, until the wreck was discovered five years later. A second example cited by Blanchard, Clochard and Rodier concerns the deaths of sub-Saharan Africans who clashed with Spanish and Moroccan armed forces while trying to scale the border fences surrounding Ceuta and Melilla. Despite images of the clashes being televised around the world, authorities have refused to release the names of the dead, and even estimates of the numbers remain imprecise, ranging from 14 to 21. Similar accusations have been made by the SIEV X campaigning group that the names of some of the dead have been withheld by the AFP. Although Cohen argues that liberal demo-cracies rarely engage in literal denial, a different picture emerges in relation to non-citizens, especially those who are victims of what the UN High Commissioner for Refugees has described as 'lawless areas, where human life has no value' (cited in Blanchard et al., 2008, p. 32).

Moreover, in the case of border control, where the witnesses may have illegal immigration status, there is a powerful option available to governments to suppress inconvenient information by removing the observers themselves. In the case of the alleged sinking of a dinghy in April 2008 by the Moroccan navy, the Moroccan NGO Association for Families of Victims of Migration claimed that survivors were expelled to the remote desert location of Ouja to prevent them from giving evidence (Carling, 2007). Survivors of an incident in which Mexican police were said to have shot at a vehicle carrying 45 illegalized migrants, killing three, were reportedly 'repatriated' to Central America within days to prevent them from participating in a criminal investigation (AI, 2010). Similar accusations of the rapid removal of potential witnesses have been levelled at the British Government in relation to the fire at the Yarl's Wood Immigration Removal Centre in 2001 (Webber, 2004) and other serious disturbances in immigration detention centres, although none of these incidents involved fatalities. Furthermore, according to Fekete (2009b), not one of the 12 deaths that occurred during deportation from Europe documented by the IRR since 1993 has resulted in a successful criminal prosecution. The fact that no proactive effort has been made by the EU or its member states, or by the Australian Government, to monitor border deaths systematically, or to publicly account for the fatalities, suggests that democratic governments can operate under conditions of far weaker public accountability in relation to their treatment of those outside their sphere of protection than would be possible in relation to their own citizens.

Cohen considers *interpretive* denial to be more common than literal denial in the case of liberal democracies confronted by accusations of human rights abuses. According to Cohen, interpretive denial occurs where raw facts are admitted, but the interpretation adopted by complainants is rejected in favour of terminology that is 'less pejorative' to governments. Interpretive denial is fundamentally a *rhetorical* strategy. There is considerable evidence of interpretive denial in the discourse surrounding border deaths and border control more broadly. For example, the international obligation of *non-refoulement* creates an incentive for democratic governments to mask the coercive nature of forced removal and the degree of resistance encountered. The bureaucratic language of 'removal targets' deliberately sanitizes the reality of coerced removal. The violence of the process is described in more honest terms here by a British immigration officer who has seen the practice first-hand: 'people struggle to go sometimes, you know, and they're tied up and handcuffed and you think, well what happens to these people when they get back to their countries?' (Weber & Gelsthorpe, 2000, p. 100). Similar arguments have been made about official masking of the punitive effects of detention and other enforcement measures through the use of the term 'administrative':

> You might say I am cheating, that this is not crime and punishment but administrative detention. But when people are subjected to routine fingerprinting, when they are locked up, when they are restrained

by body belts and leg shackles and thirteen feet of tape, or forcibly injected with sedatives to keep them quiet as they are bundled onto aircraft, it seems reasonable to ask: what have they done? The answer is that they have tried to come to western Europe, to seek asylum, or to live here with their families, or to work here. And the whole panoply of modern policing, *with its associated rhetoric*, is applied against them. (Webber, 1996, emphasis added)

Another rhetorical strategy noted by UNITED is the avoidance of the term 'deportation' by governments of continental Europe, where the word still evokes powerful memories of the deliberate transportation of excluded populations during the Holocaust with the intention of causing their deaths.

When media talk about 'expulsion orders' and 'repatriations', they make a wide use of euphemism. When it comes to countries where human rights are daily violated, where life is not respected, where minorities are persecuted, countries in war or famine, repatriation becomes a euphemism for deportation. (UNITED, 2008)

Equally, deliberate policies of destitution, described in firm yet euphemistic terms by the British Home Secretary as intended to make life 'uncomfortable and constrained' for asylum seekers, are given a far more 'pejorative' interpretation by critical commentators. Fekete (2009b) describes the abject conditions faced by rejected asylum seekers not merely as 'uncomfortable', but as 'designed to break their will and resolve', leading increasing numbers to make so-called voluntary departures to their countries of origin.

Cohen's final category, of *implicatory* denial, applies where governments actively seek to justify harmful actions, or at least deny moral responsibility for them. Events may be attributed to natural forces beyond human control, or responsibility may be displaced onto non-state actors, the victims themselves or, increasingly, onto those who support them (Fekete, 2009a). In relation to border deaths, it might be admitted that people did perish *en route* or die in custody, but the events can be easily construed as tragic accidents or attributed to the wrong-doing of deviant others such as people smugglers or private security companies. Jamieson and McEvoy (2005) refer to this process as a technique of 'othering', which enables states to obfuscate their responsibility. Citing Cohen, they claim that 'othering strategies have been designed to put political distance between the state and more obvious or heinous abuses, to give space to the possibility of plausible deniability' (Jamieson & McEvoy, 2005, p. 519). The media focus on the responsibility of people smugglers for the asphyxiation of the 58 Chinese asylum seekers at the British port of Dover mentioned earlier is a case in point. In the US, it has also been noted by Anderson that 'pointing the fingers solely at the coyotes and gangs is convenient', although the responsibility, he claims, is a 'shared one' arising from the failure of governments to provide legal avenues for travel (Anderson, S., 2010, p. 9). Exemplary here is the death in 2003 of 19 immigrants, including a five-year-old child, trapped without air inside a truck in Texas, which (Anderson S., 2010, p. 6) argues 'sparked consciences but no change in policies'. Not to be outdone, the Australian Government has adopted the phrase 'evil people smugglers' as something of a mantra in any discussion of border control. In the wake of the 2010 Christmas Island tragedy, Prime Minister Julia Gillard, while showing sympathy for the victims, repeatedly referred to the doomed vessel as a 'people smuggler vessel' and vowed to 'take out of the hands of people smugglers the very evil product that they sell' (*Age*, 2010a). This strategy was set in train when the incoming Labor government sought to distance itself from what it described as the Howard government's punitive policies, declaring that it 'rejected the notion that dehumanising and punishing unauthorised arrivals with long-term detention is an effective or civilised response' (Bowen, 2008). People smugglers then became a substitute target for demonization, and numbers in long-term detention have soared since. Michalowski (2007, p. 62) notes that the 'most common narratives in the United States about migrant deaths typically frame them, at best, as the unfortunate consequences of individual decisions to risk hazardous journeys, or at worst, as appropriate punishments for breaking US immigration law'. The ready attribution of blame to the victims is also apparent in the following statement from eminent political theorist David Miller, who recounts here his personal response to the fatal shootings of sub-Saharan migrants in Melilla mentioned earlier:

> I find my sympathy for the young African men who are trying to cross the fence tempered by a kind of indignation. Surely, they must understand that this is not the way to get into Europe. What clearer indication could there be of the proposition that illegal immigrants are not welcome than a double fence up to six metres tall with rolls of razor wire along the top? Do they think they have some kind of natural right to enter Spain in defiance of the laws that apply to

everyone else who might like to move there? (cited in Cabrera, 2009, p. 112)

While it is true that illegalized travellers may defy efforts to pre-empt their arrival or expel them, be treated with cruelty and indifference by unscrupulous facilitators, take additional risks to invite rescue, and/or take their own lives, the role of border policies in creating conditions that lead to avoidable deaths remains wholly unacknowledged in purely individualized accounts. The capacity of governments and populations to shift blame and responsibility for border deaths entirely onto the victims of restrictive border controls and other third parties follows from the processes discussed earlier, particularly *distanciation*, which obscures the links between events and their underlying causes. Yet there may also be a powerful motivation to allow this separation to stand. As Butler (2004, p. 5) has argued in relation to the 'War on Terror', '[i]solating individuals absolves us of the necessity of coming up with a broader explanation of events'. Moreover, Jamieson and McEvoy (2005) claim that the post-September 11 security environment has emboldened liberal democracies to violate human rights more brazenly, often without perceiving the need to resort to obfuscation strategies. Preferred frameworks for understanding disturbing events, whether terrorist violence or the violent effects of border controls, serve to preclude certain questions and historical inquiries and limit the starting point for explanatory narratives. Thus, events come to be apprehended from the moment of their occurrence, not as the outcome of a long chain of causation. Counting bodies provides a starting point, but does nothing to illuminate the determinants of these fatal journeys towards, and encounters with, the border.

Conclusion

This chapter has identified a number of ways in which border-related deaths may be normalized by populations and denied or obscured by governments. This is an important step in understanding the systemic processes that prevent these deaths from being recognized as large-scale human rights abuses that can be linked to the border protection policies consciously adopted by states of the Global North. Counting deaths has been identified as an important 'truth recovery process' (Jamieson & McEvoy, 2005, p. 521). This process has the potential to transform the 'war on migrants from the metaphorical level to a context where consequences must be documented' (Blanchard et al., 2008,

p. 33). Still, Cohen argues, '[t]he empirical problem is not to uncover yet more evidence of denial, but to discover the conditions under which information is acknowledged and acted upon' (Cohen, 2001, p. 249). Although Cohen attributes denial to the 'subversion of logic by belief', privileging logic may not be all that is needed to make the deaths of illegalized border crossers 'count'. Their deaths must not only be knowable through logical and systematic processes of counting and the construction of explanatory narratives. We contend that they must also be made grievable. It is to that complex and essentially human question that we now turn.

3
Accounting for Deaths at the Border

[W]ho counts as living and who does not, how are we to count the war dead? If a war brings with it crimes of war, targeted and collateral destruction of populations, how do such populations count when the rationale for the destruction is that they do not count at all? The reporting of the number of war dead, including civilian losses, can be one of the operations of war waging, a discursive means through which war is built, and one way in which we are inscripted into the war effort. Numbers, especially the number of war dead, circulate not only as representations of war, but as part of the apparatus of war waging. Numbers are a way of framing the losses of war, but this does not mean that we know whether, when, or how the numbers count. We may know how to count, or we may well rely on humanitarian or human rights organizations to count well, but that is not the same as figuring out how and whether a life counts. (Butler, 2010, p. xx)

[T]he crude and brutal arithmetic of migrant death has too often been seen by policy makers and the media as no more than a side effect of border control, without any recognition that each missing or dead migrant is an individual with rights and family relationships. (Grant, 2011a, p. 69)

We argued in the previous chapter that the process of counting border-related deaths is an inherently political act which makes (implicit or explicit) political claims about the border that align most closely with established accounts of border enforcement. This chapter considers the possibilities of developing a richer picture of death at the border to counter predominant managerialist methods of counting death, one that may not be easily co-opted by those invested in promoting the conditions that allow such deaths. Fundamentally, this chapter seeks to identify counter-narratives of death at the border, and explore the extent to which they might *account* for deaths (and life). We argue that many of the key planks that underpin the process of accounting for deaths (including processes of naming, grieving and memorializing) do not necessarily challenge official knowledge production of the nature, causes and consequences of deaths at the border; however, they do lead to the beginnings of powerful counter-narratives of border deaths.

Accounting for deaths at the border is the first step towards identifying chains of accountability. While it does not deny the agency of those who risk their lives to cross borders, this approach does acknowledge the role played by governments and their agents in shaping this global matrix of risks. From the standpoint of a weak but developing global human rights framework we will consider the obligations that governments owe to those who are not their citizens or lawful residents, and what claims can reasonably be made by those who seek to cross the global frontier in the face of determined efforts to keep them out.

Using the continuum model of state crime developed by Kauzlarich et al. (2003), we consider whether the task of accounting for border-related deaths can be assisted by classifying border protection practices adopted by governments of the Global North as either implicit or explicit acts of omission, or implicit or explicit acts of commission.

Accounting for the body

Forensic anthropologists and scientists offer ever more sophisticated techniques and approaches for identifying and recording the bodies recovered proximate to borders. This has most notably been applied on the US–Mexico border. In a recent special issue of the *Journal of Forensic Science*, an accurate account of the cause of death and process of dying constituted an *accounting* for deaths that occur on the border. The guest editors defined their work in pragmatic terms, and by its attention to objective detail:

> The US Government appears incapable of closing our border with Mexico, whatever the reason. As long as this is true, people will continue to die crossing it. It is our duty as forensic scientists to invest-

igate these deaths as competently as possible. (Anderson & Parks, 2008, p. 6)

As noted in the previous chapter, if the border cannot be hermetically sealed, then the above approach suggests that the least we can do is offer precise and detailed accounts of the deaths that occur in the crossings. Yet this 'accounting' does not raise questions about the causes that lie beyond the border, or their impacts. The border is seen as fixed and stable, and any rationale for this remains undisturbed. This reasoning is but one of three commonly offered as to why the identification of a body is important: 1) it enables a name to be given to an otherwise unknown person; 2) it enables family closure/grief or alternatively hope for a survivor's relative; and 3) it improves the knowledge base for understanding who dies from what and where. As Grant (2011a, forthcoming, p. 60) has noted, 'loss or abandonment of identity is a common characteristic of irregular travel'.

By contrast, Coalición de Derechos Humanos uses the act of identifying bodies on the US–Mexico border as a means of bearing witness to these deaths. The recording of this information is thus a political act of solidarity:

> In an effort to honor every life that has been lost on our borders, Coalición de Derechos Humanos records the number of bodies that are recovered on our border. With the cooperation of Arizona county officials, as well as the Consular offices of México, Guatemala, El Salvador, Honduras, and Brazil, and the Binational Migration Institute, we are attempting to put names to our migrant sisters and brothers, and bear witness to the deaths of those unknown, of whom there are hundreds buried in our communities. (Coalición de Derechos Humanos, 2007)

In this regard, locating and identifying bodies, or indeed noting the absence of bodies as a result of drowning, exposure or other means that result in the total loss or disintegration of human remains, has been an important part of developing a counter-narrative of the loss of life at the border. The identification and retrieval of a body gives physical form to a person who then requires a name, and through an account of their death an account of their life can then be produced. In the wake of the SIEV X disaster in Australia, Marg Hutton (2002) argued:

> As long as these victims remain nameless it is easy to discount this huge tragedy that took place on our doorstep a year ago. 146

children, 142 women, 65 men – their bodies were never recovered from the ocean; they were never buried. Every single number represents a person. We need to know their names.

Hutton's plea to the Australian Government came in response to its decision to suppress the names of those of whom it had evidence of being on board the SIEV X. Perera (2006) describes the namelessness of the bodies as a reflection and result of contemporary political violence. Remaining nameless renders the dead unnamed collateral damage.

It has been argued that, without names, refugees become faceless 'others', part of the commonly represented 'sea of humanity'. Refugees are often photographed without name or specific marker, and as Malkki observes they stop being specific persons and become pure victims in general: 'universal man, universal woman, universal child and, taken together, universal family' (1996, p. 378). Their helplessness is read through the anonymity of their massing or easily consumable caricatures of starvation or deprivation waiting to be acted upon (Harrell-Bond, 1985); and being nameless is central to this. The largely unquestioned iconography of refugees – a refugee aesthetic of the passive and the pitiable (Campbell, 2007) – is often a female or a child, or both, as in the case of Steven McCurry's portrait of 'the Afghan Girl' which appeared on the cover of *National Geographic* in 1985. The girl remained nameless until 17 years later when the photographer found her, and her name: Sharbat Gula. She refused to have anything to do with the ongoing use of her image, which can now be found on numerous websites of famous and even iconic portraits. In contrast, representations of refugees within criminology tend to be universalizing, such that the refugee is positioned as either deviant or criminal (Pickering, 2001); in some contexts depictions of victimhood are replaced by nameless, faceless depictions of the deviance of unauthorized arrival. Either way, the visual representation of refugees has become a 'singularly translatable and mobile mode of knowledge about them'. Malkki (1996) provocatively suggests that a 'vigorous, transnational and largely philanthropic traffic in visual images has emerged in the second part of the twentieth century', and argues that images of refugees often function to establish the bare, raw nature of refugee life. They also often fail to communicate the true histories of individuals, which can bridge the gap in understanding between the consumer of the image and the person depicted, or fail to move beyond depicting a general sense of humanity rather than the specific details of a life. At the same time, the disinterest of the international community in large-scale refugee situations has been attributed to the absence of photographic witness, such as in the case of Darfur where news of this distant place remained unknown and unimaginable without visual devices (Campbell, 2007). In terms of its representation of life and death, photography and associated technology is increasingly regarded as no less than a form of geopolitics (Campbell, 2007).

The need to identify the names of the dead links to the desire to 'give a face' to suffering, such as the faces of the three children printed on the front page of *The Sydney Morning Herald* following the sinking of the SIEV X (and subsequently reprinted in many other newspapers and news services). This may have served to quench the thirst of a media constantly in search of a visual, but also as a way to engender particular kinds of responses: to honour the memory of the children who died and to compel a common and simplified response – one of horror, indignation and empathy. Those marginally concerned with the pernicious effects of border control might thus be stung into action by making the deaths real – through the naming of bodies, and naming the faces of dead children, women and men. Where words failed to adequately convey the enormity of the deaths of SIEV X passengers, perhaps these photographs of the three children were able to communicate some account of the lives lost that did not rely on highly politicized public conversation and/or the rationalization of border protection. Yet the nature of these photographs, removed as they were from the images of their dead bodies, reflects the distance between the average Australian consumer of the photographs and the children's deaths, which occurred unseen by any camera thousands of kilometers off the Australian coast, albeit within the Australian surveillance zone. In bringing the reader closer to the children who died, the photographs simultaneously kept the reader at a distance from the reality of their deaths.

In this study we felt that the absence of any systematically recorded details of those who have died while attempting to avoid the various Australian border control practices meant that we lacked important information about the nature and scale of life lost – information required to name those who have died. In short, we needed to attempt a count in order to produce the account of death at the border presented in the second part of the book. A ledger of names may also invoke a process of adding up the loss of life – making possible some reconciliation of cause and effect.

Yet the existence of an individual's body, and their name, is not the whole story. Coronial inquiries into the causes of death are part of the legal process undertaken to identify such causes, which includes gathering findings regarding responsibility and making recommendations for prosecution. This process depends on the availability of the dead body to be subject to the allegedly objective process of forensic pathology. However, as Scott-Bray has argued, there is significant dissonance between the '(medico) legal discourse and remembering, or memorializing, the dead in a culture' (2006, p. 42). In arguing that there is ambivalence around representing the dead, she points to the highly subjective aspects of the accounts of death offered by forensic pathology. Scott-Bray concludes that managing death raises all kinds of difficulties that are only partially resolvable by the law. For those who have died on the Australian mainland, the coronial inquest has remained the official mechanism for managing death and naming not only the person, but also the circumstances of their death.

The process of naming a body is arguably a requisite component of what Butler describes as 'apprehending a life as precarious', although such apprehension does not in turn guarantee that individual lives are then afforded protection, rights or entitlements. She argues:

> [I]f we are to make broader social and political claims about rights of protection and entitlements to persistence and flourishing then we will first need to be supported by a new bodily ontology, one that implies the rethinking of precariousness, vulnerability, injuribility, interdependency, exposure, bodily persistence, desire, work and the claims of language and social belonging. (2010, p. 2)

For lives to be apprehended, Butler argues, they need to be recognized as belonging to all persons *as* persons. How do some persons become recognized as subjects while others do not? In Butler's terms, how do we shift this process to produce 'radically democratic results'? She argues that this change necessitates that we first understand *apprehension* as a mode of knowing that is 'not yet recognition', and as *intelligibility* that is constituted through the information we are able to communicate. Butler's argument is that a life needs to be intelligible *as a life* if it is to become recognizable (2010, pp. 6–7). Retrieving, naming and seeing (via photographs) the bodies of those who die form part but not all of the process of rendering knowable, recognizable subjects.

In the Australian context we rarely see pictures of the bodies of asylum seekers. Deaths occurring at sea remain largely invisible. Yet there are exceptions. When SIEV 221 broke up on the rocks off Christmas Island, images from mobile phones and portable recording devices were relayed worldwide showing refugees clinging to the boat as it was destroyed. These recordings show waves rolling in and people clinging to debris, and the next wave leaving only the debris, as the people came adrift and presumably drowned. On the US–Mexico border images of bodies discovered are more common than in Australia. In Europe, as we have argued earlier, photographs of dead bodies washed up on beaches represent complex portraits of distanciation which is effected through conceptual, rather than geographical, distance. Exemplary here is the well-circulated image known as The Indifference of the West, taken by Spanish photographer Javier Bauluz at Tarifa in the south of Spain. The image shows a couple relaxing under a beach umbrella, seemingly oblivious to or disinterested in the lifeless body of an illegalized traveller washed up a little further down the beach.[1] An image taken some time later shows the same couple playing beach tennis in the background as Spanish police carry the body away in a coffin.[2] The photographs clearly depict indifference, and in doing so show the ease with which normal life can continue in the presence of actual dead bodies.

Photographs – and the processes of naming they invite – may move us, in an emotional or empathetic sense, but they do not demand an interpretation (see Sontag, 2003; Butler, 2010). The photographs of named dead people on our borders are a case in point. While they make significant contributions to our knowing and recognizing harm, such images have not compelled questions regarding responsibility or accountability. Nor does the retrieval and naming of bodies necessitate protection, entitlement or rights. Knowable bodies, named and seen bodies, build pictures of the lives, the subjects, the people who have died.

Accounting for the life: Bearing witness, making memorial

Obviously the survivors of this incident are traumatised and they're receiving all the care and support we can provide. An imam met with survivors yesterday and arrangements are being made to hold a memorial service that is likely to be on the 19th or 20th of December. A memorial service or services and they [sic] will be for the purpose of recognising the loss of life and allowing people to grieve.

Obviously we are very mindful as well of the needs of the people of Christmas Island at this difficult time. Counselling services have been offered to Christmas Island residents who participated in the rescue or witnessed the incident. A shopfront has been established on Christmas Island with professional counsellors to provide immediate assistance to community members who feel they need that assistance. (Gillard, 2010)

Behind the security wire at one of Christmas Island's detention centres, survivors of last week's boat disaster have held a memorial service for those who died. (Eastley, 2010)

In the wake of the Christmas Island shipwreck, common to the public statements of politicians and commentators alike were expressions of grief at the tragedy. The dramatic image of the boat being smashed on the craggy rocks of Christmas Island with passengers adrift in the raging sea for a fleeting moment disciplined a united official response: to recognize the loss of life. The shipwrecked SIEV 221 was witnessed from land. There was a swift recognition of the loss of life and a businesslike approach to the need to memorialize.

The above quotations show memorial being used as a salve by powerful actors to locate the loss of life as a tragedy, to act as a remembrance of life rather than a consideration of the circumstances of death. In the quotation above from Prime Minister Gillard, grief is constituted through a public statement of support for those who grieve – namely those who survived and those who witnessed the deaths first-hand. Support is the appropriate official gesture for those who grieve, and is activated through the outsourcing of counsel to an unnamed imam. Yet the Prime Minister herself does not grieve; her acts do not remember. Rather, recognition, grief and mourning for lives lost are proximate to the incident: borne by the survivors and the local residents. The survivors are kept proximate for they are in immigration detention on Christmas Island, close by the scene of the shipwreck. Their memorial is organized for them, and it is formal, religious, and carried out soon after the event. Commercial type arrangements for the provision of counselling are made for the comfort of locals who experienced trauma as a result of their attempts to aid the rescue, and their witness of death and survival. The memorial is official, swift and does not involve the nation, its leaders or its people. It is unseen and leaves no mark on the physical landscape. Arguably such a memorial is more about going through the motions of forgetting, and moving on.

Ware argues that the memorial can be understood as an expression of positive attitudes whereas what has become known as the 'anti-memorial' affirms and celebrates a more 'inclusive and potentially subversive range of states within the diverse operations of memory' (2008, p. 62). Her work points to the fluidity of memory and memorials, and how the latter can embrace the contradictions and complexities of memory. She draws on Young's interpretation of anti-memorials – a category in which memorials for deaths at the border would easily fit – as aiming not to console but to provoke, not to remain fixed but to change and demand interaction. Most of all they 'invite their own violation and not to accept graciously the burden of memory but to drop it at the public's feet' (in Ware, 2008, p. 62). In this sense, anti-memorials (or popular commemorative practices) can contribute to social change and may be viewed as a form of political activism, as well as a vehicle for the expression of grief. For the purposes of this book, their potential to engender what Khalili (2005) calls counter-hegemonic commemorative practices is of particular importance.

Counter-hegemonic commemorative practices can incorporate competing political narratives about events and histories. Histories of illegalized travellers are full of narratives of pain and suffering connected to privileged discourses of rights and refugee protection above other migrants, while also speaking of common histories of suffering (Khalili, 2005). Because of the vast maritime and desert spaces, the lack of commemorative signs or plaques for those who die on the border militates against commemorative narratives in context (Khalili, 2005). Therefore, sites need to be appropriated, as in the case of the memorial gathering detailed by Michalowski on the US–Mexico border:

CANDLES GUTTERED IN THE BREEZE. IN THE BACKGROUND, PALE RIBBONS DRAPED the aging adobe walls of El Tiradito, a small folk shrine in Tucson's historic barrio district. As the setting sun painted March storm clouds red and orange, 15 people formed a semicircle facing the shrine, each holding a small sheet of white paper. Most of the faces were Anglo; a few were Latino or Indian.

After a brief invocation, a woman read the name written on the paper in her hands. As her voice faded, the group responded in unison with the word '*presente*' ('I am here'). One by one, those gathered read the name on the paper they held, sometimes fluidly, sometimes stumbling over an unfamiliar Mexican or Indian pronunciation, or sometimes simply saying *desconocida* or *desconocido* – indicating an unidentified woman or man. Each reading was followed by a collective *presente*. As names accumulated on the evening breeze, some in the group wept softly. After all the names were read, the readers approached the shrine's crumbling walls and pinned what was now their sanctified piece of paper to one of the ribbons.

This ritual was repeated throughout the 2006 Lenten season. By Easter, the ribbons draping El Tiradito held over 800 names of those who where known to have died in recent years attempting to cross the desert that separates the US–Mexico boundary from first-stop cities like Tucson and Phoenix. (2007, p. 62)

Sharing the grief of survivors and loved ones of the dead and honouring the dead are common elements of memorials to deaths at the border. In the case described above the memorial is about being present, remembering and witnessing the living and passing of life at a time on the Christian calendar that is meant to be about recognizing suffering, death and life.

On the Italian island of Lampedusa, a very different memorial has been erected as a first step towards *accounting* for those whose names and exact place of death will never be known:

In 2008, a memorial was dedicated to thousands of migrants who had died or gone missing at sea trying to reach Italy; the deaths were 'often without burial and therefore without pity'. The memorial is built on the island of Lampedusa, in the shape of a door facing the sea, and represents the gateway to Europe. It commemorates the women, men and children who lost their lives 'in search of a better life'.

The memorial does not list the names, or even the nationalities, of those who died, because they are unknown, and there were often no bodies. Nor can it explain why they embarked on such dangerous journeys, what caused their deaths, or whether these were the result of misfortune or human agency. By leaving these questions unanswered, the memorial points both to the dimensions of this human tragedy, and to the fact that there has been no systematic attempt to identify or account for the thousands of migrants who have died attempting to cross international borders in the last two decades. (Grant, 2011b)

The sinking of SIEV X and SIEV 221 were significantly different yet similar events in the public gaze. The most notable difference was in the nature and extent of the media coverage they each received. SIEV X struggled to gain significant media attention. The loss of 353 lives, unseen, made it a difficult (non-visual) story for the media to cover, and the SIEV X was never seen by ordinary Australians. The boat, the sinking and the bodies could not be seen so far out to sea. Much of the reaction to the sinking was inevitably shaped by questions of how such a tragedy could occur beyond the reach of our gaze (despite some observers highlighting the impossibility of being able to know with any certainty such a large maritime area). Memorial activity around the SIEV X has been marked by a desire not to forget an incident that ordinary people never knew was occurring at the time. Memorials to the SIEV X are thus attempts to remember what we should have known but could not witness. By contrast, memorials to the Christmas Island shipwreck have been marked by attempts to ease the trauma of witnesses and rescuers who from all reports went to considerable lengths to save lives.

In, around and far from the borders we discuss in this book are a range of memorials for people who die while attempting to cross borders. The photograph of stones erected on Christmas Island in memorial to the SIEV X shows an act of remembering from land as proximate to the point of the sinking.

Memorials to the SIEV X have taken a number of forms, including online condolence books. Most prominently was the memorial built on the shores of Lake Burley Griffin in the Australian capital, Canberra. The organizers went out to schools to invite designs, and settled on a depiction of the SIEV X using a series of painted poles – taller poles to represent the 207 adults and shorter poles to represent the 146 children who died. The poles were then assembled into the shape and dimensions of the boat, with lines of poles leading out at either end: in one direction to the water of the lake and in the other up further onto the land. The memorial was set up only for one day because of restrictions limiting the conduct of memorials on the shores of the lake (see Ware, 2008). In October 2006, on the fifth anniversary of the sinking, a memorial was held as a form of remembrance, as an invitation to all to participate and grieve, and as a form of protest. The Chief Minister of the Australian Capital Territory, the Honourable Jon Stanhope, spoke to the occasion:

> The story of SIEV X – a boat full of people hoping to escape hardship and to find in Australia a life of their dreams, only to find themselves caught up in a maritime disaster of terrible proportions – is one of great loss. Three hundred and fifty-three people – 146 children, 142 women, 65 men – lost their lives that day. Just 42 survived – some of whom are now living in Australia.
>
> The story also resonates here because this was an Australian loss. In a sense, although they never reached their destination these were

Memorial on Christmas Island to the 146 children, 142 women and 65 men who died when the vessel codenamed the SIEV X sank between Australia and Indonesia on 19 October 2001
© Michael Sinclair-Jones

Crosses in memory of named and un-named migrants who died while attempting to cross the Arizona desert
© Raymond Michalowski

members of our community, because that was what they wanted so badly to be.

But the story while unutterably sad is also one of great strength, and of hope. Strength, in those who did survive to tell the tale. Strength, in those who lost loved ones and demanded that their story be told. And hope – considerable hope – in the movement which has been building to remember the event that took so many lives on October 18, 2001. (Stanhope, 2006)

In fact only a minority of the survivors now live in Australia. The rest, while identified as refugees under the Refugee Convention to which Australia is legally bound, were resettled in other countries. Nevertheless, the 2006 memorial was an attempt by officialdom to acknowledge the loss. Other such attempts were made by political leaders, most notably by Senator John Faulkner, a much respected elder of the Australian Labor Party. In 2002, in arguing for the importance of acknowledging the cause and responsibility for the loss of life, Faulkner publicly made the link between the sinking and border control disruption activities:

Were disruption activities directed against Abu Quassey[3]? Did these involve SIEVX?

I intend to keep asking questions until I find out. And, Mr Acting Deputy President, I intend to keep pressing for an independent judicial inquiry into these very serious matters.

At no stage do I want to break, nor will I break, the protocols in relation to operational matters involving ASIS [Australian Secret Intelligence Service] or the AFP. But, those protocols were not meant as a direct or an indirect licence to kill. (Faulkner, 2002)

The comments of political leaders provided above are notable for being part of a memorial to honour the dead – a group of people who as refugees had been subject to intense vilification and criminalization (Pickering, 2001, 2005). While these people had come from war-torn countries they were not war heroes of the kind that are the routine subject of memorials. The SIEV X memorial has been considered a democratic space within which national values and ideals have been contested (Ware, 2008).

However, the founders of the SIEV X Memorial Project are cautious about political positioning, instead taking a neutral political position as to the cause of the sinking and issues of accountability. The website includes the following statement:

> An important statement from the people building the SIEV X memorial
>
> Ever since the news first broke about the SIEV X tragedy, questions have been raised about the role of the Australian Government in the sinking.
>
> These have included allegations that our government knew about the voyage beforehand, that it failed to mount a rescue which could have saved many lives, and gravest of all, that Australia paid agents to disrupt and sabotage people-smuggling vessels, and this might have caused the tragedy. Some of these implications were lent authority by Labor Senator John Faulkner following the Certain Maritime Incident enquiry in 2002 and detailed in three speeches to the Senate.
>
> The people building the SIEVX Memorial do not make any allegations of Australian culpability in the deaths of 353 people on the SIEVX. We are ordinary citizens and do not have any special knowledge of the events of October 2001. Nonetheless we feel that a tragedy on this scale and with so many unanswered questions merits an independent judicial enquiry, or a Royal Commission, to establish just what was the truth about the voyage and its outcome.[4]

This neutral stance adopted by the SIEV X Memorial Project leaves some ambiguity around its motives for presenting these memorials. The project would not endear itself politically by being onside with the comments made by Senator Faulkner, but through their very mention (rather than their absence) the group seemingly aligns itself with his comments; indeed. Arguably, this may be aimed at creating a distinction (and a link, literally) between the memorial project itself and the explicitly political activism of the SIEV X website. The website calls for a Royal Commission into the sinking, and is at times more explicitly political. Indeed, it routinely cites the comments of Senator Faulkner on its homepage to highlight its concern over the disruption activities of Australian agencies generally, and any alleged involvement of Australian officials in the sabotage of boats leaving Indonesia for Australia. The website also publishes witness statements. The information produced and accumulated functions, on the one hand, to honour those who died and, on the other, to detail the events and the role of the Australian Government in them. Both aims culminate in a call for an independent inquiry into the sinking of the SIEV X as the ultimate way to honour the lives lost and attribute blame. The act of bearing witness transcends expressions of grief and reaches into the political and arguably legal realms to seek attributions of responsibility.

State crime

AFP Commissioner Keelty confirmed the more active nature of the disruption activities when he said that their purpose is to 'prevent the departure of a vessel ... either by the arrest or detention of individuals or by ensuring that the individuals do not reach the point of embarkation', if that was known.

It is not clear whether disruption extends to physical interference with vessels. It is not clear what, if any, consideration is given in the planning and implementation of disruption to questions of maritime safety, to the safety of lives at sea. (Faulkner, 2002)

We had nothing to do with it, it sank, I repeat, sunk (sic) in Indonesian waters, not Australian waters. (PM John Howard cited in Kevin, 2004)

Attempts to memorialize and remember the lives of those lost are commonly replete with both explicit and implicit assertions of state responsibility or accountability for border-related deaths. This includes public histories, academic studies, and the work of solidarity and political action groups. In relation to the SIEV X, Perera asserts government accountability for the 353 deaths, but direct chains of responsibility are difficult to establish. Thus, she considers the incident to be '[a]n act of violence for which the Australian body politic is accountable' (2006, p. 638). Criminology can draw on a rich vein of state crime research to include a theoretically rigorous consideration of responsibility for border-related deaths that moves beyond mere assertion. This does not render the contribution any more significant than the work of numerous human rights lawyers, cultural theorists and other academic commentators. However, for criminologists there is an onus to consider not only crimes committed by the weakest members of society, but also those committed by the powerful which are routinely found to cause greater and more extensive harms (Michalowski, 2007). Considering state responses to irregular migration as forms of state crime has been the focus of a nascent body of criminological work, including that of Green and Grewcock (2002), Pickering (2005), Weber (2005), Grewcock (2009) and Michalowski (2007).

Attempts to *account* for border-related deaths have largely built on collective attempts to remember and honour the lives lost. These forms of *accounting* often foreground attributions of responsibility and accountability. However, as noted above, this can be difficult for a range of reasons that may best be summarized as the difficulty to ascertain direct and short chains of responsibility between deaths and those in positions of power who may have caused or contributed to those deaths, as well as the diffusion of responsibility in the perpetration of systemic harm. In the coming chapters we present our substantive accounts of deaths at the border, which are broadly organized around the concept of degrees of state culpability. This draws on some aspects of the 'complicity continuum' of state crime proposed by Kauzlarich et al. (2003), applied in association with key components of cognate theorizations of state crime that remedy their overly legalistic definition being concerned with acts/omissions deemed criminal by domestic or international law.

The complicity continuum proposed by Kauzlarich et al. (2003) is based on a linear model that follows from implicit omission to explicit omission to implicit commission to explicit commission (see Table 3.1). While noting the limitations of a linear model, Kauzlarich et al. argue that the continuum should be understood as a 'submerged' manifest-latent continuum:

> This relationship highlights how action or inaction relates to larger state goals such as legitimacy, hegemony, and elite ideology, the requisites for the support of fundamental matters of political economy. As one moves to the right of the continuum, the crimes are more likely to be a manifestation of specific, proximal and material state goals. As one moves towards the left, the two categories of crimes are more implicit, signifying a less direct or causally distal relationship between the crime and the state's goals. (2003, p. 246)

In usefully identifying the range of ways states can be complicit in the perpetration of crime, Kauzlarich et al. (2003) define the four

Table 3.1 Dimensions of border harm

Global matrix of risk	Continuum	Audiences	Intentionality	Othering	Neutralization
Structural violence	Explicit acts of commission	From above	Intentional harm	Othering perpetrators	Literal denial
Suspicious deaths	Implicit acts of commission	From within	Unintended but reasonably foreseeable	Othering victims	Interpretive denial
Suicide and self-harm	Explicit acts of omission	From without	Unintended harm		
	Implicit acts of omission	From below			Implicatory denial

points on the continuum as follows. *Explicit Acts of Commission* are regarded as overt, purposeful actions aimed at achieving material state goals. These include some of the most egregious forms of state crime, and contain most of the examples studied by scholars of state crime, including genocide and ethnic cleansing. These are considered highly proximate and direct forms of harm perpetrated by the state. *Implicit Acts of Commission* include the tacit support of criminal or socially harmful actions by state actors or institutions. In this case, the role of the state is less direct and less proximate, and these acts tend to facilitate rather than directly contribute to state organizational goals. Typically these include the actions of private institutions, or organizations with quasi-state authority, and are often represented in the literature in the form of state/corporate crime or non-state activities that yield direct benefits to the state. *Explicit Acts of Omission* are often the result of state failures to act or of state negligence, including bureaucratic failures and organizational cultures that are unable or unwilling to protect groups from harm. Typical examples include inadequate or poorly executed safety arrangements. *Implicit Acts of Omission* are regarded as the most contentious category, for it includes the state's failure to act to remedy practices that are 'inequitable, harmful and marginalizing' (Kauzlarich et al., 2003, p. 250), and state negligence is often diffuse and difficult to identify. Often related to broad social problems around race, gender, or social and economic inequity, this may be considered the most 'catch-all' category in the continuum, and the one that is most difficult to ascertain with any certainty. This kind of catch-all category is also emblematic of Schwendinger and Schwendinger's (1975) definition of state crime as any violation of human rights.

Kauzlarich et al.'s continuum functions as an initial organizational framework for applying a definition of state crime. The literature is broadly unanimous regarding the need to include both acts and omissions by the state, state agents, state or state-sponsored institutions, or state proxies in the commission of crime. In essence, there is broad agreement on what comprises the state, and this increasingly includes both state and non-state agents. However, debate remains about how to define the 'crime' referred to; some question the utility of a crime label in comparison to a more nuanced or flexible idea of social harms (see Michalowski, 2007). Early definitions of state crime were based on broader interpretations (for example, Schwendinger and Schwendinger's [1975] focus on human rights and Friedrichs's [1995] 'harmful activities'). More recently these have been extended to include more precise definitional forms of state crime. For example, Green and Ward have argued that state crime occurs as a result of the violation of human rights and of state-organized deviance. Importantly, they argue that state crime can be censured by a range of social audiences (from both within and outside the state, and both powerful and less powerful groups). In our view, Kauzlarich et al. (2003) unnecessarily disagree with Green and Ward's consideration of social audience in arguing that a definition of state crime needs to be more objective, thus relying on a legalistic framework in which to ground their definition. In considering border-related deaths we utilize the continuum of state crime for its simplicity in detailing different kinds of state crime, and Green and Ward's definition of state crime for its ability to explain a greater range of activities occurring in complex and fluid circumstances. Green and Ward's work also has some resonance with Stan Cohen's theorization of denial which explains some of the mechanisms used to deny crime and suffering to which a (multiple) audience response is critical. As Green has argued:

> The important question when assessing the criminality of states in relation to asylum policy and practice is not so much the potential illegality of states in these processes but the extent to which state activities in relation to refugees and forced migrants can be understood as deviant and subject to sanction by audiences external to the state's own formal legal mechanisms. (2006, p. 162)

Sympathetic to Tilly's position on the primary importance of violence and war-making to the state, we begin from the standpoint that states can systematically engage in deviant behaviours that are central to their foundation and maintenance, rather than being simply opportunistic; however, we acknowledge that opportunism is also important to the operation of state power. The challenge for criminologists is how to clearly trace the lines between criminal activity and omission and the development and implementation of state policies – in this case in the field of illegalized migration. This task is made more difficult for the location of our study – at the edges of the sovereign state (often played out on, beyond and within the territorial border), where understandings of deviancy, acts, omissions and human rights occur in uncertain and exceptional places that are often 'beyond' the reach of the law (see Arendt, 1968; Agamben, 2005). Our project is therefore also sympathetic to the views of Jamieson and McEvoy (2005), who argue that conceptualizations of state crime need to be less monolithic and more subtle in their account of different modalities of proxy agency which do not depend on international and national criminal laws. They base their argument on the analysis of the practices carried out in spaces where sovereignty is exercised in conflicting ways, including in extra-territorial spaces.

For the purposes of this book we need to consider that all the complications attached to applying ideas of state crime in both the domestic and international context are present as we attempt to unravel the chains of responsibility for deaths at the border. The concept of legitimacy of state action becomes the lynchpin from which to expand on the attempts to account for deaths outlined above through memorializing and the identification of counter-narratives of border-related deaths, for these attempts are about the expression of often unspoken shared social values regarding the interdependence of life. The act of coming together to recognize the loss of life demands the names of those who die, and to honour lives lost is to declare that the loss of life is illegitimate. The acts detailed above are also examples of voices 'from below' that can function to censure a deviant or criminal act.

Therefore, in the following chapters we consider how particular cases fit the continuum proposed by Kauzlarich et al., which perhaps better suits jurisdictionally discrete situations. We then turn to explore how cases drawn from Europe, North America and Australia can be understood through Green and Ward's conception of multiple audiences, precisely because it is from a diverse range of audiences that forms of accounting for deaths have emerged. We also consider Jamieson and McEvoy's (2005) proxy state crime model to understand deaths at the border where conceptions of the state are less fixed, and to identify practices and processes that distance state crime from an easily recognizable sovereign territorial state. We couple this with reference to Cohen's work on denial, specifically on neutralization, as discussed in Chapter 2.

Conclusion

Throughout this book we focus on those border practices that have been developed and sustained and increase the risks to illegalized migrants. Accounting for bodies is not the same as accounting for the lives lost and the human desire to grieve and honour those lives. This includes the need to bear witness not only to juridical functions of culpability around harm and crime, but also to social and communal needs to memorialize. Our intention in the next section is not to produce a list of actions that fit the various tests and criteria that have been set to define state crime. We do, however, want to account for harms perpetrated both directly and indirectly that may fall within the ambit of state crime definitions. In doing so, we routinely draw on the sensitizing concepts contained in Table 3.1 in ways that best serve the purpose of accounting for border deaths, in particular how they may be censured or discounted by different audiences. We seek to identify state culpability in ways that lead to determining accountability and enhancing the prevention of harms rather than focusing on the specifics of labelling and categorizing criminal acts and omissions.

Part II

Border Inquest: Misadventure or Death by Policy?

> An inquest is a court hearing in which the Court gathers information to assist in determining the cause and circumstances of death and if appropriate, to make recommendations that may prevent similar deaths occurring in the future. The Court calls witnesses to give evidence of what they know about the death. An inquest is not a trial, rather it is an investigative process to shed light on the cause and circumstances of a death. (Courts Administration Authority South Australia, South Australian Coroners Court information sheet)

Following the identification of the body and determination of *how* a person has died comes the explanation, pursued through juridical rather than medical means, of *why* they died. The chapters in Part II present our substantive *account* of deaths at the border. The effects of specific border control policies will not only be seen in the size of the human death toll, but will also be reflected in *who* dies, *where* they die and *how* their lives are lost. Evidence of the effects of the deterritorialized border will be found in deaths occurring *en route*, in encounters with officials at physical borders, and at sites of border enforcement within destination countries, such as detention centres, designated places of dispersal and sites of illegal work and arrest. Our analysis reveals how border control policies influence the age, gender and nationality of those who die by shifting the burden of risks associated with illegalized border crossing in particular places and moments in time. In doing so, we demonstrate how border deaths, far from being random and unforeseen events, are significantly shaped by particular border policies and practices that have both local inflection and global significance.

91

The chapters in this part are grouped according to the presence or absence of an obvious 'suspect'. In Chapter 4 we explore border-related deaths which appear, on the surface, to be tragic accidents. However, in following the trail of evidence we identify border control policies as 'invisible actors' that contribute both explicitly and implicitly to the deaths of illegalized migrants. In Chapter 5 we discuss border-related deaths that can be attributed to the actions of specific individuals, but discover upon further examination that government policies and institutions are complicit in the circumstances leading to such deaths. In Chapter 6 we consider instances in which illegalized border crossers ostensibly die at their own hands, and find these cases to be 'assisted suicides' driven by circumstances of unbearable desperation and despair.

We find many of the 'sensitizing concepts' discussed in the previous chapter to be useful in discussing these different categories of border-related death. Our 'ice-core sampling' reveals examples of both intended and unintended harm; attributes direct and indirect roles played by governments; and identifies a variety of audiences, some of whom oppose border policies, some of whom attest to their legitimacy, and others who undertake to enforce them, whether in a professional or voluntary capacity.

4
Structural Violence

Galtung was one of the earliest to publish in the Western academic press an expanded definition of violence which identified and distinguished between direct and indirect actions, and also identified 'invisible' actors such as institutions, systems and structures rather than simply human beings acting directly. Violence, then, could be committed directly and deliberately, but could also be conducted indirectly and largely unintentionally, by structures populated by humans ... Violence was to be understood as a force that unintentionally prevented humans from realizing their actual potential. (Roberts, 2008, p. 19)

My hope to make life in your country really is finished. And when I leave here I don't know what will happen to me in Iran but I know death in my land is much better than dying in this detention or this hell. I lost everything. I lost my life, my love, my family and now I think maybe if I stay here I lose my mind.
(Letter from Australian asylum seeker reproduced in Burnside, 2003, p. 171)

Illegality and exposure to death

The passage from Roberts cited above encompasses within an 'expanded definition of violence' a broad range of harmful actions which may be either intended or unintended, and can be perpetrated through either direct or indirect means, by individuals or institutions. Structural violence is characterized primarily by the absence of visible actors and is associated with forms of violence that are largely unintended. In this chapter we identify many aspects of border control as examples of structural violence. It might be objected immediately that the harms inflicted by borders are far from unintended. Deterrence-based policies rely on the threat of harm to deter others; and while inflicting harm on those who are not deterred is evidence of policy failure, some measure of pain is fully anticipated in return for the expected compliance of the majority.

In the examples that follow, it will sometimes be apparent from official statements and from the very design of the policies themselves that harm to some illegalized travellers is foreseen and deliberately intended. At other times, the full extent to which border policies could lead to suffering and death, rather than compliance, may be unforeseen, although not unforeseeable. The inability to anticipate the fatal consequences of border control policies may be an ideologically determined error made by those who imagine a world of individual choice, and are blind to the circumstances and imperatives of others who are situated very differently from themselves. Cutting across the dichotomy of intended versus unintended harms, Khosravi argues that 'borders do not kill or want immigrants to die but are willing to tolerate casualties' (Khosravi, 2010, p. 29). A purely punitive mentality towards border protection, in which causing pain and death becomes the explicit and primary purpose of border control, is the province of extreme ideological positions. The Italian politician Umberto Bossi, cited in Chapter 2, who expressed his willingness to 'let the cannons roar' in order to prevent the arrival of illegalized travellers, occupies this space on the spectrum of intentionality.

It is the *invisibility* of human culprits, rather than the presence or absence of intention to cause harm, that best defines structural violence. As explained by Roberts (2008, p. 20, emphasis added): 'These structures are rarely easy to imagine. Nor do they readily take concrete form. Many of the structures surrounding our lives may appear benign when in fact they can be unintentionally (*or intentionally*) malignant.' This is not to say that structural violence represents a less culpable form of harm. That assertion does not follow from the identification of institutions and systems as the means by which violence is perpetrated. The structures themselves have been constructed by human agency and they are 'human-inhabited' (Roberts, 2008, p. 24). However, once systems intended to deter or expel targeted groups are in place, they may become self-perpetuating so that the harms arising cannot be readily traced to their original source. Moreover, those who are part of the system may misperceive their own role and culpability in the routine production of serious harm (Weber, 2005). These displacements are typical of processes mediated through large organizations, particularly indirect modes of neoliberal governance effected through chains of disparate actors. What Roberts refers to as 'global structures of violence' are the primary means through which the production of harm is magnified and promulgated far beyond the ranks of those who would individually inflict direct suffering on others. Once the violent implications of these structures are unmasked to potentially critical audiences, the political task of challenging the ideologies that legitimize them, and the competing interests that motivate them, can begin. This task is likely to be hindered by the power of the law as a symbol of assurance, which supports fantasies about its potential to deliver justice even in the face of evidence that indicates otherwise (Fan, 2008). These fantasies about the law may help to shore up the structural violence of border controls, even after their systemic harm has been made visible.

As outlined in Chapter 1, contemporary border controls are a hybrid of deterrent and risk-reducing measures. Operating within a bureaucratic framework, visa regimes often present a façade of legitimacy and non-violence – they do not depend, in the first instance, on harsh rhetoric or military force against targeted groups. The exclusionary power of visa regimes works behind the scenes, ensuring that whole categories of travellers designated as 'high-risk' are denied access to any legal means of travel. The identification of these 'invisible actors' and the harm that they produce requires the adoption of a structural violence perspective. Measures such as the imposition of visa regimes intended to reduce real or imagined risks for settled populations actually do so by shifting risks onto excluded groups. In the following passage, immigration barrister Frances Webber describes the amplification of deviance and risk resulting from selective visa controls targeted at refugee-producing nationalities: 'the combination of visa controls and carrier sanctions makes legal travel to western countries impossible for refugees and other forced migrants, and forces them into lying to embassy officials so as to obtain visit or study visas, or buying false documents, or travelling clandestinely so as to by-pass immigration controls' (Webber, 2004, p. 136). Viewed from the perspective of state officials, the process manifests as a spiral of increasingly duplicitous and subversive behaviour exhibited by illegalized travellers; however, it is experienced by the travellers themselves, to varying degrees, as an increasing spiral of risk. This transfer of risk constitutes an act of structural violence. In the words of Khosravi (2010, p. 27): 'This is the main feature of contemporary border politics.

It *exposes* the border transgressors to death rather than directly using its power to kill.'

The attribution of illegal status to individuals who have successfully crossed borders but have no legal entitlement to stay is another means by which the structural violence of borders is perpetrated. Nevins (2010, p. 119) notes that the discursive category 'illegal' as a way of denoting unwanted immigration did not exist in the US until around 1950, but is now the 'term of choice'. Dauvergne (2008, p. 10) observes, with some concern, that 'illegal' has become a noun. Despite its apparent normative power, she argues that it is a label that is empty of content, circumscribing an individual's identity solely in terms of their relationship to the law. It is increasingly the legal/illegal distinction, Dauvergne argues, that defines the boundary between inclusion and exclusion, access and denial, protection and exploitation, and sometimes between life and death: '"Illegal" is now established as an identity of its own, homogenizing and obscuring the functioning of the law and replicating layers of disadvantage and exclusion … For extra-legal migrants seeking legal protection or redress for harms, the status of "illegal" has been almost insurmountable' (2008, p. 19). In fact, Dauvergne equates 'illegality' in contemporary times with the status of 'civil death' – a juridical category used historically to mark individuals as excluded from protection under the law. There may be room for debate about the extent of this exclusion in particular jurisdictions. However, Fan (2008, p. 727) also characterizes 'illegals' as 'sacrificial migrants' who are 'literally banned from the symbolic order of law's promise of benefits, security and succor, rights and entitlements'.

Since 'illegality' is often a taken-for-granted condition, it is important to unmask its politico-juridical nature. This unmasking reveals that the process of illegalization is a key technology for the expression of the internal border. Dauvergne (2008, p. 15) notes that '[e]ach extension of the law regulating migration increases illegal migration through defining increasingly larger categories as being outside the law'. In fact, illegalization does not always simply serve to mark those who are destined for exclusion. It may also be productive as a tool of neoliberal governance (Hiemstra, 2010), creating a subordinate workforce of insecure and rightless workers, who are disciplined not only by the threat of losing their jobs, but also by the ever-present possibility of deportation. This possibility needs to be continually reinforced to a range of audiences. De Genova (2002, p. 437) notes that the '"[i]llegality" effect of protracted and enduring vulnerability has to be recreated more often than on the occasions of crossing the border'. The consequences of this categorization for those labelled as illegal can vary enormously across time and place, depending on specific configurations of 'illegality' (De Genova, 2002), and on the resources deployed by particular states at particular times and localities to define and defend their borders (Hiemstra, 2010). Willen notes in relation to those marked as 'illegal' (2007, p. 2) that:

> At best they are tolerated; at worst they are hunted down and forcibly deported. In everyday terms, most such migrants are consigned, either temporarily or permanently, to spaces that are structurally as well as geographically, socially, and politically peripheral. Within these marginal, abject zones, their everyday lives are framed by the experiential consequences of their peripheral status, variously epitomized as 'illegality', 'irregularity', 'invisibility', and 'non-existence'.

The incorporation of employers into surveillance networks through the threat of criminal sanctions, the announcement of targets for large-scale deportations, or the deployment of state police to identify those without legal status inscribe the border ever more deeply on the bodies of those marked by their 'deportability'.

Against this spectre of abject marginalization it is important to recognize that illegalized migrants still seek to participate in social and economic life within the limits of their politico-juridical status, to form alliances with sympathetic groups, and sometimes to actively resist the confines of their illegality. While it might be tempting to argue that 'illegality' has become what proponents of criminological labelling theory would call a 'master status', this is not necessarily confirmed by ethnographic research. Illegalized migrants often engage in complex social relations with legal residents, and live in close relations with them as spouses, neighbours and co-workers (De Genova, 2002). This is not to say that their illegal status has no meaning. Chavez (2007, p. 193) describes the overall treatment of illegalized migrants in the US as 'schizophrenic', since, on the one hand, they have some success in obtaining jobs and accessing services, while on the other their illegality 'undermines imagining undocumented immigrants as part of the larger society'. Therefore, while it is important to recognize the spaces in which illegalized migrants can exercise their agency, it is also true that these spaces can be sharply circumscribed by border policies and other factors such as the availability or lack of informal networks of social support. If unsupported, illegalized migrants may experience the impact of their illegality through hunger, unemployment, exploitation and violence, and social or even physical death (De Genova, 2002).

As with exposure to the risk of death through taking dangerous routes and forms of travel, the deprivations associated with illegal status can also be identified as a form of structural violence that shifts risks onto excluded groups for the benefit of those who are included:

> The benefits from the structured inequalities and violence inherent in the condition of illegality accrue to citizen members of the societies in question, who gain value in the commodities immigrants produce and the services immigrants provide. Nationals also gain because of the symbolic value and material privileges that accrue to them as 'citizens'. (Chavez, 2007, p. 193)

In the remainder of this chapter we consider some examples of the fatal consequences of illegalization: first, as experienced by those trying to cross borders without authorization; and second, as experienced by those forced to live under the mantle of illegality.

Deadly displacements

Geographical displacement

The risks faced by illegalized travellers that are most hidden from view arise from offshore interdictions at airports. In these interstitial spaces, critical audiences capable of monitoring state practices are noticeably absent. Savitri Taylor has pointed out that the fate of 'inadequately documented passengers' intercepted by Australian immigration liaison officers posted at airports along transit routes to Australia is undocumented and simply unknown (Taylor, 2008). In contrast, geographical displacement into more hazardous routes by land and sea has been relatively well documented, and has become the subject of contentious debate. A 'funnel effect' has been clearly discernible resulting from the fortification of the US–Mexico border (Rubio-Goldsmith et al., 2006, 2007), and Fekete (2003, p. 3) has argued that in Europe, 'EU policy is, quite literally, funnelling people to their deaths'. The European NGO Migreurop, in collaboration with geographer Olivier Clochard, has produced an Atlas of Migrants in Europe which documents the evolution of European border controls and represents their sometimes fatal consequences in a series of analytical maps (Migreurop, 2009).

Figure 4.1 dramatically depicts the rapid rise in the number of deaths at sea that occurred alongside the build-up of external border controls.

Figure 4.1   Evolution of the number of deaths at Europe's doorstep

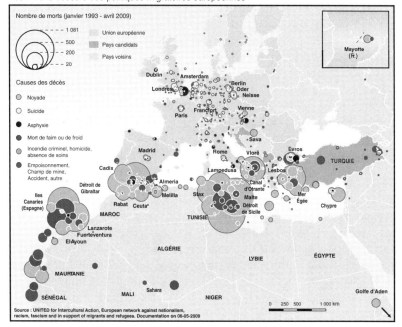

Les miroirs obscurs des politiques migratoires européennes

Source: Atlas des Migrants en Europe, p. 118 © Migreurop, 2009

The key policy referents depicted in the map series are the introduction of the Schengen Treaty; the implementation of SIVE patrols between Spain and Gibraltar; agreements reached at the Seville and Rabat Summits; and the externalization of migration controls through a series of bilateral agreements, notably with Libya. The Migreurop analysis is based on the data collected by the NGO UNITED, and thus carries with it all the limitations identified in Chapter 2 in relation to that data. The UNITED data records 9470 deaths occurring in the Mediterranean and Atlantic oceans from 1988 to 2009. This represents 70 per cent of the border-related deaths recorded over that period across Europe and is likely to be a significant underestimate because of the unknown rate of recovery of bodies at sea. The map of deaths for 1998 to 2002 clearly depicts the opening up of the dangerous Atlantic people-smuggling route to the Canary Islands, initially from Mauritania, then later from Senegal (Spijkerboer, 2007) as Spanish SIVE patrols across the narrow straits of Gibraltar were stepped up. By 2003, bodies were said to be 'piling up' in the 'nautical graveyards off Gran Canaria' (Fekete, 2003). Carling (2007) reports that interceptions by SIVE patrols on the Canary Islands route increased from 12 per cent to 59 per cent of total interceptions in the first two years of operation, suggesting a marked geographical shift.[1] Moreover, the destination point in the Canary Islands shifted from Fuerteventura to Lanzerote, adding a further 50 per cent to the journey's length, in response to the instigation of SIVE patrols around Fuerteventura (Carling, 2007). According to the Migreurop maps, by 2006–09 deaths in the Atlantic were far outnumbering those in the heavily patrolled Straits of Gibraltar, while the Libya–Malta route and the land and sea borders between Greece and Turkey – notorious for border violence, unexploded mine fields and treacherous mountain and river crossings – were also beginning to claim more lives. Notably, deaths in the Sahara have begun to be recorded as the effects of EU border externalization have pushed still further into the African continent. For example, Spijkerboer (2007) reports that in October 2005, following the storming of the boundary fence by sub-Saharan Africans at the Spanish enclave of Melilla in which more than a dozen people were killed outright, Morocco 'rounded up' migrants and dumped them in the desert several hundred kilometres further south, without food or water. Not discernible from the aggregate data depicted in the maps is the reduction in the recorded number of deaths in the Atlantic from 2007 to 2008, which the Spanish Government has attributed to its efforts to prevent departure. This may appear to be good news; however, any decrease in deaths in this location may well have been offset by increases in other locations, and the fate of those whose journeys are cut short in Africa is not known. Migreurop concludes: 'Surveillance in the Gibraltar, Otranto, and Sicily straits as well as surveillance that was established further south to limit the movement of people assumed to be about to leave for Europe have certainly altered migratory paths, but nothing proves that they have lowered, or even contributed to controlling these "fluxes"' (Migreurop, 2009, p. 116). The question of whether the overall risk of death for illegalized travellers has increased or decreased as a result of border fortification and externalization will be considered in Chapter 7. That discussion will also take into account the most recent data on deaths and apprehensions by Frontex patrols, which indicates that further changes may have occurred in the patterns of illegalized border crossings and deaths.

The displacement of border-crossing deaths to far-flung locations such as the Atlantic coast of west Africa ensures that border-related fatalities are 'hidden even further from the European gaze' (Fekete, 2003, p. 4). As well as the attendant dangers of longer voyages through more inhospitable terrain, the risks arising from geographical displacement may be compounded by other, more subtle effects. For example, Carling (2007) has argued that displacement to less intensively monitored times and places may concentrate illegalized arrivals in areas where there is less humanitarian support available. At the time of writing, this description could be applied to Greece, through which the majority of unauthorized arrivals in Europe are now being funnelled. In the midst of its own financial and political crisis, and with no established history of refugee processing mechanisms, Greece has proven itself unable to meet the legal and humanitarian needs of asylum seekers and other illegalized travellers, particularly unaccompanied minors. This has prompted the Council of Europe (2011) to take the extraordinary step of making a public announcement calling on Greece to respond immediately to allegations of poor conditions and mistreatment in immigration detention raised repeatedly by the European Committee for the Prevention of Torture (CPT, 2011). In fact, Greece is considered to be so unsafe for illegalized travellers that the European Court of Human Rights ruled in January 2011 that returning an asylum seeker to that country under the provisions of the Dublin Convention would expose them to torture, inhuman or degrading treatment – thereby striking a major blow against the practice of routinely returning asylum seekers to their first country of arrival in Europe (*M.S.S. v Belgium & Greece*, reported in European Council on Refugees and Exiles [ECRE], 2011). Reports are also emerging of anti-immigrant violence building in villages along the eastern border of Greece (Daley, 2011), adding further to the threats faced by illegalized travellers *en route*.

It is important to recognize that countries that are often seen merely as transit locations on the journey to the Global North may themselves be attractive destinations for some migrants. However, geographical displacement due to externalized border controls may take the form of immobilization at staging points along the way, where different kinds of dangers arising from local hostility may be encountered. It is believed that 26,000 illegalized migrants were prevented by Moroccan authorities from crossing into Europe during 2006 alone (Spijkerboer, 2007). Carling notes that many sub-Saharan Africans become 'de facto immigrants' in North Africa when they find they cannot pay the inflated cost of illegalized travel to Europe, and cannot return to their countries of origin, so have no choice but to remain 'in a desperate situation under appalling conditions' (2007, p. 319). A similar pattern has been observed among illegalized travellers from Central and South America, and beyond, who become stranded in Mexico due to controls along the US–Mexico border. The direct risks faced by these groups, primarily at the hands of hostile and exploitative third parties, will be discussed in the next chapter.

When the US Government began building border walls and checkpoints that divided towns on the US–Mexico border, and fortifying the border with additional armed patrols, it expected that the forbidding terrain of the Arizonan deserts and the fast-flowing waters of the Rio Grande would deter illegalized crossings in these isolated areas. A doubling of the numbers of border-crossing deaths from 241 in 1999 to 472 in 2005 suggested otherwise (GAO, 2006). Michalowski (2007, p. 66) argues that this litany of deaths and injuries was far from unforeseen:

> For the immigration policy planners behind Gatekeeper, the death and injury of migrants was not something to be avoided, but rather a useful 'deterrent' to other potential border crossers (U.S. Border Patrol 1994). Contradictorily, it is also true that Border Patrol agents in the Tucson Sector (as elsewhere) devoted considerable time and effort to assisting migrants in distress, often saving lives in the process. These honest efforts, however, take place within a perverse policy framework that deliberately increases the chances that migrants will be subject to injury and death while simultaneously directing Border Patrol agents to provide 'humanitarian' assistance to the very migrants the government has forced into high risk crossings.

The implementation of the South West Border Strategy in California in 1994 was already known to have altered the course of most border crossings into more remote locations. Increased fatalities in the All-American canal were observed as early as 1997, as Californian crossings were deflected away from urban areas (Eschbach et al., 1999). The busy San Diego crossing reportedly accounted for one third of all deaths along the US–Mexico border in 1990, but only 8 per cent by 2003, as crossings (and deaths) were funnelled elsewhere (GAO, 2006; Hill & Kelada, 2010). By the mid-2000s, the relentless border build-up had left fewer and fewer options open for relatively safe crossings. Drawing on data from a number of official sources, the US GAO found that 94 per cent of the increase in deaths from 1998 to 2005 was accounted for by the arid Tucson sector, providing convincing evidence of the displacement of border crossings into more dangerous areas. One particular route through the lands of the Tohono O'odham Nation claimed 229 lives in seven years, becoming known as 'the deadliest migrant trail in the US' (Jimenez, 2009, no page). The changing nature of the risks faced by illegalized migrants was reflected in the changing causes of death, with a significant increase noted in deaths due to environmental exposure, accompanied by a relative decline in deaths from homicide and road traffic accidents (GAO, 2006). Moreover, local variations in border control technologies could sometimes be linked to specific changes in the risks experienced by illegalized border crossers. In the San Diego region, Hill and Kelada (2010) linked increased injuries caused by falling from the border wall – which were observed despite significant decreases in the number of crossings – to an increase in the height of the wall in that location.

Deadly demographics

Specific border policies can also affect *who* is exposed to the risks of illegalized border crossing. Sub-Saharan Africans trying to reach Europe are widely considered to be more at risk than North Africans for a number of reasons, including the long and arduous journeys they must make, and a widespread inability to swim. However, they may also experience a heightened risk at the hands of North African facilitators arising from the greater 'returnability' of Moroccans following a bilateral agreement between that country and Spain. Carling (2007) reports that, in response, boats carrying sub-Saharans began to be used as decoys to engage the attention of maritime patrols, enabling the smugglers to land their Moroccan passengers in relative safety. Moreover, Carling argues that increased surveillance in the Mediterranean has coincided with a shift in the composition of passengers undertaking illegalized voyages towards those who do not depend on crossing borders without being detected. He notes that, when arriving *pateras* (fishing boats) are approached by rescue workers in Spain, 'it is common for the sub-Saharan Africans to sit waiting on the beach while the Moroccans try to run away and hide' (Carling, 2007, p. 328). Moroccans reportedly use other strategies, such as sending unaccompanied children, for reasons explained here by Carling (2007, p. 328):

> Since the late 1990s, several thousand unaccompanied minors have entered Spain without documentation every year, either in *pateras* or by other means. It has not been possible to repatriate them unless their families in Morocco have been located, and after six months, they have been given residence permits in Spain. This makes the

crossing more worthwhile than for adult Moroccans, who are often repatriated within 48 hours.

The arrival of unaccompanied minors of a range of nationalities is a relatively new yet growing phenomenon in Europe. Migreurop (2009) estimates that around 10,000 unaccompanied minors may be present across Europe, many of whom face an uncertain future, while others do not survive the journey. Reports of the deaths of children, travelling with or without their parents, appear regularly in the UNITED data on European deaths. The list makes distressing reading. An unknown boy fell from under a lorry onto a motorway in France in 2001. In the same year, the decaying bodies of two African children were found in the hold of a Panamanian vessel bound for Spain, and an Algerian minor died of cold and exhaustion while attempting to swim to Ceuta. Five Iraqi Kurdish minors suffocated in a truck in Italy in 2002. In 2003 the frozen body of a young Congolese boy was found in the undercarriage of a plane flying from Brazzaville to Paris. Children appear in the records of those drowned, starved or asphyxiated during ill-fated boat crossings in incidents too numerous to list. Among them, a Sierra Leonean toddler is said to have died of starvation on a sea voyage in 2006; the small body was consigned to the sea by the child's parents.

According to Carling (2007), a growing number of pregnant women are also making illegalized journeys into Europe – a trend he links to incorrect beliefs about the protections women and their children will be offered under the nationality laws of European countries once they give birth. This explanation presupposes that pregnancy precedes the decision to travel illegally to Europe. Given the incidence of rape experienced by women making these long and hazardous journeys, it is likely that the temporal order of these events is reversed in some cases (Pickering, 2010). One estimate suggests that 60 per cent of women trying to cross into the US through Mexico without legal protection are sexually assaulted along the way (AI, 2010). Women as a group have also been found to be at higher risk of death during illegalized travel in the US–Mexico borderlands. It is often reported that women and children are more likely to be left behind by guides if they cannot keep up. The differential risks of illegalized travel for women and children have even been quantified:

Women are 2.87 times more likely to die of exposure than men. Children are 3.4 times more likely to die in a motor vehicle accident than adults since families prefer paying smugglers the higher fees for transporting children in motor vehicles rather than exposing the children to the harsh conditions of the rugged terrain or deserts. Only with respect to homicide do women fare better than men. (Jimenez, 2009, no page)

Women and children, like men, are also liable to be summarily returned over the border by the US Border Patrol, often into areas where violence is pervasive. NGOs have complained that children are often not handed over to proper authorities or provided with appropriate support. A study by a working group within the Mexican Congress found that 15 per cent of the 90,000 minors who were transported over the border from the US in 2008 remained in the border areas to which they were returned, and did not travel back to their places of origin. Among those interviewed for the research, 70 per cent of the young people said they would again try to cross the border (Jimenez, 2009). Yet prospects for young people attempting to cross the US–Mexico border illegally are highly precarious. Jimenez reports that an estimated one in five smuggled children never makes contact with relatives awaiting their arrival in the US.

In addition to the elevated risks they face, there is also evidence that women are embarking on illegalized journeys in greater numbers. The US GAO has noted that deaths of women during border crossing were consistently lower in number than deaths of men, but increased from 9 per cent of all deaths in 1998 to 21 per cent in 2005, with a significant proportion of the increase centred around Tucson (GAO, 2006). The decision to undertake an illegalized border crossing is likely to be influenced by conditions in the women's home countries. Schrover et al. (2008) note that women often experience discrimination in their countries of origin in terms of mobility and access to labour markets, so that even the uncertainties of illegalized travel may be viewed as an improvement in their lives. Analysts have also identified specific changes in US immigration policies which have led more women and children to undertake dangerous journeys. Formerly, under the Bracero programme, migration from Mexico to the US was highly 'masculinized', as single males and putative heads of households were constructed as the idealized labour migrant (Boehm, 2011). This regime encouraged the formation of transnational families maintained by frequent, legal border crossings. However, as Fan (2008, p. 708) explains, border fortification 'disrupted a formerly cyclical process of migration, causing migrants to remain in the United States and send for their families rather than risk the costly and dangerous journey back and forth across the border'. Other analysts agree that restrictive immigration policies that have closed avenues of legal entry for reasons of 'family unity' are directly implicated in the increased numbers of women and children making dangerous, illegalized journeys (Jimenez, 2009).

In Australia, the introduction of Temporary Protection Visas (TPVs) by the conservative government of John Howard has also been associated with a deadly change in border-crossing demographics. TPVs were explicitly introduced as a deterrent against unauthorized boat arrivals. When the policy was implemented, government spokespersons explained that it was intended 'to reduce the attractiveness of Australia for those seeking to enter illegally and claim asylum' (reported in Burnside, 2003, p. 170). From October 1999, asylum seekers arriving by sea without visas were ineligible for permanent refugee protection, and were offered, at best, only temporary protection visas with limited entitlements. Significantly, TPV holders have no option of family reunion. Ultimately, the vast majority of TPV holders were granted permanent residence (Phillips & Spinks, 2011), but the policy was seen by lawyers and refugee supporters as harsh and inhumane. When it came to power in 2007, the Labor government abolished TPVs, which they acknowledged had caused enormous suffering to those living with uncertainty and unable to reunite with their families. When the immigration debate ramped up again around 2009, as boats began to arrive once more, the Opposition laid the blame for the arrivals on the government for weakening Australia's border defences, and pointed to the abolition of TPVs as one cause of the increase. NGOs weighed into the debate by refuting a link between what they described as 'more humane' immigration policies and overall arrival numbers, arguing that:

> There is no credible argument that has been put forward to corroborate a link. What we do know is that the increased number of arrivals witnessed over recent months is consistent with international trends and with deteriorating situations in a number of countries, resulting in greater numbers of people being displaced and attempting to flee persecution. (Refugee Council of Australia, 2009)

A recent analysis by Parliamentary Library researchers has also concluded that there is no statistical evidence that TPVs reduced the number of boat arrivals (Phillips & Spinks, 2011). While the deterrent power of TPVs and other restrictive border controls is disputed, links have been made between the introduction of TPVs and the age and gender composition of passengers undertaking risky voyages by boat to

Australia. These criticisms were brought into sharp relief when 146 children were among the 353 people who died in the sinking of the SIEV X vessel. The tragedy marks one of the darkest periods in the annals of Australian border control. Immigration lawyer Robert Manne (2003) wrote:

> The astonishing cruelty of the temporary visa laws was finally understood by the general public following the incident late in 2001 when 353 asylum seekers on their way to Australia drowned ... Three of these were daughters of an Iraqi man who had been granted refugee status but who had been refused the right, under the new temporary visa regime, even to apply for reunion with his family. As it happens, although his daughters died, the man's wife survived after a day in the ocean. The man was informed by the Minister that, although he was perfectly at liberty to leave Australia to visit his grieving wife in Indonesia, if he did so, because of the conditions attached to his temporary visa, he would, unfortunately, be unable to return.

Information posted on the DIMIA website in 2000 acknowledged that there had been a change in the pattern of arrivals, although no link was made with any particular policy. The unauthorized vessels were said to be larger than before, and to be transporting 'complete family units, which have included pregnant women and young children' (DIMIA, 2000). Using official data collated on the SIEV X website showing the numbers of adults and children arriving on unauthorized boats between 1989 and 2003,[2] it can be calculated that the proportion of passengers who were classified as children increased from an average of 19 per cent before the introduction of TPVs in October 1999, to an average of nearly 22 per cent afterwards. Figures quoted by former Minister for Immigration Chris Evans, which also include women, show a shift from 25 per cent women and children before the introduction of TPVs to around 40 per cent afterwards (Phillips & Spinks, 2011).[3] These before and after calculations obscure the trends that were occurring immediately prior to and following the policy reform. Figure 4.2 reveals that the percentage of children among those arriving on unauthorized boats had also been high in the mid-1990s, but was starting to decline in the years immediately prior to the introduction of TPVs. The year 1999 marks the beginning of a distinct shift in this trend towards increased proportions of children among boat arrivals.

Figure 4.2   Percentage of children among unauthorized boat arrivals to Australia, excluding boats where breakdown by age group unknown

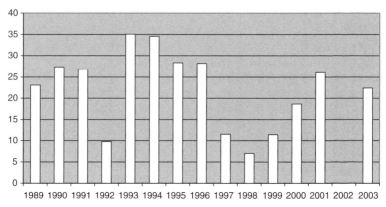

Source: Database of Asylum Seeker Boats http://sievx.com/dbs/boats/

Ten years later, images of the lost children and grieving parents are still displayed on the SIEV X website. Yet we must ask: has the Australian public really understood, as Manne suggests, the connection between a policy aimed at deterring illegalized arrivals and the loss of so many young lives? If it did, the link appears to have been forgotten by 2009, when the number of boats arriving began to increase again. Assertions by conservative politicians, who were then in opposition, that a return to the previous government's policies, including the use of TPVs, would once again succeed in 'stopping the boats' seemed to strike a chord with large sections of the population. Breakdowns of the ages of asylum seekers arriving without visas by boat are no longer publicly available; however, it would appear that large numbers of women and children are once again risking the sea voyage that has continued to take more lives since the sinking of the SIEV X. The Australian Broadcasting Commission reported in March 2011 that almost half of the children in mandatory immigration detention at that time had arrived without their parents, and that most of them were Afghan boys (ABC News Online, 2011a). It was also noted that the increase in unaccompanied minors arriving had occurred alongside a decrease in the issuing of family reunification visas. This could suggest, while not spelled out in the report, that a reduction in the realization of family reunion rights is being effected through unannounced administrative procedures rather than through an explicit change in visa entitlements.

Transporting risk

The range of means by which illegalized travellers seek to cross borders into the Global North is a testament to their determination and resourcefulness. It is also too often a ticket to death. Illegalized migrants die in sealed shipping containers and concealed beneath commercial loads in airless lorries; they lose their grip while clinging to the under-carriages of trains and trucks; they are crushed, frozen or fall from the sky during terrifying journeys in the wheel compartments of planes; and they miscalculate when trying to jump from bridges onto the roofs of moving trains. More routinely, they are packed into overcrowded and inherently unsafe boats and vehicles, made more unsafe by the efforts of their drivers to evade detection. No statistical analysis is needed to realize that these are not the modes of transport chosen by people who have a better option. Only those who are compelled by the need to evade detection resort to using such methods. The displace-ments discussed in this section are the shifts into deadlier modes of travel which are direct responses to particular border control tactics designed to prevent arrival. Tragically, these 'non-arrival' policies often achieve their ultimate promise, when the failure to arrive is literal and permanent.

Spijkerboer (2007, p. 128) notes that '[i]rregular migrants who choose to reach Europe by sea cannot afford to pay for the forged documents that are necessary for air travel and, in many cases, for travel by land'. Intensified maritime surveillance introduces further risks into sea cross-ings as facilitators seek to avoid interception by deliberately departing in poor weather or unloading passengers at sea without lifejackets to avoid the risk of going ashore. According to Carling (2007), the nature of smuggling operations between Morocco and Spain changed with the advent of intensive SIVE patrols. Whereas traditional *pateras* had pre-viously been the most common mode of transport, more organized smugglers began to use cheap, purpose-built craft that were often less seaworthy and sometimes designed with the intention of being sacrificed. To add further to the risks, inexperienced migrants have often been put at the helm in heavily monitored areas to ensure that facilitators evaded capture, greatly increasing the danger faced by those on board.

Similar tragedies result from efforts to evade detection along land routes. In June 2000 the grisly deaths by suffocation of 54 men and four women from Fujian Province in China who were found concealed in a lorry travelling from Zeebrugge to Dover demonstrated in dramatic fashion the dangers routinely faced by illegalized travellers. Dutch lorry driver Perry Wacker was later convicted on 58 counts of man-slaughter, his personal culpability increased in the eyes of the jury and public by claims that he had closed the air vent to avoid detection by immigration officials (BBC News, 2003). Around the time of this inci-dent, port authorities at Dover were proudly displaying their enhanced capacity to detect stowaways using sniffer dogs, carbon dioxide detec-tors, scanning devices and heartbeat monitors. Seven Chinese nationals were later convicted for people smuggling. As with the SIEV X tra-gedy, questions are still being asked about whether Dutch and British authorities or Europol had the smuggling group under surveillance, but allowed the journey to go ahead as a so-called controlled delivery (Statewatch, 2001).

In the US–Mexico borderlands, concealment in vehicles has also increased as an alternative, or sometimes as an adjunct to, arduous crossings through remote terrain. The increase in border patrols, cou-pled with the post-September 11 expansion of roadside checkpoints on arterial roads up to 100 miles inland from the Canadian and Mexican borders, has created the conditions for riskier clandestine travel. Unlike many other border security tactics, this measure is visible to a wide range of audiences who may protest its illegitimacy. The American Civil Liberties Union (ACLU) has described the establishment of the roadblocks at which Border Patrol officers deploy powers to stop and question individuals which are normally associated with physical borders as the creation of a 'Constitution-free zone' (ACLU, 2008). The appeal to civil liberties principles attests to the potentially wide-ranging impact of these measures on citizens and legal residents as well as illegalized travellers. Even so, the practical and symbolic significance of these dislocated border sites will be experienced very differently by those with legal status and those without.

The checkpoints have been linked to an increase in vehicle accidents resulting from Border Patrol pursuits. An online map produced by the NGO Humane Borders shows border-related deaths from 2000 to 2007 occurring in clusters within desert regions, but also fanning out along arterial roads.[4] An article in *The New York Times* (Archibold, 2006) reports that US–Mexico border patrols had seen a 'surge in vehicle deaths in 2003', coinciding with the start of a major push in border enforce-ment. The number of vehicle deaths was found to have jumped from 22 in 2002 to 42 in 2003. This was attributed to the new transportation methods being used by people smugglers in attempting to maximize their profits and minimize the risk of detection (Archibold, 2006). On 7 August 2006, nine migrants died in the Yuma Border Patrol sector when a vehicle carrying 21 Mexicans, said to be 'stacked in like cork-wood', lost control on a Border Patrol spike strip after speeding away from a highway checkpoint (Archibold, 2006). Arrests of people smuggled in cars tripled to a little fewer than 50,000 in 2005, up from 19,000 in 2001, although this trend was said to be reversing. Nevertheless, Michalowski (2007, p. 65) reports that during the time he spent in the Tucson borderlands from October 2005 to May 2006, 'rarely a week passed when at least one van, horse-trailer, or pick-up truck did not run off a road, overturn, or strike another vehicle, tree or bridge, resulting in serious injuries to migrants packed inside. In many instances, these crashes were the result of pursuit by Border Patrol vehicles'.

Death by degrees

Arguably, the slowest and cruellest deaths are those experienced once illegalized travellers have reached the Global North and, by virtue of their illegality or insecure status, are subjected to various forms of immiseration. Most critical commentators decline to equate the condition of illegality with a state of 'bare life' as described by Agamben, whereby individuals are stripped of *all* legal rights and protections (Agamben, 1998). Michalowski (personal communication) describes the circumstances facing illegalized migrants in the US as 'barely life', where access to social goods and essential services is severely restricted. Fan (2008, p. 725) agrees that '[m]igrants are thus not exactly bare life, denuded of all rights and protections, but theirs is a starkly *basic* life, denuded of the political and social entitlements that make the good life sweet'. Clearly, the situations of illegalized migrants will vary according to time and place, and according to the resources they can muster. However, in certain times and places, policies of deliberate destitution and indefinite detention have placed illegalized migrants in positions of such marginalization as to constitute forms of social death, exposing them to heightened risks of physical death as well.

Killed in the spirit – policies of deliberate destitution

Across the Global North, governments are increasingly engaged in efforts to reduce the access of illegalized migrants to public services and regulated labour markets. In Europe, Australia and North America, eligibility restrictions on the provision of essential housing, health and education services, and legal sanctions on employers who hire undocumented workers, are being systematically introduced. These measures may be intended to encourage departure or deter arrival by making the lives of undocumented migrants unlivable, or to enhance the capacity to detect and remove those who are not authorized to stay. Either way, these two dynamics of the internal border work together so that increased emphasis on detection may result in illegalized migrants avoiding access to essential services, whether or not there is a specific prohibition on their legal entitlement to them. Núñez and Heyman (2007) argue that illegalized migrants can be caught in 'entrapment processes' that severely limit their access to essential services such as housing, healthcare and education due to self-imposed limits on mobility. They cite immigration checkpoints as a major factor. In the wake of the passage of Senate Bill 1070 which empowers local police to investigate immigration status, undocumented migrants in northern Arizona told researchers they were already beginning to avoid public places like the local library – an essential service for their children's education – because of increased fears of detection (McDowell & Wonders, 2009/10). Ethnic community liaison officers working for police in New South Wales have reported that migrants with illegal or uncertain immigration status are often afraid to access police services, leaving them particularly vulnerable to harm from familial violence (Weber, 2012). In Germany, where healthcare workers are effectively criminalized for assisting illegalized migrants, Castañeda (2009) has found illegality to be a 'medical risk factor', preventing individuals from seeking assistance in a country that otherwise boasts universal healthcare coverage.

Against this backdrop of the increasing marginalization of illegalized migrants, it is a tragic irony that those who bring themselves to the notice of authorities in order to seek the protection of refugee status are particularly vulnerable to government policies deliberately designed to create conditions of dependency and destitution. In Britain, a comprehensive framework for asylum processing has been erected over the past decade with the aim of deterring supposedly 'bogus' asylum claims. In fact, similar policies introduced previously in Europe were found to create conditions for asylum seekers that were so dangerous and demoralizing as to encourage them to live illegally rather than apply for asylum (Webber, 2004). Granted the legal status of temporary admission into Britain while they await the outcome of their applications, asylum seekers who are not detained are barred from working legally and must rely on a system of financial support that is much more restrictive than the mainstream welfare system. Researchers from the IRR in London describe the circumstances faced by asylum seekers in the UK in the following terms: 'Asylum seekers inhabit a parallel but second-class world on the margins of society. They rely on an entirely separate system of benefits, housing and, increasingly, health services to survive. If you do not understand this, then you will never know which questions to ask and to whom' (Athwal & Bourne, 2007, p. 110, citing an unnamed refugee caseworker).

This marginal space has been deliberately created through multiple waves of restrictive policy reform implemented since 1996, aimed at reducing entitlements, controlling mobility and creating docile subjects who can be closely monitored by welfare systems. Ensuring minimal integration into the community also minimizes the potential for barriers to removal that can sometimes be mobilized by asylum seekers who have amassed community support (Webber, 2004). Asylum seekers are denied the right to work; granted minimal support (delivered in part through demeaning tokens); subjected to compulsory dispersal (often into run-down accommodation in deprived areas far from legal and social support, and where hostility to outsiders may be endemic); and deprived of all entitlements 21 days after their asylum application is rejected, creating extreme hardship where a decision is made to pursue an appeal.[5] Thus, the system is clearly aimed at 'starving out' (Webber, 2004) even those with strong claims, and forcing 'voluntary' repatriation through the sheer weight of hopelessness and despair. It is, in fact, forced deportation in another guise. The fact that an estimated half a million 'refused asylum seekers' are believed to still be living in the UK with no official support and no access to legal work (British Red Cross, 2010) attests first to the failure of that system as a border control policy, and second to the extent of the social problems it has fostered.

The policies of the UK Government have been contested by many external audiences: sometimes from a politicized point of view, which deplores the deliberate intent of the destitution programme and the departure this represents from the UK's obligations towards refugees under international law; and often from a humanitarian point of view, which is more deferential to the prerogative of governments to exercise border control. NGOs and faith groups have stepped in to fill gaps in welfare, as evidenced by the formation in Scotland of a 'Refugee Survival Trust' which provides small grants to destitute asylum seekers and, along with the Red Cross, attempts to work cooperatively with the UKBA which administers the asylum seeker support system (Refugee Survival Trust/British Red Cross, 2009). A report published by the Red Cross in 2010 goes further in its criticism, describing incidents of destitution as 'shameful' and challenging the refusal of permission to work which underpins the current system. More critical commentaries identify the structural violence inherent within the asylum support system

and point to the system's deadly outcomes. New enforcement strategies announced in 2007 by British Home Secretary John Reid, aimed
in part at unsuccessful asylum applicants, were openly designed 'to
make living and working illegally ever more uncomfortable and constrained' (Home Office, 2007). However, the intention of these policies
has been described in stronger terms as 'designed to break their will
and resolve' (Fekete, 2009b). Those living without legal status and
support face physical and mental health problems, loss of dignity and
self-worth, exploitation in the illicit economy, and exposure to violence at the hands of hostile citizens, fuelled by denigrating rhetoric
about 'bogus asylum seekers' and 'immigration offenders'. The conditions faced by destitute asylum seekers are made even worse by their
circumstances of entrapment, as explained here by the Red Cross:
'Most refused asylum seekers feel safer being destitute and homeless in
the UK than returning to their home country despite being at risk of
violence and exploitation' (British Red Cross, 2010, p. 19). One asylum
seeker spoke for many when he told the Red Cross, 'I have no hope. If I
have to go back home I will kill myself' (British Red Cross, 2010, p. 25).

Research by the IRR has identified a number of fatalities spanning the
17 years prior to 2006, which the researchers attribute to the iniquities of
the UK asylum system (IRR, 2006). The 'roll call of death' reported by the
IRR included the following: five deaths due to denial of healthcare for
treatable problems; one death directly due to destitution; 32 deaths (considered the tip of the iceberg) as a result of dangerous work in the 'black
economy'; and 18 deaths at the hands of violent racists, some of which
followed dispersal to conflict-ridden areas, notably in Glasgow, Liverpool,
Manchester, Newcastle and Bristol. A follow-up report four years later
identified a further seven deaths linked to the denial of healthcare, three
deaths as a direct result of destitution or unsuitable housing, four deaths
associated with illegal employment, and seven deaths through racist violence (Athwal, 2010). The IRR also reported that deaths of asylum seekers
in the community, particularly suicides, were increasing and averaging
one known death a month. Some examples of documented deaths associated with Britain's internal border are included in Table 4.1.

Comparisons with the holocaust may incur the objection that asylum
seekers in Britain have not, as yet, been subjected to the complete denial
of the 'right to have rights' (Arendt, 1968) – the form of *civil* death that
preceded deliberate killing of whole population groups in Nazi Germany.
Nevertheless, anyone who has witnessed directly, or read about, the state
of abjection into which many asylum seekers are placed will find some
resonance with the powerful testimony of Auschwitz survivor Primo Levi

Table 4.1 Examples of known asylum seeker deaths attributed to UK policies of destitution and dispersal

2002: Iranian asylum seeker Mohsen Amri (27) commits suicide at his home in Birmingham after his asylum application was rejected 'on a technicality'. He had made repeated requests for a work permit as he did not want to work illegally. *

2004: Twenty-three undocumented workers, mostly from Fujian province in China, drowned after being caught by a rising tide while working in the dark on dangerous mudflats in Morecombe Bay. It is believed most were awaiting asylum decisions and had been forced to work by a gangmaster who withheld their wages. *

2004: Iraqi asylum seeker Razgar Rassool Hamad (24) is found dead, probably from hypothermia, in a disused factory in West Bromich, having arrived in the UK the previous year from the Sangatte refugee camp in Calais. *

2005: Zimbabwean asylum seeker Star Engwenya dies in Hull Hospital, having lived 'from place to place' for several years. She had been unable to access treatment for her mental health problems and had also suffered a stroke. *

2006: Sri Lankan Yadav Krishnakumar (20 months) dies in Fairfield Hospital, Bury, of dehydration due to diarrhoea and vomiting. The Coroner describes the dispersal of his asylum seeking parents to an area without any support network as 'incomprehensible and inhumane'. ○

2006: Ethiopian Djere Kebede-Tulu (25), an elite long distance runner, and torture survivor, is found dead in his flat after continuing to train while living on £25 a week. He had been granted indefinite leave to remain three weeks before his death. ○

2007: Rejected Iraqi asylum seeker Solyman Rashed (28) is killed by a roadside bomb two weeks after making a 'voluntary return'. He had endured homelessness and destitution, followed by more than a year in detention where repeated bail applications were rejected. ○

2008: Iraqi Mohammed Ahmedi (18) dies in Gloucester Royal hospital as doctors and social workers attempt to clarify his immigration status. His family and lawyer claim he was not treated adequately because his status was unclear. ○

2008: Asylum seeker Lucy Kirma is found dead in her house in Birmingham. Friends believe she shut herself inside and 'just starved herself to death' after her application was rejected and her support discontinued. ○

2010: Rejected Ukrainian asylum seeker Yurij Skruten is found hanged in a disused pub in Brentford after living rough following the rejection of his application. His body is badly decomposed so the exact cause of death is difficult to determine. ○

Sources: * IRR (2006) *Driven to desperate measures*, Institute of Race Relations, London.
○ Athwal, H. (2010) *Driven to desperate measures: 2006–2010*, Institute of Race Relations, London.

who describes being 'killed in our spirit long before our anonymous death' (Levi, 1995, p. 61).

The invisible border that deliberately subjects asylum seekers to crushing destitution and welfare surveillance is sustained by a mentality of deterrence and by the primacy accorded to border protection which is not dislodged by the rising toll of death and suffering. The tragic death of 39-year-old Ghanaian woman Ama Sumani is just one example of this mentality taken to its logical conclusion, and one that galvanized at least some sections of the British medical community in protest. Ama Sumani died in hospital in Accra in 2008, after being deported from the UK while receiving treatment for cancer at the University Hospital of Wales. She was reportedly taken from the hospital in a wheelchair by five immigration officers and driven to Heathrow Airport (Athwal, 2010). In an editorial in the *Lancet* which refers to this tragedy, the editor strikes a critical tone in describing the failure of the medical fraternity to provide treatment for those in desperate need, and their complicity in authorizing 'fitness to travel' (*Lancet*, 2008). In doing so, he identifies the medical profession as a crucial, and potentially critical, audience capable of bearing witness to the human impacts of border control policies. Moreover, the editorial notes that Ama Sumani's solicitor was inundated with offers from members of the public to provide funds for treatment, and even from those offering to donate their bone marrow, observations that highlight the silence of medical professionals as all the more culpable. It concludes: 'To stop treating patients in the knowledge that they are being sent home to die is an unacceptable breach of the duties of any health professional. The UK has committed an atrocious barbarism. It is time for doctors' leaders to say so – forcefully and uncompromisingly' (*Lancet*, 2008, p. 178).

Dying inside: The impacts of indefinite detention

While zones of social exclusion can be created around individual asylum seekers living within the community through policies of immiseration and entrapment, detention centres represent the ultimate in purpose-built spaces of putative non-existence. Administrative detention is another means by which governments seek to deter asylum seekers from arriving, and to assert control over them if they manage to breach border defences. In Australia, asylum seekers who arrive by sea without a prearranged visa are subjected to mandatory and indefinite detention in isolated facilities without recourse to adequate legal assistance or review by the courts. Indefinite detention has been likened to an existence so extrapolated from the normal experience of personhood as to approach a form of social death. Australian novelist Bernard Cohn has described the mandatory detention regime in the following terms: 'In those places, you see, they are not really in Australia. They are in the empty ungoverned space of their bodies, I guess, confined within not-Australia' (cited in Perera, 2002, p. 10). This state of near non-existence strikes a chord with Bauman's description of refugees as people who 'do not *change* places; they lose a place on earth, they are catapulted into a nowhere' (Bauman, 2002, p. 112). To be detained indefinitely, writes Butler, 'is precisely to have no definitive prospect for re-entry into the political fabric of life, even as one's situation is highly, if not fatally, politicized' (Butler, 2004, p. 68).

So much has been written about immigration detention that the arguments about its inhumanity, its contravention of international human rights prohibitions against arbitrary detention, and its failure as a deterrent cannot be recounted in detail here (but see Grewcock, 2009; Weber, 2002; Welch & Schuster, 2005). The structural violence of indefinite detention manifests as systemic racism and brutality, and in routine, sometimes catastrophic failures in duty of care that are made all the more controversial by the contracting out of detention centre management to transnational global security corporations. Recurring themes in this regard within the academic and NGO literature have included the psychological harm of indefinite detention (Coffey et al., 2010; HRC, 2001; McLoughlin & Warin, 2008; Steel et al., 2004), especially to women (Stop Prisoner Rape, 2004), children (HREOC, 2004; Hutchinson & Martin, 2004; Steel et al., 2004) and victims of torture (Pourgirides et al., 1996; Silove et al., 2007; UKBA, 2011b); failures in duty of care, notably in the provision of medical treatment (FIAC, 2009; HMIP, 2006); systemic racism (PPO, 2004); and breaches of international human rights law prohibitions against torture, and inhuman or degrading treatment (CPT, 2011).

Although presented to the public as places for the restoration of control, detention centres are frequently places of protest, desperation and violent disorder, and sometimes death. Deaths in detention have most often been categorized as suicide (discussed in Chapter 6), but also arise from a lack of access to medical care and, occasionally, from violent altercations with guards. In 1991, Omasase Lumumba, the nephew of deposed Zairean Prime Minister Patrice Lumumba, died of a heart attack after being inappropriately restrained by prison guards at Pentonville Prison in London (IRR, 2006). In 2010, Eliud Nguli Nyenze, a 40-year-old Kenyan man, suffered a fatal heart attack in the Oakington Removal Centre in England after having repeatedly requested medical care but received none. His death triggered serious disturbances which led to the transfer of 60 detainees to prisons (Athwal, 2010). In Australia, ten or more deaths from medical conditions are known to have occurred in detention centres since 2000, some of which raise issues about lack of access to medical facilities in remote detention locations (see Appendix 1). In 2003, a 29-year-old Afghan woman, Fatima Irfani, died in a Perth hospital from bleeding to her brain after being transferred thousands of kilometres by air from offshore detention on Christmas Island. Detainees can also die needless and lonely deaths in urban detention centres. In 2001, the harrowing life of a young Thai woman Puangthong Simaplee, who had been trafficked into Australia at the age of 12, was brought to a premature end when she died of complications from heroin addiction while being held in the Villawood Detention Centre in Sydney. If we add to these physical deaths the lifelong impacts inscribed on the bodies and minds of those who have endured long periods of social death through indefinite detention, the death toll from confinement in these 'empty ungoverned places' rises much higher. In the words of one refugee detained in a remote Australian detention centre, 'I think Australian regime and Talaban are no different. Talaban killed people suddenly but this regime is killing people slowly, slowly' (Burnside, 2003, p. 48).

Conclusion

In this chapter we have identified border control policies as 'invisible actors' that condition the risks faced by illegalized travellers and migrants. External border controls expose illegalized travellers to an elevated risk of death through the geographical displacement of travel routes and substitution of dangerous modes of transport, in both cases necessitated by the importance of avoiding detection. The specific details of border controls, such as opportunities (or lack thereof) for family reunion and hierarchies of 'deportability', also shape the demographics of border fatality by creating perverse incentives for vulnerable groups to attempt dangerous border crossings. Internal border controls may create conditions of life for asylum seekers and illegalized migrants, both within and outside custodial environments, that are so marginalized as to constitute a form of 'social death'. Ultimately, we contend, many deaths of illegalized travellers, whether in transit or in the context of coping with 'unlivable' lives, take external policies aimed at non-arrival and internal policies aimed at non-existence to their logical conclusion.

5
Suspicious Deaths

> Mary Bale became a hate figure for dumping a cat in a bin. She
> was under investigation, then charged and finally fined. While
> we wait for the truth to come out on Jimmy [Mubenga]'s
> death, we – the sons and daughters of Africa – are wondering
> whether the British authorities value a cat more than a person
> from Africa.
>
> *Extract from speech by Adalberto (Rosario) Miranda,*
> *Union of Angolans in the UK*[1]

In this chapter we discuss instances where illegalized border crossers
are believed to have died directly at the hands of others, including
state agents, private contractors working for the state, people smugglers, border vigilantes and other private individuals. Although the
chains of responsibility leading to these deaths may be more clearly
discernible than the examples of 'death by policy' discussed in the previous chapter, they must also be understood as products of the social,
legal and political context in which they are embedded. Roberts (2008)
points out that even direct and deliberately inflicted violence may be
mediated by wider ideological structures that shape what could otherwise be interpreted as isolated, individual actions. The real-world
example he gives is the killing by a lone extremist of a prominent
female politician in Pakistan for refusing to wear a veil, which is clearly
a product of the broader sociopolitical context in that country as well
as the individual motivations of the killer. With respect to border
control, official depictions of irregular migrants and asylum seekers
as deviant, dangerous and illegal create the ideological context in
which government, commercial and private actors operate, and which
sometimes leads to migrant deaths. The attribution of responsibility to

individuals for such deaths may satisfy entirely legitimate demands for equity and justice; and this is of course an important part of accounting for these avoidable border-related deaths. However, attributing individual responsibility may leave unquestioned the complex of laws, policies, economic interests and beliefs that determine the behaviour of both illegalized travellers and those who may ultimately bring about their deaths.

This is not to argue that culpable individuals should be absolved of moral responsibility; there is a delicate balance to be found between acknowledging the power of authoritative structures and demanding that individuals continue to exercise both practical and moral judgement within the bounds of such structures. We might also expect to find individual differences among agents working either officially or unofficially on behalf of the state, in terms of their interpretation of and adherence to the framework of rules and expectations governing border control. Kelman and Hamilton (1989) have established that individual differences in orientation to authority influence how actors working within hierarchical organizations respond to directions that may cause harm to others. These ideas about 'crimes of obedience' have been applied by one of the authors to empirical research into border control. Interviews conducted at UK ports revealed that some border officials were found to be positively disposed towards detaining asylum seekers at the point of arrival, believing it to be their duty, while others considered the deliberate or unthinking detention practices of many of their colleagues to be illegitimate (Weber, 2005).

While we assert that attributions of responsibility that focus *solely* on individual actions (whether those of official agents or illegalized travellers) are partial and therefore inadequate, it is also important to acknowledge that there are considerable barriers to the recognition of individual responsibility in the first place, particularly where the allegations refer to official actors. The politico-legal framework of border control, with its elevated status as a 'transcendent mission' essential for protecting the security of lawfully present populations, attaches a *prima facie* legitimacy to the actions of those charged with implementing border control policies that is persuasive for many audiences. This makes it difficult to cross the contested legal boundary that separates lawful from unlawful killings when judging the actions of state agents. Even when viewed from a human rights perspective, agents of the state tend to be accorded a certain 'margin of appreciation' in recognition of their responsibilities and special status as the state's repository of coercive force. These protections for the state and its representatives complicate the process of accounting for deaths that result from risky, but officially sanctioned activities, such as interdicting illegalized border crossers to prevent their arrival, holding them in custody, or forcing them aboard aircraft for deportation.

Deadly deportations

The violence of forced deportation

While their numbers are not large compared with the catastrophic loss of lives at sea, deaths during deportation[2] are highly visible and violent. Moreover, they often involve people who have established networks of community support, whose deaths are therefore particularly socially divisive and politically controversial. Deaths during deportation usually arise from the use of unsafe methods of restraint, including adhesive tape or gags, resulting in suffocation or cardiac arrest. The British public was alerted to the violence of deportation in 1993 when a 40-year-old Jamaican woman, Joy Gardner, was asphyxiated after being bound and gagged in her home by police who were assisting immigration officials to deport her. Ms Gardner had been in England illegally since overstaying her visa in 1987. She left behind a five-year-old son who was born in England, and who witnessed the events leading to his mother's death. Six officials had been sent to the north London flat, which was occupied only by the mother and son. Three Metropolitan Police officers were later tried and found not guilty of the killing, despite it being established that they had wound 13 feet of sticking tape around Joy Gardner's head, reportedly to prevent her from biting them (BBC News, 1999). According to media reports, four independent pathologists found the cause of death to be 'hypoxic brain damage' caused by oxygen starvation, but differences of opinion emerged over whether this was caused by the gagging (Kirby, 1993). A Police Complaints Authority inquiry and a ministerial inquiry described as 'informal and secretive' were conducted into the circumstances surrounding Joy Gardner's death (Torode, 1993). However, no disciplinary action was taken against the police officers involved, and their supervisor was cleared in court of any wrongdoing (Fekete, 2005). No coronial inquest was ever held, apparently on the grounds that the facts of the case had been thoroughly examined during the criminal trial.

Joy Gardner's death came to symbolize wider concerns about the violence of forced deportation. After this case, forced deportation became an issue of great concern to the Council of Europe. In October 2003, a meeting of the European Committee for the Prevention of Torture and Inhuman or Degrading Treatment or Punishment (CPT) considered the issue of the deportation of foreign nationals by air (CPT, 2003). In the report that emerged from this meeting, the CPT noted, without qualification, that 'deportation operations by air entail a manifest risk of inhuman and degrading treatment'. As well as reminding EU Member States of their obligation to avoid the *refoulement* of individuals to locations where they risk being subjected to torture or ill treatment, and of the prohibition on any form of assault, the Committee reiterated the guidelines it had previously set for the lawful use of force in deportations. Underpinning these rules are the standard human rights tests of lawfulness, appropriateness and proportionality. Specifically, the CPT warned against prolonged application of body weight or bending the detainee forward, which are known to lead to 'positional asphyxia', and urged an immediate ban on the use of gagging or other devices that could obstruct airways. Preventing deportees from using toilet facilities, and forcing them to wear nappies, was identified as a degrading practice according to Article 3 of the European Convention on Human Rights. The Committee also expressed concern about the treatment of detainees *en route* to airports, and recommended that guards should be trained in manual control techniques in order to avoid the use of incapacitating gases or medications. Finally, the CPT report highlighted the importance of allowing deportees time to arrange their affairs and prepare for deportation – no doubt with the escalating practice of 'dawn raids' clearly in mind – noting that unnecessary anxiety and trauma were likely to increase the agitation of those being forcibly removed.

Soon after the CPT recommendations were issued, a report published in the UK by the Medical Foundation for the Care of Victims of Torture (Granville-Chapman et al., 2004) highlighted the urgent need for the CPT recommendations to be adopted. The Foundation's study of the excessive force used in unsuccessful attempts to remove 14 rejected asylum seekers revealed a litany of abuses (see Table 5.1). The study relied on a small sample of individuals who successfully resisted deportation. It is inherent within the nature of deportation that the violence suffered by individuals who are successfully returned remains undocumented. While admitting that their sample was small, the report's authors identified patterns suggestive of a systemic problem, notably: the use of unsafe and inappropriate methods of instrumental force; apparently punitive applications of force away from the public view; the unnecessary continuation of force after the deportee was restrained; and the misuse of handcuffing, much of it apparently deliberate. Analysis of the case files

Table 5.1 Injuries found by Medical Foundation doctors to be consistent with reported use of force

---

Injuries to limbs:
Cuts over wrist from handcuffing
Nerve injuries from handcuffing
Thumb fracture
Abrasions on shins due to kicking
Fluid on knee from twisting

Injuries to head, neck and face:
Sprained neck from head being forced down
Tenderness over cheekbone from blow to face
Abrasion over cheekbone from being dragged
Lip laceration from head being forced down
Bruised jaw and larynx from fingers pressed to throat
Temple laceration from striking head against object

Injuries to torso:
Tenderness over ribs from pushing, punching, kicking
Tenderness around scrotum from squeezing
Abdominal wall tenderness from punch to abdomen

Source: Granville-Chapman et al. (2004), p. 15

provided by the Medical Foundation doctors who examined the victims led to the conclusion that each of the cases established *prima facie* instances of breaches of Article 3 of the European Convention on Human Rights, for which the government was accountable, and probably constituted grounds for criminal charges and/or civil actions against the perpetrators. The report recommended *inter alia* that all individuals subject to a failed removal attempt should be referred for medical examination, and should not be thereafter subject to removal if a case for legal action were subsequently established. Around the same time, based on a different body of evidence, the Home Affairs Committee recommended that the role of Visiting Committees established to monitor the day-to-day management of detention centres should be extended to include the observation of removals (Home Affairs Committee, 2003). It seems that neither of these recommendations was adopted.

Turning people into removal statistics

Since the publication of these critical reports, politically populist removal targets have been adopted by governments throughout Europe (Fekete, 2005, 2009b). Britain alone reportedly spent £100 million in the period 2005–10 on deportations (Milmo, 2010). A UK National Audit Office

(NAO) report on returning failed asylum applicants claimed to identify efficiency improvements which could release a further £28 million per year to be used to increase removal numbers (NAO, 2005). Repeated financial crises have subsequently created further incentives to accelerate deportation programmes as cheaper options to the construction of more detention centres (ERA, 2010). An examination of developments in deportation policies from 2009 to 2010 by the ERA led the organization to conclude that the pace of deportation was accelerating across northern and eastern Europe in particular, while the emphasis in the south remained on preventing arrival. The ERA researchers reported that, of the €5866 million allocated by the EU to so-called solidarity and management of migration flows for the period 2007–13, nearly €3000 million is allocated to external border controls and returns. A further €500 million has been allocated to the European border agency Frontex over the same period (ERA, 2010, p. 2). This compares with only €628 million allocated to dealing with refugees, of which ERA claimed nearly 30 per cent is spent on voluntary returns, and an unknown amount on removals under the Dublin Convention. Deportation is clearly a growth area for Frontex, which was initially deployed primarily to secure the external perimeter of the EU. The agency's Program of Work for 2011 refers to the management of joint deportation operations to supplement the efforts of Member States as a relatively new role for the organization (Council of the European Union, 2011).

A growing number of bilateral agreements between countries of the southern perimeter of Europe and governments across Africa's northern and Atlantic seaboard have ushered in an era of targeted, large-scale returns. Although the information base is limited, Fekete (2009b) observes that deaths arising directly from forced deportation seem to be disproportionately occurring among Africans, notably Nigerians. This suggests that sub-Saharans are subjected to higher levels of physical control, or are more likely to be involved in forced deportations, or both.[3] Deportations are also being systematically targeted at groups that were previously given temporary refuge after fleeing armed conflict in their home countries. For example, in March 2001 the UKBA announced a resumption of charter flights in collaboration with Frontex and the Swedish Government to return 'failed asylum seekers' to Iraq, against the express advice of the United Nations High Commissioner for Refugees (UNHCR) (Bowcott, 2011). Removals to Iraq which had formerly been running at around 50–60 a month had been on hold after a ruling by the European Court of Human Rights against returning Iraqis to danger (Bowcott, 2010). Thousands more Iraqis are believed to be facing deportation from Britain. While scheduled commercial flights may still be used for individual deportations, sometimes engaging the intervention of critical audiences, charter flights are spaces from which external audiences are excluded. According to ERA (2010, p. 5), UK charter flight removals to Afghanistan 'take place every other Tuesday evening under the codename Operation Ravel'.

This acceleration of the expulsion effort has been widely associated with the increasing use of force against deportees. Fekete (2009b, p. 3) argues that removal targets, with associated performance indicators for border police and security guards, create a 'callous culture' conducive to violence in which the humanity of those targeted for removal is neutralized. HM Chief Inspector of Prisons Anne Owers (cited in Youseff, 2011, p. 12) has described the accelerated removal process in Britain as 'dehumanising', noting that '[s]ome of those we observed in detention had been dealt with by immigration authorities as though they were parcels, not people; and parcels whose contents and destination were sometimes incorrect'. Categories of exclusion are also expanding, notably through a focus on criminal deportees whose legal right to residence has been revoked following a criminal conviction in their country of residence. The increasingly 'criminal' nature of the population of deportees then becomes a basis for inflated risk perceptions and provides justification for still higher levels of force. The fact that the process has been accelerated itself brings added risks, in reducing access to legal reviews and increasing the chances of 'mistakes' (ERA, 2010; Home Affairs Committee, 2003, p. 13). This in turn increases the likelihood of deporting those in abject fear of return, and concomitantly, one might surmise, raising the likelihood of resistance.

In 2008 a UK legal practice, a medical NGO and a campaigning group together compiled a list of assaults at the hands of private security guards which were reported to them by deportees (Wistrich et al., 2008). The authors considered the 300 cases in their dossier to represent the 'tip of the iceberg'. A third of the cases involved women, and many of the violent incidents were witnessed by children. Eighty per cent of the cases involved a person from sub-Saharan Africa. Documented abuses included many of the practices recorded in 2004 by the Medical Foundation, such as hitting and kicking, dragging and tight handcuffing. However, this study added to the catalogue of abuse reports of shackling, tying of legs, slamming doors onto hands and feet, denial of medical care, and eye gouging – all often said to be accompanied by racist abuse. Table 5.2 summarizes the locations and types of injury described in the 2008 report. The authors concluded that the abuses

Table 5.2 The use and misuse of state-sanctioned force during detention and removal

Abuse experienced – all reports		Injuries reported	
Assaulted/beaten	108	Bruising/swelling	92
Punched	59	Head/neck/back pain	55
Kicked	52	Cuts/bleeding	54
Choking/gagging	47	Fractures/dislocation/organ damage	23
Overzealous restraint	46	Psychiatric damage	21
Racist abuse	38	Self-harm	4
Dragging	27	*Location of assault (where known)*	
Kneeling/sitting on	26	Airport	93
Children witnessed abuse	13	On plane awaiting take-off	46
Children assaulted	5	Escort van on way to airport	23
Sexual assault	7	Escort van on return to detention	14
Pregnant women assaulted	4	Detention centre	12
		On plane after take-off	5
		During stopover	2

Source: Wistrich, Arnold et al. (2008) Appendix 1

were systemic and widespread, and accused the Home Office of 'out-sourcing abuse' through a failure to properly monitor the actions of contracted security staff. The UKBA appointed Baroness Nuala O'Loan, a former Police Ombudsman from Northern Ireland, to investigate these allegations and others that were circulating in the press. The Baroness declined to conclude that abuse was 'systematic' – a claim which she apparently sought to investigate by looking for repeat accusations against individual officers (O'Loan, 2010).[4] From the limited documentary evidence available to her in relation to 29 cases, she concluded, rather elliptically, that 'there was inadequate management of the use of force by the private sector companies' (O'Loan, 2010). It does not appear that arrangements were made for the individuals who made the allegations to present their cases, and a large number of those alleging assault were likely to have already been deported.

Her Majesty's Inspector of Prisons (HMIP) conducted a thematic review of detainee escorts and removals in 2009 (HMIP, 2009). Based on interviews with detainees awaiting deportation at Heathrow Airport, and observations which she admitted were liable to influence the behaviour observed, Chief Inspector Anne Owers concluded that there were 'significant gaps and weaknesses in the systems for monitoring, investigating and complaining about incidents where force has been used or where abuse was alleged' (HMIP, 2009, p. 5). While she noted that most escorts were said to be polite and friendly, reports of excessive force were also received. She found that serious problems occurred regularly in relation to language difficulties, lack of access to medication and refusal to allow deportees to bring their possessions, all of which exacerbate anxieties and risks. The Chief Inspector made the important observation that 'in most cases the use of force did not assist removal, but in fact led to its abandonment' (HMIP, 2009, p. 6). She noted that medical examinations were not routinely carried out after failed removal attempts, even where injuries had occurred.

Fatality on British Airways Flight 77

In October 2010, the tragic death of Jimmy Mubenga on British Airways (BA) flight BA77 pointed emphatically to the 'inadequate management of the use of force' by the UKBA. Unlike Joy Gardner, the Angolan father of five had committed a crime. He had spent two years in prison for a serious assault, after which time his leave to remain in the UK was revoked. That two-year prison term proved to be a death sentence. Passengers on board flight BA77 reported hearing Jimmy Mubenga shouting for ten minutes or more that the guards were trying to kill him and saying repeatedly that he could not breathe, as guards from the private security firm G4S leaned heavily on him. He eventually collapsed and paramedics were called to the scene. At the time of writing, there was yet to be an official inquiry, so the available evidence consists only of eyewitness accounts reported in the British press.

The UKBA initially released statements to the effect that a passenger on flight BA77 had been 'taken ill'. They temporarily banned the use of restraint, but later reversed the decision, attracting criticism from the Chair of the Home Affairs Select Committee in the House of Commons (Lewis et al., 2010). Representatives from G4S were questioned by the Home Affairs Committee on 2 November 2010 to 'address concerns about the rules governing removals from the UK', but no report from that meeting has been posted on the Committee's webpage.[5] Jimmy Mubenga's family, assisted by the charitable group Inquest, campaigned for a wider inquiry (Inquest, 2011), supported by calls from a number of MPs who were clearly appalled by this glimpse of the brutality of the deportation system. The three guards were questioned in relation to manslaughter charges and released on bail, and media reports suggested that Scotland Yard was investigating a range of assault charges against other deportation escorts (Lewis et al., 2010). In a further development, it was reported that a rarely used corporate manslaughter charge was being considered against the G4S company, assisted by unidentified whistleblowers within the organization. These dissident employees reportedly told the Home Affairs Committee that the company ignored repeated warnings about potentially lethal practices (Lewis & Taylor, 2011). The broadening of the prosecution, and the grounds that have so far been publicly stated, strongly suggest the recognition of systemic problems related to the excessive use of force within the deportation system, and deficiencies in the oversight of contracted security guards effecting forced removals.

The *Guardian* newspaper was instrumental in identifying eyewitnesses to Jimmy Mubenga's death. Flight BA77 was full of engineers returning to their jobs with mining corporations in Angola. The accounts published by the newspaper offer some worrying insights into how a protracted event such as this can be allowed to unfold without intervention from bystanders (Lewis, 2010). One witness, a 29-year-old engineer, told the *Guardian* that 'most passengers were not concerned' at the shouting. A 51-year-old oil worker, who reportedly came forward after hearing what he considered to be misleading accounts put forward by the Home Office and G4S, said he did not get involved because he was afraid of losing his job, but added that he would be haunted by that decision for the rest of his life. Another passenger of Eastern European origin also expressed his deep regret for not taking any action, and attributed the widespread inaction to what Kelman and Hamilton (1989) would describe as obedience to authority:

> I would never ever imagine the situation like this could happen in the civilized world. Maybe that is because in the UK the authority of police and security is so high? I believe in my country, where police is not so much respected, people would be much more willing to do something witnessing situation like this. (Witness 4, quoted in Lewis, 2010)

This passenger also expressed his dismay at the inaction of the aircraft crew, both before and after Jimmy Mubenga had collapsed, adding that they were ultimately responsible for the safety of everyone on board, 'including handcuffed, isn't it?'.

It remains to be seen whether the death of Jimmy Mubenga will invite the level of scrutiny and criticism of the deportation system that was applied to the London Metropolitan Police following the racist murder of black teenager Stephen Lawrence (Macpherson, 1999). Writing in the *Guardian*, immigration adviser Anna Morvern (2010) claimed that it was time to 'look at ourselves and ask how we became a society that will now effect deportations by almost any means possible'. She added, 'we'd do well to channel our grief at Mubenga's abuse into vocal resistance of the odious immigration controls, as they provide an inherent justification for the crushing and accelerating apparatus of forced deportations'.

Judging from similar events in recent history, it seems that such a fundamental questioning by populations and governments is unlikely. Fekete (2005, p. 14) has argued that meaningful engagement by European governments with well-established human rights standards guiding the use of force has been glaringly absent, even in the face of the 'embarrassment of high-profile deportation cases which ended in deaths or injury'. Following the death of Joy Gardner in 1993, the main response from the UK Government was to seek to improve police training in restraint techniques. This was also the primary thrust of the recommendations of the O'Loan report in response to allegations of excessive force by private security guards. In relation to 12 European deportation deaths she examined, Fekete (2009b, p. 4) describes state responses as 'going through the motions of accountability', while avoiding any fundamental questioning of the morality of state-sanctioned violence applied in the process of removal. None of the 12 cases resulted in any charges being proven. In what seems to be a worst-case scenario, the Spanish Government apparently responded to the asphyxiation death of Osamuyi Aikpitanhi by recommending that resistant deportees be fitted with straightjackets and helmets. This was despite the fact that 'deportation helmets' designed to immobilize the lower jaw and to be attached to plane seats had already been banned in Germany in 1999 after being found to have contributed to the death of Sudanese asylum seeker Aamir Mohamed Ageeb (Fekete, 2009b, p. 4).

The death of Jimmy Mubenga drew attention once again to the political risks of using commercial flights for the deportation of illegalized migrants. Moreover, after the death, a BA long-haul pilot reportedly told the *Guardian* that airline crews are legally responsible for passenger safety on board, and that the option of restraining someone for many hours was not feasible in practice (Milmo, 2010). This observation may highlight the rationale for governments' increasing use of charter flights, not only because of the greater efficiency for deporting large, single-nationality groups, but also for the assurance it brings that their expulsion projects will not be impeded. Apart from the temporary ban on the use of restraint following the death of Jimmy Mubenga, the primary action taken by the Home Office has been to decline to renew the G4S deportation contract (Lewis & Taylor, 2010). At the time of writing, there appeared to be some prospect of a criminal prosecution which recognizes Jimmy Mubenga not merely as a commercial risk for a global security corporation, but also as a human being. The outcomes of police investigations are no doubt eagerly awaited by Jimmy Mubenga's family, the Union of Angolans in the UK, and other 'sons and daughters of Africa'.

Frontier violence

Border warfare

Critical commentators may resist the tendency to depict the US–Mexico border as a lawless frontier typified by shoot-outs between drug gangs and law enforcement officers, fearing that this will serve to justify harsher policies. Still, it must be recognized that parts of that border have become sites of open conflict, protest and pervasive danger. In the remote areas in which many illegalized travellers now lose their lives, danger mostly takes the form of unrelenting heat or cold, of fast-flowing rivers and of uncharted terrain. Danger may also take on a human guise in borderland communities that are now cut in two by a fortified border fence, where

US–Mexico border fence in Organ Pipe Cactus National Monument Arizona
© Cook and Jenshel

Border fence divides the town of Nogales on the border between Sonora and Arizona
© Ryan Bavetta

once their populations mingled freely. Interpersonal violence in these locations may be fuelled by two kinds of US border war: the war against drugs and the war against illegal immigration. Both wars are pursued by means of legal prohibition and enforcement, both have fuelled criminal markets and led to escalating violence of varying kinds on either side of the border and beyond, and both have inevitably intersected, although not fully converged, creating a hybrid space of criminality into which illegalized border crossers may be drawn.

Border militarization has increased the risks for illegalized travellers on the US–Mexico border. In a 2006 report to the UN Human Rights Committee (Border Network for Human Rights, 2006), the El Paso NGO Border Network for Human Rights noted that the Joint Task Force-Six (JTF-6), ostensibly created to support drug interdiction operations, had been used primarily by the Border Patrol to deal with illegalized border crossers. The NGO argued that this build-up of military presence led to several injuries being inflicted on migrants and border residents in the late 1990s during covert 'exercises'. While the report's authors acknowledge that military patrols were suspended thereafter, in 2006 the Bush administration sent 6000 National Guard troops with the explicit goal of assisting the US Border Patrol, overwhelming the populations of some borderlands communities with military personnel. Border militarization is not limited to the presence of actual military forces, as argued by the Border Network for Human Rights (2006, p. 7): 'Militarization of the border is not simply indicated by the presence of military personnel, but by the entire border enforcement strategy which utilizes military language, military training of civilian agencies, military technology and equipment to seek out undocumented immigrants at the border.' The US has a long history of armed policing, and the weapons capability of the Border Patrol appears to be upholding this tradition. According to a shooting enthusiasts' website, US Border Patrol officers swept the field in the National Police Shooting championship in 2010, taking the first three positions in the competition (Accurate Shooter, 2010). Despite this capability, or perhaps because of it, the job of a Border Patrol officer is not without its dangers. Annual memorial ceremonies are held in Washington DC to honour 'fallen heroes', and the Border Patrol announced in its 2008 fiscal year review that assaults on agents had increased by 11 per cent from 2007 (US Customs and Border Protection, 2008).

Carpenter (2006) has argued that women face particular threats arising from border militarization. Noting that rape has always been part of the 'price' women pay for crossing borders without the protection of the law, Carpenter argues that militarization of the border significantly shifts power relations in favour of gendered violence by changing the nature of the border into a 'war zone'. While there is no statistical data to determine whether the numbers of rapes are increasing, Carpenter notes that many of the reported rapes at the US–Mexico border documented by Falcon (cited in Carpenter, 2006) display an element of the misuse of government authority. Falcon's research documents cases of rape by border officials, in which women have been released into US territory after being raped. This leads Carpenter to conclude that rape is not being used in an instrumental way to keep women out, but rather for punitive purposes in order to 'keep them in their place'. In other contexts researchers have found that rape may become the 'currency' for purchasing cross-border mobility in the absence of legally protected border-crossing options (Pickering, 2010; see also Khosravi, 2010).

Mexican authorities have been active in identifying killings and other human rights abuses arising from US border control. Mexico's Ministry of Foreign Affairs reported 117 cases of human rights abuses by US Border Patrol officials against Mexican citizens from 1988 to 1990, including 14 deaths (Border Network, 2006). The Border Network for Human Rights NGO has documented the following examples of death at the hands of Border Patrol officers. Nineteen-year-old Juan Patricio Peraza Quijada was shot and killed on an El Paso street on 22 February 2003 when he fled from a document check. This case aligns with a long history of the permissive use of lethal force in American criminal law enforcement in relation to 'fleeing felons' (Kleinig, 1996). On 4 June 2003, 22-year-old Ricardo Olivares Martinez was shot five times while climbing *back* over the border fence, after reportedly throwing rocks at Border Patrol agent Cesar Cervantes. This was the sixth report of a fatal shooting in response to rock-throwing since 1996. Throwing rocks as a protest against segregation and disempowerment is a familiar scenario from situations of occupation, notably Palestine, where the protests of dispossessed youths may also be met with deadly force. These examples suggest that the border wall is a generator of violence in itself. In a tragic reversal of the usual rock-throwing scenario, two women and a teenage girl drowned in the Rio Grande as US Border Patrol members reportedly threw rocks at a group of six migrants who had crossed safely, in order to force their return (Border Network, 2006).

More recently, the Mexican Ministry of Foreign Affairs has reported that 17 Mexican nationals were killed or injured in 2010 in use of force incidents – up from 12 in 2009 and five in 2008 (*Sydney Morning Herald*, 2010). A particularly controversial incident took place in June 2010, when 15-year-old Hernandez Guereca was shot by US Border Patrol officers on the Mexican side of the border fence near El Paso, Texas, allegedly after he had thrown rocks. This followed soon after the death by beating and tasering of Anastasio Hernandez Rojas at the busy Tijuana–San Diego crossing in May of the same year, apparently while he was resisting deportation. The shooting of a minor, particularly on Mexican soil, was bound to be inflammatory. President Felipe Calderon expressed his grave concern about the 'surge of violence against Mexicans' (*Sydney Morning Herald*, 2010). Syndicated news reports in January 2011 stated that the family of Hernandez Guereca had filed a lawsuit against the US Government seeking $25 million in damages (Associated Press, 2011). Media reporting around this incident often states that border agents are permitted to use lethal force against rock throwers (see, for example, Marosi, 2008) – a claim that, if true, would amount to sanctioning and systematizing the use of disproportionate force.

Away from the borderlands, deep inside Mexican territory, the effects of the fortification of the US–Mexico border reverberate. Many illegalized migrants travelling from the Americas and beyond use freight trains as their preferred mode of travel towards hoped-for jobs in the north. Here they are easy targets for interdiction by Mexican immigration officers, often assisted by military personnel. The Mexican Human Rights organization Comisión Nacional de los Derechos Humanos (CNDH) has documented instances of the use of excessive force by Mexican naval personnel during these operations. It criticizes in particular the 'pattern of surprise' adopted by officials, which CNDH argues encourages the use of force. Citing the CNDH data, Amnesty International urged the Mexican Government to refrain from using military forces that were untrained for the role and not legally empowered to perform immigration checks (AI, 2010). Amnesty noted that a rhetoric of danger, which classifies the trains as conduits for drugs and arms, has been used to justify military-style interdictions aimed at overcoming a dangerous enemy. In the same report, Amnesty documented several fatal attacks carried out by state police. On 9 January 2009, Chiapas state police opened fire on a truck carrying around 45 illegalized travellers from El Salvador, Guatemala, Honduras, Ecuador and China, when it failed to stop in response to a police order. Three passengers were killed and eight were seriously wounded. The state prosecution authorities investigated the incident and, according to Amnesty, found that police had shot at their own vehicle in order to later claim that the migrants had opened fire. Three police officers were arrested and charged with murder and wounding. A similar incident in the same state on 18 September 2009 resulted in the death of one migrant and the injury of others.

Amnesty condemned the use of lethal force in a situation where there was no threat to life, and blamed the lack of a clear regulatory framework for the use of excessive force by Mexican security and police forces.

Criminal gangs (and their accomplices)

Across the border from El Paso, Texas, Ciudad Juarez is widely considered to be among the most dangerous cities in the world (Boehm, 2011, p. 12). Where the war on the US–Mexico border and the US war on drugs collide, endemic violence has ensued. This violence has impacted residents, internal Mexican migrants seeking work in the factories built by US corporations in the northern borderlands, and illegalized travellers of other nationalities who are forced to stay or pass through violent areas on their journey towards the US border. Boehm (2011, p. 12) sees parallels between the sources of violence that affect vulnerable communities on either side of the border, since much of the violence in Mexico is driven by a demand for drugs in the US and by the supply of arms crossing the border in the other direction.

There is considerable documentation, and growing concern, about the deliberate targeting of illegalized migrants in Mexico by criminal gangs and their Mexican law enforcement accomplices. Drug-related crime has become interwoven with illegalized border crossing in a number of ways. A *New York Times* editorial claimed sardonically, '[w]e have delegated to drug lords the job of managing our immigrant supply, just as they manage our supply of narcotics' (*New York Times*, 2010). The most shocking evidence of a growing trend among organized criminal groups to kidnap migrants for ransom was witnessed in the so-called Tamaulipas Massacre, when the bodies of 72 murdered migrants were found on a ranch in the north-east border state of Tamaulipas in August 2010 (Boehm, 2011). The 58 men and 14 women came from Honduras, El Salvador, Guatemala, Ecuador and Brazil. Mainstream media reports stated that the migrants were heading for the US border when they were waylaid by a notorious drug cartel, and executed when they were unable to pay a ransom and/or refused to work as drug mules (BBC News, 2010). One of only two survivors managed to alert personnel at a military checkpoint. It was reported that Mexican marines then engaged the gang in a shoot-out in which one marine and three gunmen were killed, while all but one suspect managed to escape. According to reports, the judge involved in the prosecution and the town mayor were also murdered soon after.

The Tamaulipas Massacre was not an isolated incident. So serious is the situation that the matter was brought to the 138th session of the

Inter-American Commission on Human Rights in 2010. CNDH has estimated that 20,000 kidnappings and extortions occur each year in Mexico (*Economist*, 2010). An article in *The Economist* (2010) argued that '[m]igrants from Central and South America are particularly easy targets. Illegal in Mexico, they must evade checkpoints throughout the country and risk deportation if they report a crime'. As well as being vulnerable to interception and mistreatment during their journey, they may put themselves in danger by engaging the services of people smugglers – a strategy that has become necessary as the fortification of the US border has continued:

> Because the crossing is difficult, most migrants seek help. A 2010 report from the United Nations Office on Drugs and Crime (UNODC) estimates that human smuggling is a $6.6 billion industry in Mexico, and that 90 per cent of unauthorized immigrants crossing into the United States through Mexico hired a smuggler at some point along the journey – for food, for shelter, for a hiding spot in the back of a tractor-trailer, for guidance about where to find water on the trail: 'For many immigrants it pays off', says Nestor Rodriguez, a sociologist at the University of Texas, Austin. He notes that some coyotes are members of their communities in good standing, esteemed for having helped friends and neighbours. The problem is that other smugglers are predators, who abandon, kidnap or kill their charges. (*Economist*, 2010)

Illegalized migrants are particularly vulnerable because they are known to carry relatively large amounts of cash with them to pay for transport and the fees required to cross the border without authorization. A 2010 Amnesty International report referred to illegalized migrants in Mexico as 'invisible victims' (AI, 2010). It noted that tens of thousands of migrants travel through Mexico without legal permission every year, around 90 per cent of them from Central America. Around 20 per cent of these migrants are women, and it is estimated that six out of ten have been sexually assaulted along their journey. Mexican NGOs have begun conducting surveys on the abuses suffered. Based on interviews with 828 migrants who arrived at its shelter between May 2007 and February 2008, the Belén Posada del Migrante organization in Saltillo reported 3924 incidents of non-lethal violence (AI, 2010). Carpenter (2006) asserts that women who gather to work in the factories or *maquiladoras* in Mexico's north are particularly vulnerable to border-related violence. She notes that the city of Juarez has 1.3 million inhabitants and a concentration of 380 *maquiladoras*. Around half the population are transient residents from all over Latin America, some of whom stop to look for work in the largely US-owned factories. More than 300 women were murdered in the city environs in the 11 years prior to 2006, an unknown number of whom were illegalized migrants. Like Boehm, Carpenter finds parallels between the two sides of the border, not so much between the sources of violence, but more with respect to its purpose in relation to women. She argues that 'violent methods of social control used against women on the Mexican side of the border mirror the violence of United States border policies and technologies of enforcement' (Carpenter, 2006, p. 168).

So prevalent are deaths and disappearances of illegalized migrants that a grassroots organization Comité de Familiares de Migrantes Fallecidos y Desaparecidos (Committee of Relatives of Dead and Disappeared Migrants) has been established in El Salvador. It claimed that 293 El Salvadorans had been killed or had gone missing in the two years prior to February 2009 (AI, 2010). Under Mexican law, inquiries must be held for any death arising from accident or violence; however, Amnesty International contends that 'in the context of large numbers of violent deaths in many parts of Mexico, the investigation is unlikely to progress unless relatives are actively involved' (2010, no page). Amnesty argues that the Mexican state is obliged to investigate, prosecute and seek to prevent human rights abuses against non-Mexicans, just as it has urged the US Government to do in relation to Mexican citizens. Amnesty International's recommendations on preventing the abuse of illegalized travellers are an important step in highlighting the need for the equal protection of the human rights of illegalized travellers. However, they do not fundamentally call into question the framework of illegalization operating on both sides of the border which delivers illegalized travellers into the hands of unscrupulous criminal gangs, and traps them in violence-ridden towns on the northern borders as they wait to gather the resources needed to negotiate the difficult and expensive border crossing.

Some observers have claimed that kidnappings are taking a new turn as drug gangs become more involved: 'According to what I've been told, the kidnappers appear to belong to drug trafficking groups, which is new. There have always been kidnappings of migrants around here, but those responsible were criminals of another kind, less organised' (Manager of Home of Mercy shelter for immigrants in Mexico, cited in Cevallos, 2008). On the other hand, while it may suit both the US and Mexican authorities to attribute the violence to criminal gangs, a phenomenal 91 per cent of the 238 kidnap victims interviewed by the

CNDH (AI, 2010) claimed that government officials were directly responsible, and 40 per cent reported police collusion. The direct involvement of the police is usually to detain illegalized travellers, often by taking them from trains, and handing them over to criminal gangs. The collusion is sometimes said to spread further, involving train drivers and private security guards on trains. According to Amnesty International, no prosecution has followed in any case where the CNDH has handed over documentation about offences such as these to the authorities.

Associated with these instances of criminal victimization, there is a larger story to be told about the twin wars on drugs and illegal migration, and what Bowling (2010) has described as the 'globalisation of harm'. Bowling argues that a 'spillover' of serious armed violence and corruption into transit areas – most notably the Caribbean, but also through Mexico, Venezuela, Guyana and Brazil – has resulted from the redirection of drug trafficking routes due to the transnational prohibition against the supply of psychotropic drugs. While this violence is clearly criminally motivated, it has also been spurred by US policies which have fuelled illicit markets through an almost exclusive emphasis on the control of supply rather than an amelioration of demand, and sought to buffer American populations from the resulting violence by further fortifying the border. The above factors have exposed illegalized travellers moving along these routes to extreme dangers. Moreover, Boehm (2011) has argued that the desire to close the US border to crossings that are seen as exclusively labour-related, and to secure American populations against cross-border violence, has rendered invisible the genuine protection needs of many illegalized border crossers, from Mexico and beyond, who are seeking to escape intolerable levels of violence in Mexico.

Border patriots

The US has a long history of organized vigilantism, which emerged out of frontier conditions to fill perceived gaps in law enforcement. Just as we have observed in relation to people-smuggling operations, vigilante organizations have not been uniformly murderous and corrupt. Early vigilante movements in the US often embodied the spirit of self-help that is associated with the Republican tradition. They could be well-organized, rule-governed and considered legitimate by large sections of the local population, at least at the outset (Brown, 1991). In contemporary America, civilian patrols are once again emerging, in this case to cover perceived gaps in border protection. Cabrera (2010) notes that border vigilantism in Arizona dates back at least to the 1970s. As with any form of policing, the legitimacy of border policing groups will be differently perceived by different audiences. The best-known groups are the Minutemen Project and American Patrol – referred to by migrant communities as 'migrant hunters' (Border Network, 2006). California Governor Arnold Schwarzenegger is reported to have declared his support for the Minutemen Project (Cevallos, 2005).

The Minutemen emerged in April 2005 when several hundred volunteers, some carrying side-arms, began to stand watch along stretches of the south-eastern Arizonan desert where the border was marked only by a barbed-wire fence (Cabrera, 2010). It might be argued that the iconography of the fence itself played a role in the emergence of these groups: on the one hand, building up the expectation of impermeability, while on the other, being so frequently breached. The illusion of border control sets the government up to fail in the eyes of those who demand unbreachable borders. In some locations Minutemen groups have reportedly constructed their own border fences. The *modus operandi* of the Minutemen is said to be to 'pursue and hold' illegalized border crossers and deliver them to the Border Patrol, although Cabrera notes that their methods have sometimes been suspected of being more violent. In terms of the role they play, Cabrera likens these self-appointed groups to the slave patrols of earlier times – the recognized forerunners of the Ku Klux Klan – as both the old and new seek to fill perceived gaps in law enforcement against specific groups. Although there are marked differences in the circumstances of slaves and contemporary border crossers, runaway slaves were also seeking to cross borders without authorization in order to escape to freedom and safety. In relation to both slave patrols and border vigilantes, Cabrera concludes: 'In both periods, the presence of non-professional civilians who have little formal oversight in their efforts to enforce the law magnifies the risks to those crossing borders' (2010, p. 229). While he notes that the Minutemen have been 'adamant that their volunteers are neither violent not racist, citing strict self-defense protocols and screening processes' (2010, p. 229), Cabrera points out that juries have made awards of around $100,000 in a number of cases to migrants or Hispanic Americans who have established that they have been abused by civilian border patrol members in Arizona and Texas.

The Border Network for Human Rights (Border Network, 2006) has also alleged that organized civilian border patrollers and armed ranchers frequently harass illegalized migrants. It cites reports by the American Civil Liberties Union that a request for official records revealed a disturbing number of incidents related to vigilante activity on the US–Mexico border in which migrants reported being 'shot at, bitten by dogs, hit with flashlights, kicked, taunted, and unlawfully imprisoned' (Border Network, 2006, p. 8). The Border Network filed a petition with the Inter-American Commission on Human Rights regarding instances of vigilante violence, claiming that 'when the local sheriff publicly praises vigilantes, justice can be hard to find' (Border Network, 2006, p. 9). At least one such incident ended in a fatality. Seventy-six-year-old rancher Samuel Blackwood shot and killed Eusebio de Haro in May 2000, after the young man stopped at his ranch to ask for a drink of water. After failing to 'subdue' him for the Border Patrol, Blackwood is said to have pursued the young man for some time in his pick-up truck and then delivered the fatal shot (Border Network, 2006). The incident prompted the United Nations to dispatch a special envoy to investigate what was at that time a spate of violent incidents along that stretch of the border (McGirk, 2000).

In May 2009, vigilante violence in the Arizonan borderlands took a sinister new turn when Shawna Forde, a founder of the Minutemen American Defense Group, allegedly orchestrated the point-blank shootings of Raul Flores and his young daughter in their own home. Flores's wife was also shot, but survived. The prosecution case is that Forde made a deliberate plan to steal money from Flores – who was said to be a suspected drug trafficker – in order to fund her civilian militia group. The plan allegedly included the killing of all witnesses, including the execution of the 9-year-old girl (AOL News, 2011). The trial was ongoing at the time of writing.

Young Americans in border regions seem to be rising to the challenge of protecting America's southern borders, if a 2009 article in *The New York Times* is anything to go by. The article, entitled 'Scouts train to fight terrorists, and more' (Steinhauer, 2009), includes a photograph of a group of serious-looking uniformed teenagers holding compressed airguns which look like semi-automatic rifles. The young men and women, some as young as 14, are members of the Explorers programme run by a sheriff's deputy in Imperial County California, which trains young people in the 'skills used to confront terrorism, illegal immigration and escalating border violence'. It is reported that Border Patrol agents who contribute to the programme consider it to be a training ground for future employees. Deputy Sheriff Lowenthal is quoted as saying the programme 'is about being a true-blooded American guy and girl'. When asked what she likes about the programme, a young participant, Cathy, answered, 'I like shooting [the guns]. I like the sound they make. It gets me excited'.

Conclusion

It is easy to find trails of evidence which link border control policies to the deaths of illegalized travellers that occur at the hands of official border enforcers, those who take this role upon themselves, and those who exploit the vulnerability created by illegal status. The precise relationship between border controls and these suspicious deaths will vary across these categories and can operate at multiple levels. Official policies and practices that allow the use of potentially lethal forms of force to restrain deportees or in response to rock-throwing youths betray a failure in duty of care. These deaths also demonstrate the cycle of violence set in train by a politics of resistance to perceived injustice. Deaths caused by vigilante violence may be perceived by some as arising from the failure of governments to provide adequate border security. However, we contend that government culpability is manifest most clearly in these cases, through promulgation of the myth of the border as an unassailable site for the production of security. Other third-party deaths arising from workplace exploitation or victimization by criminal gangs may initially appear to be attributable to individual criminality. Yet on closer examination they engage complex arguments about the false promise of borders as sites for the regulation of labour supply and drugs. Underlying all these disparate scenarios is the process of illegalization itself which provides the structural foundation on which border-related violence is built.

6
Suicide and Self-harm

> The self-harming was so prevalent and so pervasive that no child would have avoided seeing adults self-harming .... There was very visible self-harm, constant talk of it. The children for example when I arrived would have seen people in graves ... Some of the children – it was their parents or people they knew. They knew why the parents were doing this. They knew that the parents were talking about possibly dying. They were on a hunger strike. There was visible self-harming on the razor wire. People were taken to the medical centre at regular intervals having slashed. People taken to hospital. There were attempted hangings that these children would have seen (quoted, HREOC, 2004, p. 405; cited in Grewcock, 2010).

The above quote is not depicting a situation in a country experiencing war or conflict, or a region plagued by poverty or civil upheaval. Rather, it is describing the conditions inside immigration detention centres in Australia in 2003. If detention and deportation are the bodily sanctions imposed by the current migration regime (Khosravi, 2010), then suicide and self-harm are the means by which those bodies are (self)-marked as excluded and unwanted.

Internationally, suicide as a form of border-related death is mostly discernible in relation to failed asylum (or equivalent) applications, and experiences of immigration detention centres and impending deportation. It is most clearly identifiable in the European and Australian contexts through a direct link to asylum determination processes and coronial investigations. Most border-related deaths recorded in the US are not related to asylum processes, yet suicide is a feature of immigration detention, most recently observable in the release of figures from the US

Immigration and Customs Enforcement (ICE) regarding deaths in ICE custody. This chapter considers suicide as a form of death at the border and the ways in which it manifests in the landscapes of border enforcement in Australia, Europe and North America.

Suicide as a means of dying makes up a minority subset of deaths currently counted as border-related deaths. For the period January 1993 to January 2011, UNITED recorded 14,037 border-related deaths in Europe, of which 334 were recorded as suicide. However, the identification of suicide in some cases is the result of official investigations such as coronial inquiries, or of the determinations of UNITED researchers based on the available information on the incident. In the Australian data we collected (Appendix 1), 11 people committed suicide in the period 2000–11. Of these 11, five occurred inside Villawood Detention Centre in Sydney, the majority of which followed the individual receiving notice of commencement of deportation proceedings. Figures on suicide as a form

Table 6.1 Border deaths: Suicides (compiled from UNITED data) and total number of border-related deaths in Europe 2003–2010

Year	Suicide	Number of deaths
1993	17	60
1994	18	109
1995	26	179
1996	27	513
1997	10	334
1998	18	398
1999	13	514
2000	23	687
2001	11	433
2002	20	800
2003	16	1297
2004	33	1093
2005	17	814
2006	19	2051
2007	29	1750
2008	10	1323
2009	16	1417
2010	11	208
Total	334	13980

Table 6.2 Australia: Border-related suicides 2000–2010

Date	Personal Details	Incident Details
2000	Villiami Tanginoa, Tongan, male, 52	Died after plummeting from basketball pole at Maribyrnong Detention Centre, Melbourne, reportedly after being bullied by guards.
2001	Shahraz Kayani, Pakistani, male, 48	Set himself on fire outside Parliament House, Canberra, because family's application to migrate was denied.
2001	Avion Gumede, South African, male, 30	Killed himself after arriving at Sydney Airport and being detained in Villawood Immigration Detention Centre, Sydney.
2002	Thi Hang Ley, Vietnamese, female	Killed herself after being put in Villawood Immigration Detention Centre, Sydney, for overstaying visa. Third suicide attempt.
2003	Dr Habuibullah Wahedy, Afghan, male, 46	Killed himself at Murray Bridge, South Australia, after the Immigration Department said his TPV would soon expire and encouraged him to return to Afghanistan.
2008	Mr Zhang, Chinese, male	Committed suicide after being deported to China, feared persecution and torture in China.
2010	Josefa Rauluni, Fijian, male, 36	Jumped off a roof at Villawood Immigration Detention Centre, Sydney, hours before he was to be deported.
2010	Ahmad al-Akabi, Iraqi, male, 40	Committed suicide at Villawood Immigration Detention Centre, Sydney, after refugee application was rejected twice.
2010	David Saunders, British, male, 29	Committed suicide in Villawood Immigration Detention Centre, Sydney.
2011	Miqdad Hussain, Afghan man aged 20	Found dead in detention centre in Weipa, near Queensland by staff. Suspected suicide.
2011	Mohammad Asif Ata, Afghan man, aged 19	Found dead in detention centre in Curtin, Western Australia by other detainees. Suspected suicide.

of border-related death in the US are more difficult to collate and analyse largely because of the state-by-state enforcement of the border in conjunction with federal border protection activities, resulting in disparate (or no) processes of data collection. A snapshot of suicides is available from the recently released figures on migrants in ICE Custody (detained in a range of immigration detention, local, state and federal prisons).

Based on this limited quantitative picture we can only undertake an initial reading of trends in relation to the practice of suicide as a border-related death. Similar to the broader data on suicide, the limited data on suicides of illegalized migrants suggests that it is a practice more likely to be carried out by men than women, and often as a result of ongoing frustration with asylum processes. Beyond this, the quality of this data precludes any rigorous attempt to identify trends regarding where, when and why people suicide as a form of death at the border.

Suicide is, on the one hand, representative of a small proportion of border-related deaths. Yet it is important to note that there are significant shortcomings in how states identify and classify suicide and self-harm in the context of illegalized migrant death, and therefore the existing quantitative picture is deficient. On the other hand, suicide is arguably the most emblematic form of border-related deaths: an act often performed in the context of imminent return or indefinite detention, and one seen as indicative of the punitiveness of migration systems and the helplessness and hopelessness of detainees.

Suicide in immigration detention

Suicides in immigration detention centres often fall outside the scope of official mechanisms of counting deaths for two main reasons. First, most developed nations have official processes for counting deaths in custody, but immigration detention often remains outside this form of official oversight of state practices. Second, the recording of suicides in immigration detention often results in indeterminate findings, in particular that coronial investigations are inconclusive as to the cause of death. For example, there are inconsistencies between the UNITED data on deaths by suicide, presented in Table 6.1 above, and official coronial findings which are inconclusive on the cause of death.

According to Cohen (2008), our understanding of the extent and circumstances of asylum seeker suicide and self-harm is seriously undermined by the lack or inadequacy of data. For example, coroners in the UK are not required to record asylum seeker status or ethnicity, and community-based programmes aimed at the prevention of self-harm are not required to report on asylum seeker status and ethnicity. In Australia, coroners are also not required to record the visa or migration status of the deceased, making identification and classification within coronial records across jurisdictions difficult. This renders problematic the process of identifying coronial findings in relation to such cases, or collating across common factors, such as immigration detention and impending deportation. Cohen (2008) argues that not only should such data be recorded, but also that it should be subject to independent audit.

In Australia, suicides that occur in immigration detention are not recorded as part of the government-sponsored programme officially charged to monitor and record deaths in custody: the Australian Institute of Criminology (AIC) Deaths in Custody database and annual reports, set up following the Royal Commission into Aboriginal Deaths in Custody. Moreover, deaths in immigration detention were again confirmed as being outside the remit of the reporting process in 2010. The most recent report of the AIC noted:

> This report analyses deaths occurring in custodial settings, such as prison and juvenile detention, as well as police custody and related operations, such as sieges and motor vehicle pursuits. It does not consider deaths in detention centres under immigration legislation. Since it was established to monitor issues relevant to Indigenous people in custody as explained below; the question of the future scope of the monitoring program will be considered in a planned review of this program. (Lyneham et al., 2010)

The Royal Commission into Aboriginal Deaths in Custody found that the high number and frequency of indigenous deaths in custody was due to too many Aboriginal people being in custody, and too often. For the purposes of improving the quality of data on deaths in custody (and hence contributing to the future prevention of these deaths), immigration detention is determined not to be 'in custody'. The AIC collections were set up to operate only within the context of police and prison custody.

Recent reports indicate that 27 people have died in Australian immigration custody since 2000, compared to one death between 1991 and 2000 (Ting, 2010). The definition used by Singh in the collation of this data reported by Ting (2010) goes beyond custody in the context of immigration detention centres to arrangements that include being in the care and control of immigration enforcement officers. This number may include deaths attributable to natural causes (Ting, 2010). From the data collected and verified for our count of Australian border-related deaths we were able to confirm that 11 suicides have occurred in Australian immigration detention since 2000. The AIC maintains that the decision over what to count as a suicide in custody is one for the government to make, and notes in its most recent report that it does not include people detained under immigration legislation. Yet in a recent newspaper report, DIAC claimed that it is a matter for the AIC to 'determine what statistics are relevant for a particular piece of research' (Ting, 2010). Somewhat paradoxically, deaths inside immigration detention centres *are* routinely investigated by the majority of state-based coroners who define their remit in such cases on the basis of whether the death has occurred in custody. This highlights the disjunction between differing legal and statistical definitions of custody. With the exception of Western Australia, all state-based coroner's Acts are interpreted to include immigration detention deaths as deaths in custody, meaning that inquests are mandated for deaths that occur inside immigration detention centres.

The administrative classification not only of death, but also of what counts as a state responsibility in relation to non-citizens, has facilitated a distancing of federal government policy from suicides in immigration detention. In a television interview (ABC, 2002) given in 2002, then Immigration Minister Philip Ruddock was questioned following the release of a UN Report on Human Rights and Immigration Detention in Australia which was highly critical of the use of mandatory detention and geographically isolated and poorly equipped centres to detain those Australia deemed to be 'unauthorised arrivals'. The interviewer (Tony Jones) was attempting to solicit information from the Minister as to the number of suicides occurring, as well as the relationship between the policy of mandatory detention, self-harm and suicide:

TONY JONES: Have there been actual suicides in detention in Australia? PHILIP RUDDOCK: Well, we don't know, but there have been I think seven deaths in detention, and I think a number of them were from natural causes. I think two were from falls, and whether they were suicide or accidental, the coroners haven't determined. One was a Tongan, I believe, in the Maribyrnong centre, who was on the basketball hoop and fell. The other was a Vietnamese young lady who was not very well, but it was off a balcony at Villawood. But in terms of the centres like Woomera, Curtin, Port Hedland, I don't believe there have been any suicides there. There have been suicide attempts, and I think in terms of the number of incidents in a period of about nine months they numbered around about 230 involving something like 90,000 detention days. So I don't know that you can call it a particularly rampant depression. Some people suffer depression, and they're treated for it.

Thus, according to the former Minister for Immigration, suicides are reducible to individual factors. Complex chains of causation are absented, and the context of the hopelessness of detention is thereby erased. The visible and invisible, the immediate and distal factors contributing to this incident, go unacknowledged.

Case study: When suicide is not suicide

The death of 53-year-old Viliami Tanginoa in December 2000 received some media coverage following live reports on radio that he had climbed a basketball ring in the recreation area of the Maribyrnong Immigration Detention Centre in Melbourne. Hourly bulletins reported on the situation throughout the day. Viliami Tanginoa stayed on top of a basketball pole for eight hours before he 'dived to his death' on the day he was to be deported. He had lived and worked in Australia for 17 years and had seven children.

The coronial investigation into the death of Viliami Tanginoa found that the death could have been prevented if the private operator of the centre had acted appropriately. Coroner Phil Byrne was highly critical of the operation of the Maribyrnong Detention Centre by Australasian Correctional Management (ACM), specifically for not calling in specialist police negotiators to deal with the situation. The Coroner heard evidence that detention centre staff did not believe he was at risk of committing suicide and therefore did not follow procedure to call in police negotiators. The Coroner remarked:

> If one action epitomises the ineptitude of the approach adopted by ACM, it is the action of David Randich, operations manager (not an underling), bouncing a basketball in the courtyard in the vicinity of Mr Tanginoa – at best unhelpful and amateurish. (Russell, 2003)

The Coroner continued:

> I remain puzzled why virtually no one appreciated Mr Tanginoa was at imminent risk of some form of self-harm … It may be due to a

fundamental misjudgement of this gentle, quiet, apparently uncomplicated man. Whatever the reason, the message was not adequately imparted. (Russell, 2003)

The Coroner concluded that the immediate cause of Viliami Tanginoa's death was his decision to jump from the basketball pole, but also noted that another cause was the inaction of the detention centre's management – thus, a failure to manage the situation. The Coroner could not determine whether Viliami Tanginoa had intended to commit suicide or was trying to injure himself to prevent his deportation. Therefore, his death was not officially recorded as suicide.

According to DIAC and the operator of the centre, all appropriate procedures were followed. In a media release following the release of the coronial findings, ACM said:

> We are pleased that the coroner found no fault with ACM's policies, staff training or the medical management of the incident, including the attempted resuscitation of Mr Tanginoa ... We note the coroner was not satisfied that Mr Tanginoa intended to kill himself. This supports the view taken by ACM staff at the time, that he was not at risk of self-harm. (Russell, 2003)

The absurdity of these statements, and the protection of corporations at the expense of a reasonable explication of the truth, is astounding. How can the act of climbing a basketball pole by a detained man, sitting up there for eight hours and then jumping to the ground be regarded as anything other than suicide?

The Coroner recommended the following: that detainees who are faced with imminent deportation be reassessed to determine whether they are at risk of self-harm, that any incident involving a detainee at risk of self-harm is to be recorded on video and audiotape, that ACM review the use of interpreters to ensure that each language group is covered, and that a protocol be developed for use by external negotiators in crisis situations. In 2005, Viliami Tanginoa's family lodged a damages claim against both DIAC and ACM.

Internationally, immigration detention is identifiable by some key shared features. It is often indeterminate; it often fails to meet expectations of standards in relation to gender segregation, educational programming and health service provision (in particular, the provision of mental health services), or to separate immigration detainees from convicted persons; and it includes as routine the detention of children. Notably, these features have been highlighted in the now significant body of literature on the psychiatric impact of immigration detention, in particular the levels of psychiatric illness and suicidal intent among detainees.

Confinement in immigration detention centres for extended periods of time has been found to have severe, psychologically disabling effects on detainees, including attempted suicide and self-harming behaviours (Sultan & O'Sullivan, 2001; PHR, 2003). A 2004 study of adults and children who had been referred to mental health services from a remote immigration reception and processing centre found that 100 per cent of the children had suicidal ideation and 80 per cent had made significant attempts at self-harm (Mares & Jureidini, 2004). Another study of adults and children found that 100 per cent suffered from at least one psychiatric disorder, with 26 different disorders identified among the adults, and 52 disorders among the children (Steel et al., 2004). In this study, all child respondents reported seeing people self-harm and make suicide attempts. The study concluded that immigration detention is injurious to the mental health of detainees.

Over a decade ago, reports to the UN delegation sent to visit Australia for the Report on Australian Immigration Detention noted above included evidence that identified the use of suicide as being qualitatively different within immigration detention centres than in other closed or open detention settings. For example, it was suggested that suicide and self-harm in immigration detention centres more often involved children and young people and the methods of suicide and self-harm included hanging, throat-slashing, deep wrist-cutting and drinking shampoo. Immigration authorities were noted as responding to such incidents as a 'form of protest'.

The most recent study of suicide and self-harm among asylum seekers was undertaken by Cohen (2008) in the UK. She argued that it is widely known that suicide rates inside prisons far exceed the rate for general populations, and this holds across jurisdictions from which accurate information is available. So while the actual incidence of self-harm or suicide in immigration detention remains unknown, it is reasonable to assume that the rates are likely to at least mirror, if not exceed, those of similarly organized and operated closed institutions such as prisons. Cohen (2008) found that the rate of self-harm in Immigration Removal Centres in the UK was 12.79 per cent, while comparable UK prison data reported rates of self-harm of between 5 and 10 per cent.

Importantly, Cohen identified the distorting impact of gender on these figures. For example, in UK prisons women suffer almost 50 per cent of self-harm but comprise less than 6 per cent of all prisoners. Data disaggregated by gender is not available for Immigration Removal Centres but women are known to comprise 10–14 per cent of all those detained. The data becomes less clear when it is considered that some failed asylum seekers and those awaiting deportation in relation to criminal conviction are in some jurisdictions kept in prisons, while in others they are held in immigration detention, making it difficult to identify cases across institutions (this is especially the case in the US). Damningly, Cohen has been able to conclude that, similar to suicide in prison, the suicide rate increases as the size of the detained population increases.

There is a dearth of academic research on suicide and self-harm in US immigration detention facilities. One of the few available studies, conducted by Keller et al. (2003), surveyed 70 detained asylum seekers and found that 18 (26 per cent) participants reported having thoughts of suicide while in detention, and two reported having attempted suicide. Reports by non-government and human rights organizations mirror the issues identified in the Australian and UK contexts (AI, 2009; Women's Refugee Commission, 2010). ICE recently released data on deaths of undocumented migrants in ICE custody (Table 6.3). For the period 2003–10, 115 deaths were recorded in ICE custody, which included seven hangings. However, it is possible that some of these deaths may have been the result of suicide, but were recorded as 'asphyxiation' (of which there were six recorded cases). Of the combined 13 cases of possible suicide, two occurred in detention centres and the remainder in federal, state or local jails (the majority in local jails but all places designated immigration detention centres for the purposes of keeping the person in custody). One of the deaths was of a female detainee.

The incidence of suicide in immigration detention centres has highlighted broader concerns about the conditions within the centres, and the impact of detention on detainees (Silove et al., 2006; Silove et al., 2001). Legal interpretation of the legality of immigration detention has been marked by the avoidance (or arguably denial) by judiciaries of directly ruling on the violent or otherwise inhumane conditions inside immigration detention centres. For example, in the pivotal Australian case of *Behrooz*, in which an asylum seeker escaped from immigration detention and faced criminal charges as a result of that escape, the Supreme Court was willing to consider the conditions of detention,

Table 6.3   US border-related suicides in ICE custody

Year	Name	Gender	Country of Birth	Final Cause of Death
2004	Leyva-Arjona, Argelio	Male	Cuba	Hanging
2004	MEJIA VICENTES, Sebastian	Male	Mexcio	Hanging
2004	RUIZ TABARES, Ervin	Male	Colombia	Asphyxia
2005	HEO, Sung Soo	Male	Korea	Hanging
2005	BELBACHIR, Hassiba	Female	Algeria	Asphyxia
2005	SALAZAR GOMEZ, Juan	Male	Mexico	Hanging
2006	GARCIA SANCHEZ, Felipe	Male	Colombia	Asphyxia
2006	ARCIA MEJIA, Geovanny	Male	Honduras	Asphyxia
2006	LOPEZ GREGORIO, Jose	Male	Guatemala	Asphyxia
2006	CARLOS CORTEZ, Raudel	Male	Mexico	Asphyxia
2006	MARTINEZ RIVAS, Antonio	Male	Mexico	Complications of Hanging
2007	ROMERO, Nery	Male	El Salvador	Hanging
2008	CANALES BACA, Rogelio	Male	Honduras	Hanging

whereas on appeal to the High Court the Justices presiding did not (see Grewcock's [2010] analysis of the *Behrooz* case in 2004). By contrast, leading international and national agencies have been less reluctant to identify as state violence the acts and omissions occurring in immigration detention centres that lead to cultures of self-harm and conditions conducive to suicide. The Australian Human Rights Commission, then known as the Human Rights and Equal Opportunity Commission (HREOC), heard about the extent and impact of such practices in its 2004 research into Children in Immigration Detention (cited at the start of this chapter). The report documented the case of a 13-year-old boy and his 11-year-old sister:

> A senior child psychiatrist examined the children in May 2002, after the children had spent more than a year in detention, and made the following diagnoses: [The brother] meets criteria for major depressive disorder. More importantly, he is an acute and serious suicide risk. [His] suicidal intent is closely related to whether or not he is in detention. This should not be dismissed as some form of emotional blackmail, but recognised as a realistic reaction to his appraisal of his predicament after many months in detention witnessing the pro-

gressive disintegration of his family, and the destruction of hopes for the future. (HREOC, 2004, pp. 403–4)

In many parts of the world, including Australia and the UK, immigration detention centres are operated by private contractors. This has been found to further obfuscate information about the circumstances of suicides and self-harm and the identification of links of causation and responsibility. As Athwal and Bourne (2007, p. 110) argue in relation to the UK, 'suicide prevention is, in part, being left to market forces. Private contractors which run many of the centres have to pay financial penalties for each successful suicide. But such disincentives are clearly not working. In the last five years, fifteen people in detention have died by their own hand.'

Desperation and deportation

> It would be inappropriate for me to go into the rationale behind the refusal of the authorities of asylum, but the fact of that refusal and that he was liable to be detained and removed from the UK clearly would have operated on his own mind. I'm sure that was a factor in him formulating the decision to take his own life. (*Rochdale Observer*, 2006)

The prospect of being returned to one's country of origin has been identified as a key source of stress for asylum seekers (Mansouri & Cauchi, 2007). Ongoing uncertainty associated with precarious forms of migration status (such as various forms of temporary protection) and fears surrounding impending deportation have been identified in studies examining the high levels of post-traumatic stress disorder for the individuals involved (Steel, 2003). The prevalence of forms of anticipatory stress, such as those associated with deportation, is believed to be significant in reports of suicide and self-harm. However, it is clear that we know very little about suicide and self-harm among asylum seekers and other illegalized travellers living in the community. There is 'simply no way of knowing' how many such deaths or incidents have occurred (Cohen, 2008, p. 241).

Deportation has become a key tool in managing the border and effecting governments' desired migration outcomes. Without quality data on border-related suicides it is difficult to establish causality between the increasing use of deportation and increasing levels of suicide. Yet the reports of NGOs and others suggest that confirmation of this causal link would be possible were such information to become readily available.

The suicides of those who have overstayed their visas or who are facing impending deportation may be subject to coronial investigations. However, in Australia and the UK coronial reporting is not required to record the visa status of the deceased person. Therefore, it is not straightforward to identify border-related deaths involving suicide that occur in the community. Self-harm and attempted suicide in the community are rarely recorded in relation to migration or asylum seeker status as hospitals and similar healthcare providers are not required to collect or report this information (Cohen, 2008). For example:

> Two cases did very clearly indicate a lack of understanding of the asylum issues: in one the victim was serving a sentence for travelling under a false passport and on being told he was to be moved to a different prison, apparently believed that he was going to be removed to his country of origin. No interpreter was used when he was given this information. In another case, the victim was served with a notice to quit his accommodation but believed that this meant his claim was lost and so killed himself. In fact he had been given refugee status but had not received the letter, so although the reason he was being given notice to quit was due to the change in his asylum status he did not know this. (Cohen, 2008, p. 243)

Threatened or impending deportation is identified as a key 'stressor' in many of the cases of asylum seeker suicide and self-harm, both inside immigration detention centres and in the community. However, it is difficult to obtain accurate estimates of the extent of this causal link, simply because, similar to the examples cited above, some harm and suicide occurs as a result of poor communication, whether the result of malicious intent or operational incompetence. In this regard, poor communication with vulnerable populations in such circumstances may be interpreted as either an unintentional omission or an intentionally harmful act. It is equally difficult to obtain accurate information about pre-deportation suicides in the community, with many such individuals isolated or the deaths deemed not to be newsworthy. Some of the most notable examples of pre-deportation suicides have been documented in the UK. Most often they have occurred following an extended wait for the outcome of an asylum application.

Athwal (2010) has noted that in the UK the available information on pre-deportation deaths that occur in the community reveals that most individuals who commit suicide are young men from Afghanistan, Iraq and Iran who are without family. This finding is notable insofar as the lack of kith and kin means that questions regarding the circumstances of the death are likely to remain unasked. Moreover, the system in place to investigate such deaths, as noted above, is not geared towards recording the circumstances surrounding the death in a way that produces a comprehensive account, or towards recoding such information to enable an analysis of the factors leading to these deaths, with a view to their future prevention.

In 2005 the UK lifted the moratorium on deportations to Zimbabwe even though the UNHCR continued to recommend that all states suspend removals to that country. In August 2005, a Zimbabwean female asylum seeker facing deportation threw herself out of a fourth-storey apartment. In Zimbabwe, her husband had been disappeared by the Mugabe regime, after which she was tortured and repeatedly raped. She miraculously survived the fall but sustained serious injuries.

Khosravi (2010) documented the case of an Afghan man who attempted suicide while in the process of facing deportation proceedings in Sweden:

> In some cases, only death is assumed sufficient to testify to the authenticity of the claimed fear. In mid-February 2009, a 45-year-old Afghan man was taken to the emergency ward of a hospital in Stockholm. It was around midnight. The person who took him to the hospital disappeared as soon as the nurses showed up. Ingesting a large number of pills, the man had wished to put an end to his life. He was saved after 20 hours in a respirator. The man, together with his family, wife and three daughters, had sought asylum in Sweden in 2005. The Migration Board rejected their application twice and a deportation order was issued. I asked the man why he had attempted suicide. He said he thought that his death would help his children have a chance to stay. He assumed that the Swedish authorities would then believe that their fear of returning was genuine and well founded. When all the documents he had offered the authorities were deemed not 'enough' to prove, in the eyes of the authorities, his and his family's suffering, he thought to attest to the authenticity of their case with his death. Not even his suicide attempt helped them.

Purposive suicide and hunger strikes

Similar to the Afghan man's case outlined above is that of Manuel Bravo, whose story is arguably emblematic of the suicide–deportation nexus currently operating in the UK. Bravo's suicide shows that taking one's own life is not only an act of hopelessness or desperation, or a way for an individual to avoid deportation, but can also be a means of securing a better future for one's family, most notably one's children. Bravo fled Angola after his parents, members of an opposition group, were killed and his sister was raped. In 2001 he brought his wife and two sons to the UK. In early 2005 his wife returned to Angola with one of the sons to care for relatives and after a few months they were reported as having disappeared. Bravo applied for asylum in the UK but was refused. He was then arrested along with his 13-year-old son and taken to Yarl's Wood Removal Centre. Reports document that Bravo was terrified of being returned to Angola, and within 48 hours of being sent to Yarl's Wood he committed suicide. His suicide was reportedly captured on CCTV (IRR, 2006).

The ensuing NGO concern and activism around Bravo's death revealed that he took his life not only to avoid being returned to Angola, but also to ensure his young son would be allowed to return to school in Leeds and to remain in the UK. His suicide note included the following: 'I kill myself because I don't have a life to live anymore. I want my son Antonio to stay in the UK to continue his studies.' In a note to his son he said, 'Be Good Son and Do Well at School'. The inquest found that Bravo took his own life in the belief that it would secure his son's future in the UK.

Psychiatric studies of the impact of immigration detention have found that parents often report fears for the safety of their children as their primary motivation for fleeing their country of origin, and express guilt about bringing their children into the detention environment (Mares & Jureidini, 2004). In some reported psychiatric studies, parents have identified their own suicide as a way to improve circumstances for their children – namely, that their children can then be released from immigration detention: 'S [mother] said "Leave me in the camp to die, but please get my children out of here"' (Mares & Jureidini, 2004). The mental health impacts of immigration detention such as suicide and self-harm were recently highlighted by the Australian Human Rights Commission when it again recommended ending the current system of mandatory and indefinite immigration detention (Australian Human Rights Commission, 2011).

Grewcock has suggested that, as challenging and injurious as acts of self-harm and suicide may be, they nevertheless can be regarded as powerful messages that highlight the circumstances of asylum seekers:

> Combined with more orthodox protests and escapes they demon-strated that the detainees were prepared and able to act on their own behalf. This raises important conceptual issues for theorists of state crime regarding the levels of abuse required to satisfy definitions of state crime and the role of resistance in constructing the social audience. (2010)

Notably, governments do not often interpret self-harm and suicide as acts of high-risk resistance, but generally as seemingly predictable acts of manipulation that in themselves are representative of a broader form of deviance. As Grewcock notes, this attitude on the part of governments has proved counterproductive to their aims, with acts of self-harm and suicide, particularly in relation to detained children, proving to be a rallying point for anti-detention campaigns which have met with some level of success in Australia in recent years. In its report on Children in Immigration Detention, HREOC noted: 'It took a hunger strike, lip-sewing and a suicide pact in January 2002 before arrange-ments were made to transfer a group of unaccompanied children to home-based foster care detention in Adelaide' (2004, p. 10). However, sadly, these successes have been etched away in recent years, with over 1000 children still living in immigration detention in Australia at the time of writing.

Hunger strikes have been used by asylum seekers and other illegal-ized travellers in a range of detention and community settings. If the act of suicide is regarded as being at the end point of a continuum of self-harm, then hunger strikes can be seen as a form of self-inflicted harm used for a range of purposes – most notably in these contexts as a way to achieve expedited resolution of their claims for asylum, to be released from detention or as a reprieve from deportation.

Hunger striking is of course an ancient form of seeking redress for a wrong. Irish history reveals the use of the hunger strike by families and clans to redress a harm or crime committed against them by another family. However, the hunger strike as an act of seeking redress from the state – an act deemed so important that non-resolution will end in death – takes on additional significance when carried out in state custody. As Annas (1995) notes:

Although deaths are rare, the power of the hunger strike comes from the striker's sworn intent to die a slow death in public view unless those in power address the injustice or condition being protested about. Hunger strikers are not suicidal and would greatly prefer responses to their demands. The most intractable hunger strikes, from a human rights and medical ethics perspective, are those carried out by people in the custody of the state, usually in prisons or other detention centres.

The history of illegalized migration in Australia, Europe and North America is marked by the use of hunger strikes, which often include large numbers of participants. For example, in early 2001 almost 600 migrants went on hunger strikes in churches across Barcelona in an effort to resolve uncertainty about their migration status (García de Olalla et al., 2003). In 2010, a group of students in the US who had been brought to the country as children staged a ten-day hunger strike on the steps of a senator's office in order to advance the legalization of their citizenship status. Hunger strikes by asylum seekers in Australia have mostly occurred in immigration detention since it was introduced in 1996 (Silove et al., 2006), and have numbered up to 200 people on hunger strike at any one time (at Woomera Detention Centre in 2002). The official response to hunger strikes has largely characterized them as manipulative, and DIAC has been legislatively empowered to authorize doctors to provide non-consensual medical treatment. Silove et al. (2006) note that in 2001 the department issued approximately 40 authorizations for compulsory medical treatment in violation of international medical guidelines.

In February 2011, 300 migrant workers, mostly from North Africa, went on hunger strike in Greece. Most had lived and worked in Crete for many years and some were asylum seekers. The strike ended after six weeks, during which time over a third of the strikers were hospitalized. In 2010 and early 2011, Greece became the main entry point for unauthorized migrants, and so, in a move fuelled by the country's perilous economic state, the Greek authorities amplified the already deafening anti-immigrant rhetoric and policy. Under the Dublin II arrangements, migrants who enter Europe through Greece can only apply for asylum in Greece. Hence, migrants found in other parts of Europe who have entered via Greece have since 2003 been returned to Greece. A European Court of Human Rights ruling early in 2011 changed this. Regardless, the situation has deteriorated for people in Greece who have 'no papers'. The hunger strikers were seeking resident permits which would allow them to work legally, and to access medical care and education. In short, they wanted their migration status regularized, and to have access to services that would guard them against destitution. The BBC reported that the strike was resolved because:

> The state was highly embarrassed by images of migrants lying list-lessly in a central Athenian building surviving on sugared water. Ministers were terrified that one or more of the protesters might die. The compromise was reached after a public prosecutor instructed state doctors to take all necessary medical actions to prevent the strikers from dying. The prospect of forced feeding helped to concentrate minds. (BBC, 2011)

The following statement was given to the public by the Solidarity Initiative on behalf of the 300 hunger strikers, after a compromise was reached between the Greek Government and the strikers:

> The struggle is complete. With the documents in hand and our heads up high, we return to our homes and our work vindicated, after 44 days on hunger strike.

> The struggle continues. The announcements for an eight-year limit and the increase of work credits as prerequisites for the issuing and renewal of residence permits must become law immediately.

> The struggle is the only option. The struggle against the daily exploitation and racism's walls, the struggles for the legalisation of all migrants with no prerequisites, for equal rights between local and foreign workers, for a life with values and dignity, these are our next steps. Together with the anti-racist and migrant movement we will walk along this difficult path, the path of struggle.

> The struggle unites us. With the documents in hand and the head up high we salute and wish farewell to everyone who supports us. To the people in solidarity in Greece and all other countries in the world, the doctors and their colleagues, all who stood by our side in these days of the hunger strike, in all days when our lives and our deaths demanded vindication and freedom. (Migrants Rights Watch, 2011)

Conclusion

The limited available research on the suicide and self-harm of illegalized travellers, notably asylum seekers, reflects how little we know about the victim in this scenario (Cohen, 2008). This lack of knowledge and data has been attributed to the failure of those who control the processes and systems to ask timely and necessary questions in relation to the mental health of those in immigration detention, or to supply timely information that is understood by the recipient. The various acts and omissions surrounding the duty of care of those in immigration custody are marked both inside and outside immigration detention environments. While suicide and self-harm are always the acts of individuals, the cases and circumstances we have considered suggests that the ways borders are enforced against individuals means their actions cannot be understood apart from the border protection processes in which they are enmeshed.

Part III
From Finding Truth to Preventing Border Harm

The Coroner's Court is less formal than other Courts. It is not bound by the laws of evidence and is not too technical or legalistic. In making a decision the Court can also make recommendations to any relevant authorities that may result in changes to laws or practices in order to prevent similar deaths in the future. It is not the Court's role to establish whether a crime has been committed or to find a person guilty of that crime. (Courts Administration Authority South Australia, South Australian Coroners Court information sheet)

In the previous three chapters we identified many ways in which borders are implicated in the deaths of illegalized travellers. We undertook a forensic examination of the structural violence of borders that is manifest in risky journeys made more dangerous by the need to avoid detection, and in lives rendered unlivable by indefinite detention and policies of immiseration. We identified particular individuals who played a direct role in the deaths of illegalized travellers, whether as official enforcers of border policies or self-styled border protectors, as bystanders who failed to intervene to prevent potentially lethal enforcement practices, or as deliberate exploiters of the vulnerability arising from illegal status. In each case, we noted that border policies played a formative role in creating the conditions leading to the deaths. We have also found a clear trail of evidence leading to the border in cases where illegalized travellers make the desperate decision to take their final journey. Woven throughout this account is a subtext of resistance and rescue, of claims and counter-claims about the potential for border controls to save, rather than endanger, lives. We admit that we are deeply suspicious of the claim that border control saves lives. However, we sincerely admire the genuine efforts made by

161

many individuals, including those working in border control roles, to render assistance to those in need of rescue. Reiterating an observation reported earlier from Michalowski (2007, p. 66), we acknowledge that the 'honest efforts' of these individuals 'take place within a perverse policy framework'. In the following chapter we try to unravel the matrix of risk that exposes illegalized border crossers to deadly hazards. We examine the contradictions of risk and rescue, both qualitatively and quantitatively, in preparation for identifying possible strategies to prevent border-related deaths and promote a more mobility-tolerant future.

7
The Ambiguous Architecture of Risk

> [The Chilean mine disaster] was an example of media mani-
> pulation in which a terrible accident caused by negligence was
> seized by hungry politicians and turned into an opportunity
> to show off in front of the international media, seemingly
> acting as saviours when they were actually responsible for the
> whole situation. Rescuing them was their duty.
>
> (Chilean folk singer Nano Stern quoted in Hillier, 2011)

Although they are closeted from many of the harmful consequences
of contemporary border controls, populations of the Global North are
occasionally confronted with the violent deaths of illegalized border
crossers. Sometimes the grim reality is experienced first-hand when
unidentified bodies wash up among holidaymakers on Mediterranean
beaches, or when airline passengers observe fatal altercations between
struggling deportees and security guards. These witnessed tragedies
engender sympathy and anguish from many of these audiences. Still,
in public discourse, responsibility is primarily attributed to misguided
personal choices by the travellers themselves, or the greed of ruthless
people smugglers. Just as illegalized border crossing has been recon-
structed in terms of the organized crime of people smuggling, illegalized migrants may be readily depicted as their hapless victims. We
therefore find governments arguing that more effective border controls
are needed, not merely to protect the integrity of the nation-state, but
also to protect excluded groups from taking risky voyages in the first
place. This argument becomes self-reinforcing – justifying even stronger
measures designed to deter, pre-empt or contain, supplemented with
responsibilizing strategies (often supported by NGOs who are genuinely
concerned with migrant welfare) aimed at educating targeted groups

about the risks of illegalized travel. This hegemonic discourse leaves unquestioned the rights of states to control their borders through whatever means they choose, and ignores the unmet security needs that drive illegalized border crossers to take what appear on the surface to be irrational risks. Yet where the *needs* of illegalized border crossers are understood to be greater than their *fears* (Nevins, 2008, p. 189), both the rationality of decisions to undertake these journeys and the futility of persisting in attempts to deter them become apparent. This dynamic matrix of risk and responsibility shapes both the experiences of illegalized border crossers and the interpretations of their actions by various audiences. In this chapter we uncover a complex and ambiguous architecture of risk by telling stories of resistance and rescue, stealth and sabotage, death and deterrence; and we scrutinize claims that surveillance regimes can both pre-empt and protect would-be border crossers.

Mapping the matrix of risk, responsibility and rescue

The calculus of risk and responsibility

At the heart of this book is the vexed question of who is responsible for the risks faced by illegalized border crossers and for their often deadly consequences. The search for an embodied 'culprit' leads most readily to the modern folk-devil of the people smuggler. Yet, as the previous chapters have demonstrated, smugglers are animated by a range of motives, and many other actors may populate the spaces between border policies and their victims.

> In the process of criminalizing migration, human smugglers become scapegoats. They are held responsible for all migrant deaths at borders. The authorities represent human smugglers as criminals. The vast majority of migrant deaths, usually by drowning, in the sea along the Spanish–African borders happen in relation to interception activities by Spanish border guards. (Carling, 2007)

The variability in the motives and behaviours of individual people smugglers, and in the size and criminality of their operations, has been noted by a number of commentators (Cabrera, 2010; Weber & Grewcock, 2011). This point is reinforced by the first-hand experience of Khosravi (2010, p. 26): 'Not everyone was as lucky as I was to have had a good "guide" and "facilitator". Later in Karachi, I heard horrible stories of rape, homicide, kidnapping and blackmail of people on the borders by their smugglers.' Actions in which people smugglers may be found blameworthy range from the ruthless or reckless infliction of harm, to acts of omission (such as inadequate food supply and planning), to exposure to risky forms of travel (such as unseaworthy vessels or unsafe vehicles). Judgement about levels of culpability is complicated further by the possibility that some of the risks taken by illegalized travellers may be within the 'normal' experience of risks faced by some populations of the Global South, including the facilitators themselves. Recalling the words of Garcia Benito quoted in Chapter 2, the life prospects of the dinghy captain who ferries illegalized travellers across the sea to Europe may be equally 'wretched'.

While inflicting intentional harm in order to escape prosecution, or in pursuit of personal gain, deserves the strongest condemnation, it is the actions of governments in erecting barriers to keep out the unwanted that have created this lucrative market (Weber & Grewcock, 2011; Grewcock, 2003). Put simply, in the words of Benito (2003), '[t]he large majority of sub-Saharan and Moroccan citizens who apply for entry visas to Europe have their applications denied. With a visa, they would cross the Strait in a ferry, which would result in the problem of corpses disappearing'.

On the other hand, it remains important to position the agency of illegalized travellers within the matrix of risk and responsibility, and consider their decision-making from a personal and structural stand-point. From this perspective it may be easier to see how the imperatives of seeking economic and personal security can overtake other consider-ations such as respect for national laws and the potential risks of ille-galized travel. It is far more problematic to incorporate within our matrix of risk and responsibility acts of sabotage and other behaviours in which illegalized travellers appear to actively contribute to the risks they face. However, even these desperate and potentially destructive acts can often be linked to particular border enforcement strategies and are open to multiple interpretations.

In the notorious 'children overboard' affair, the administration of former conservative Prime Minister John Howard promulgated the story that asylum seekers aboard a vessel intercepted by the Australian Navy had deliberately thrown their children into the sea. The Prime Minister made it clear that people who would be so callous as to throw their own children into the water could not be 'real refugees' and were not wanted in Australia. Senator Ross Lightfoot took things further, referring to boat people as 'uninvited and repulsive peoples whose sordid list of behaviours included scuttling their own boats' (Wilson, 2011). No lives were lost in this incident, but it sparked a fierce political debate. Critics alleged that government statements were intentionally and maliciously calculated to discredit and dehumanize asylum seekers in the eyes of the Australian public. Others saw the debacle as a failure of communication between government, bureaucrats and naval personnel, exacerbated by a readiness to attribute blame to the asylum seekers. The inquiry that was instigated by the Opposition-controlled Senate confirmed that the story presented to the Australian public had been untrue, and attributed the failure to correct the public record to a series of systemic miscommunications, deliberate deception by some politicians, and an over-responsiveness by public servants to the political needs of ministers (Select Committee, 2002). The Committee noted the complex chain of relationships involved in whole-of-government approaches (in this case the People Smuggling Task Force which answered directly to the Prime Minister), whereby a number of agencies worked towards the same government objective, and advocated the promotion of a 'culture of responsibility' rather than thinking in terms of a 'line of accountability'. A minority report was issued by government members of the Committee, indicating the level of politicization of the incident, in which they set out the evidence for what they described as a 'pattern of conduct' of the 'potential illegal immigrants', which they believed added background and context to the events (Select Committee, 2002). Although no-one involved in the inquiry disputed that the representation of the asylum seekers' actions had been incorrect, no formal retraction was ever made, and no disciplinary action was taken with those who had misinformed the public, leaving an indelible impression of culpability.

A similar rush to attribute blame to asylum seekers attended the explosion of the vessel code-named SIEV 36 off Ashmore Reef while *en route* to Australia in 2009. In this case five Afghan asylum seekers were killed, and the lives of naval personnel on board the vessel were also endangered. More than 30 people were seriously injured and had to be flown to hospitals in Darwin, Broome and Perth. Amid attempts by the federal government to quell the speculation immediately following the disaster (Rodgers, 2009; Maley & Toohey, 2009), the Liberal Premier of Western Australia announced that the boat had been deliberately doused with petrol (Christian, 2009). Former Liberal Immigration Minister, Philip Ruddock, added further fuel to the media fire by claiming that asylum seekers were routinely advised by people smugglers to sabotage boats rather than risk being returned to Indonesia (Maley & Lower, 2009). Refugee advocates countered that the boat was being refuelled at the time of the explosion and suggested it was 'unlikely' that refugees would deliberately sabotage boats, since they had no reason to believe they would be forced back to Indonesia (Christian, 2009). Because there had been deaths in Australian waters, a full coronial inquest was conducted by the Northern Territory Coroner, at which 34 witnesses were heard. An examination of the matrix of responsibility did not fully exonerate those on board, or absolve the naval personnel of responsibility for the fatal events. The Coroner concluded that the boat had been deliberately set alight by some of the passengers, that passengers had lied about the events that were recorded on a navy video, and recommended that three of them be investigated for criminal prosecution. As to the motives for this act of sabotage, the Coroner concluded: 'I accept that whoever started the fire did not expect that an explosion would occur. What was intended was that a fire be started so that the boat would be crippled and they would be taken off the vessel and taken to Australia' (Cavanagh, 2010, p. 37).

As always, the actions of people involved in dramatic events such as these are better understood when the wider circumstances are examined. The vessel had been judged by naval patrol officers to be seaworthy and had been kept in a holding position for up to three days pending the arrival of a transport craft to take the passengers to detention on Christmas Island. Media reports suggested that the navy had towed the refugee boat in figure-eight patterns for a full day, leaving the passengers sick and disorientated (Toohey, 2009). Crucially, the Coroner criticized the navy for issuing passengers with an 'inappropriate' warning notice advising them not to enter Australian waters. Since they were already within Australian waters, the meaning of the notice was not clear and the Coroner found it had acted as 'the catalyst for the unrest' (Cavanagh, 2010, p. 20). Ultimately, it seems that failures in communication and uncertainty over their fate led to a series of desperate actions by those on board. While the Coroner was supportive of the rescue by navy personnel after the explosion, he apportioned responsibility across all parties. Other audiences were less equivocal. Refugee advocate Ian Rintoul looked beyond the actions of the asylum seekers themselves, saying 'when you look at the whole picture the blame lies much more on the circumstances that those asylum seekers were placed in'. However, the Executive Director of the Australian Defence Association condemned the actions of the passengers, saying, '[t]he bottom line here is that we've had asylum seekers coming to this country for 60 to 70 years without having to employ high levels of violence to get into the country ... Why has this suddenly changed now?' (ABC News Online, 2010b). Policies of interdiction at sea appear to have created an 'arms race' of defensive and attacking manoeuvres, greatly increasing the risks to all involved and creating circumstances in which the perceived deviance of illegalized border crossers can become a self-fulfilling prophecy.

Detention centres represent another contested border site where illegalized migrants may take individual and collective actions that endanger the lives of themselves and others. Whereas the sabotage of boats may be interpreted as largely instrumental actions intended to lead to rescue, disturbances at detention centres appear to be acts of defiance, frustration and protest. On 14 February 2001, the 900-bed Immigration Removal Centre at Yarl's Wood in England, said to be Europe's largest, was burned to the ground only a month after its opening. Miraculously, no-one was killed, although early accounts reported up to 25 asylum seekers missing, feared dead. Soon after the fires, Home Secretary David Blunkett laid the collective blame at the feet of the detainees and vowed to toughen the detention regime. The Home Secretary accused detainees of preventing the fire service from tackling the blaze, and said, '[h]aving removed asylum seekers from prison, we now find that our reward is the burning down of a substantial part of the facility' (Hardie, 2002). The unrest was triggered by the restraint of a middle-aged Nigerian woman Eunice Edozieh by Group 4 security guards. Viewing her treatment as unjust, rioting male detainees overran the centre and many escaped. In the confusion, a fire broke out. The official inquiry conducted by the Prisons and Probation Ombudsman concluded: 'There was of course no excuse for the actions of those detainees involved in the disturbance and the suffering and damage they caused. I have concluded, however, that what occurred at Yarl's Wood was the result of a series of decisions taken over the previous three years' (Shaw, 2004, p. 377).

The inquiry was extremely wide-ranging. The Ombudsman considered the impacts on the management of the centre of the presence of convicted criminals among the detainees (the explanation favoured by government), and the introduction of a more coercive removal regime (the explanation favoured by legal and support groups) (Shaw, 2004, p. 10). On the first point, he criticized the failure to instigate risk assessment procedures similar to those used in prisons, notwithstanding the non-criminal nature of the population in general. The woman at the centre of the disturbance was herself described as 'troublesome' (Shaw, 2004, p. 7), giving some succour to those seeking to attribute responsibility to individual 'troublemakers'. On the other hand, many detainees – including former prisoners and some of those later charged with damage and arson offences – were praised for their conduct before and during the disturbance. Several submissions to the inquiry suggested that some detainees had been 'contaminated' by exposure to convicted populations while being held in prisons. But the Ombudsman concluded that prison experience was a 'two-sided coin' so that ex-prisoners could also be 'more likely to be compliant given their improved environment and facilities' (Shaw, 2004, p. 334).

The inquiry also heard that aspects of detention and deportation policy at the time contributed to the disturbance, particularly the instigation of removal targets that had necessitated a massive expansion of detention capacity. The centre had been built and opened in haste in the context of a government target to remove 30,000 'failed asylum seekers' and 'immigration offenders' during 2001–02. Refugee support groups and the Firefighters Union criticized the government's decision not to fit the building with sprinklers (Athwal, 2003), a budgetary decision the Ombudsman ultimately accepted as reasonable. As part of the political communication surrounding the accelerated removals policy, a decision had been made to designate many of the detention centres as 'removal centres'. This was found to have played a role in provoking the unrest. The Ombudsman explained: 'Re-naming as a removal centre took away all vestiges of hope as detainees knew that ultimately they would be removed from the country' (Shaw, 2004, p. 342). One official admitted to the inquiry that there had been 'a complete refusal to face up to the fact that as we get better at chucking people out of the country we are actually going to provoke more non-compliance' (Shaw, 2004, p. 343).

The disciplinary regime that operated in the centre reflected the tension inherent in the incarceration of a largely non-criminal population. The deliberate policy of recruiting ex-prison staff into the Immigration and Nationality Directorate, the formal adoption of some aspects of the Prison Rules, and the instigation of a formal disciplinary system all suggest an overriding emphasis on security. The need for procedural fairness in order to promote perceptions of legitimacy was stressed by the Ombudsman, and Group 4's staffing policies came under some criticism. However, the Ombudsman focused more of his attention on questioning the wisdom of implementing what was seen as a relatively 'light' management regime. After questioning the former Home Secretary Jack Straw, the Ombudsman reported:

I asked Mr Straw how far the decision to run removal centres with a light disciplinary touch had been a Ministerial demand, and whether there had been a failure to face up to the coercive nature of the removals process. Mr Straw said that he understood and agreed that the process was coercive. He believed that the enforcement of removal would change the behaviour of other would-be asylum seekers. He said that he did not recall ever offering a formal view on the regime at removal centres, and there were no papers to suggest he had done so. Mr Straw said it had seemed to him that removal centres should have the most relaxed regime consistent with security, provided that it worked. (Shaw, 2004, p. 317)

Against this backdrop of criticisms of the management regime and policy framework, with criminal charges still pending and the Ombudsman yet to report, the government announced that Yarl's Wood was to reopen, inciting vehement criticism from supporters of the detainees: 'The Home Office showed a total disregard for human life by detaining people at Yarl's Wood detention centre in unsafe conditions operated for private profit by Group 4 ... Their responsibility for what happened at Yarl's Wood is significant' (Campaign for Justice in the Yarl's Wood Trial, 2003). The government continued its resolve to ramp up its programme of expulsions, placing more strain on the detention centre management regime. In January 2002, one year after the disturbance, and while the official inquiry was just getting underway, the government began removing groups of detainees on specially chartered flights. The inquiry heard that Operation Aardvark, as it was known, caused disruption to removal centre regimes – with large numbers of people arriving and leaving at all hours. The Ombudsman reported that the process was viewed as inhumane by some officials.

Criminal prosecutions were eventually completed for 12 detainees who were said to have damaged property and started the fires. The highly publicized trials were reported to have ended in a 'farce', with three convictions for violent disorder and one for affray, but not a single conviction for arson (Allison, 2003a). Group 4 guards reportedly gave contradictory evidence, defence lawyers criticized the Immigration and Nationality Directorate (IND) for deporting potential witnesses, and the trial judge described Group 4 as 'ill-equipped' to deal with the violence which he claimed might have been expected since 'many of the people they were sending there would be suffering from a sense of injustice' (Allison, 2003b; Athwal, 2003). Other criminal and civil actions ensued as various of the parties involved sought to reposition themselves outside the matrix of risk and responsibility. This included formal claims of mistreatment by guards lodged by some detainees, allegations of sexual assault of a female detainee by another detainee, and a controversial lawsuit filed by Group 4 against local police for failing to bring the disturbance under control. It was also reported that police had considered investigating Group 4 for corporate manslaughter, until they had established to their own satisfaction that no deaths had occurred.

In the years following the catastrophe, Yarl's Wood achieved the distinction of being the only centre to hold exclusively women, children and families. In a 2009 inspection, Her Majesty's Chief Inspector of Prisons, Anne Owers, expressed her concern over the wellbeing of the children, questioning the need for their detention, and noting the lack of meaningful activities for women at the centre (HMIP, 2010). Although the facility is still officially described as a 'removal centre', she reported that around half of the children held there in the previous six months had been released back into the community, calling into question the rationale for their detention in the first place. The centre has continued to have a troubled history. On 23 February 2010, an early day motion (EDM 919)[1] was tabled in Parliament by MP John McDonnell protesting the hunger strike of 50 female detainees who had been detained for up to two years at Yarl's Wood, and demanding an independent inquiry to address allegations of mistreatment (see also Youssef, 2011). Once again, in this very different context from the open oceans, it seems that self-imposed risk may be seen as the only viable option, undertaken in the hope of eliciting rescue.

The politics of risk and rescue

Where the possibility of rescue exists, it is most often expected from the same border control authorities that are tasked with keeping illegalized people 'out' (in the case of external borders) or 'in' (in the case of detention). In this section we consider the contradictions of risk and rescue in three contexts: at sea, where rescue of those in peril is understood to be an absolute requirement of international customary law; in remote borderlands, where rescue by border authorities and others is generally considered to be 'humanitarian'; and in detention, where the need for rescue is grounded in a more routine duty of care to preserve the safety and wellbeing of those who are not at liberty to meet their own basic needs.

The tension between orders to repel and duties to rescue came into sharp relief in the explosion off Ashmore Reef discussed in the previous section. After the harrowing events, in which naval personnel on board the sabotaged vessel were also injured, the Opposition Defence spokesperson hailed the naval personnel as 'heroes' for their efforts at rescuing the survivors (ABC News Online, 2010a). However, reports soon appeared in *The Australian* newspaper which claimed that female naval personnel had moved quickly to save the asylum seekers from drowning while a boat carrying mostly male personnel had verbally abused and physically repelled them from the rescue boats (Dodd, 2009; Toohey, 2009). These accounts by survivors were supported by unnamed others who had seen the navy's footage. The Northern Territory Coroner accepted that the actions of the navy in rescuing defence personnel ahead of asylum seekers were justified in light of official policy which supported the retrieval of naval personnel first, on the rationale that the unit is then 'more readily able to regroup and assist with the rescue operation with all available hands' (ABC News Online, 2009; Toohey, 2009). However, the Coroner noted that many of the rescuers had responded this way without realizing it was official policy (Cavanagh, 2010). The actions of the rescuers were reportedly understood by the survivors to stem from a 'culture of dislike towards asylum seekers' (Dodd, 2009), which seemed to be mediated to some extent by gender. While he rejected all criticisms about the demeanour of the defence personnel, and commended several of them for their particular bravery, the Coroner also recommended that standing orders concerning rescue should allow for a degree of 'commonsense' in rescuing civilians ahead of defence personnel where circumstances warranted.

The contradictions between interdiction and rescue are also played out in the US–Mexico borderlands. In 1998, as the body count from illegalized crossings began to mount, the Border Safety Initiative (BSI) was developed as a joint strategy between the US and Mexican governments (Border Safety Initiative 2005). It claims to be a risk-based system driven by intelligence about the location and timing of illicit crossings, and has been implemented via local partnerships in a stepwise fashion along different sections of the border. The initiative was not introduced into parts of Texas until 2010. The programme contains four elements – prevention, search and rescue, identification, and tracking and recording – all driven by an information-based approach. The goal of prevention is pursued mainly through raising awareness on the Mexican side about the risks of border crossing posed by the natural elements and the ruthless behaviour of smugglers. An example of this awareness raising is the strategic placement of signs bearing the message '*No mas cruces en la frontera* – No more crosses on the border'. More culturally ambitious strategies have embedded messages about border-crossing risks into popular Mexican folk songs to achieve maximum penetration of the 'responsibilizing' themes. This folk music strategy has also included Central American traditions, aimed at reaching intending border crossers who have travelled to the border from further south. Although these campaigns have sometimes been criticized for being deceptive – since the role of the BSI is not clearly declared – the initiative has been supported by many expatriate Mexican musicians living in the US, who clearly accept the official line that preventing illegal crossings will produce a safer environment for 'all border communities'.

The search and rescue dimension of the programme is based on the recognition that dangerous border crossings will still take place, and is intended to minimize fatalities by responding quickly to calls for assistance. Rescue beacon towers have been erected in strategic locations where distressed border-crossers can call for help from specialist BSI Search Trauma and Rescue Teams, known as BORSTARs. Customs and Border Protection has reported that BORSTAR teams rescued more than 7600 migrants from 'near certain death' from the inception of the BSI in 1998 to 2004 (*Customs Today*, 2004). The task is complicated by the need for rescues to be carried out on both sides of the border, which requires good working relations with Mexican consular officials. The BSI also has a statutory role in the identification of those for whom rescue came too late, and in the ongoing tracking and recording of data on interceptions, rescues and deaths. This information, although often in dispute (as discussed in Chapter 2), provides a resource for families and supporters seeking to locate missing people, and builds an information base to guide the 'intelligence-led' deployment of BSI resources. The initiative has spawned an industry of 'border safety lawyers' who advertise their services as go-betweens, offering to link relatives searching for missing persons to the BSI and the intelligence sources at their disposal.

The BSI does not operate in isolation. Over the same time period, a number of specialist operations have resulted in a ramping-up of control efforts through people-smuggling disruption programmes, expedited removals, and increased border checks and patrols (Department of Homeland Security, 2005). The BSI is subsumed within this broader enforcement effort. In fact, the *'no mas cruces'* message to would-be border crossers incorporates a preventive intention within an enforcement perspective by relying on the double meaning of 'cruces', which refers to both memorial crosses and people smugglers. Spokespeople from Customs and Border Protection routinely issue statements that seamlessly reconcile their rescue and control mandates. Marketing information claims that Customs and Border Protection is 'equally committed' to securing borders and saving lives, and asserts that border security is in fact the foundation for border safety, not its antithesis. The Customs and Border Protection Commissioner stated in 2004: 'Through increased enforcement efforts, the focus is to secure our border. A more secure border will reduce illegal entries, and thereby reduce migrant deaths' (US Customs and Border Protection, 2004). The statistical evidence for this claim will be examined later in this chapter.

Tensions between the duty to protect life and the requirements of border control also arise in custodial settings. In the aftermath of the Yarl's Wood fire, the British Firefighters Union reportedly criticized the decision taken by centre management to secure the detainees in 'unsafe' conditions (Athwal, 2003). Former Group 4 guard Darren Attwood is said to have testified at the trials of former detainees that guards had orders to lock detainees in the burning building during the fire (Morris, 2003). The Prisons and Probation Ombudsman conducting the inquiry into the Yarl's Wood fire concluded: 'I have not found evidence to justify the allegation that Group 4 improperly denied access to the emergency services to enter Yarl's Wood. Nor have I substantiated the claim that detainees were locked into burning buildings' (Shaw, 2004, p. 380). He did, however, question aspects of the treatment of detainees in the immediate aftermath of the disturbance in a way that suggests there was some confusion between their status as persons in need of rescue and perceptions of them as perpetrators deserving of punishment. The official Visiting Committee had been refused entry after the fire, reportedly on the basis of concern for their health and safety, which apparently took precedence over confirming the welfare of the detainees. The Ombudsman concluded: 'It is extremely regrettable that no-one thought to inform the Visiting Committee about the disturbance and fire. Even had the result not been as it was, it was likely that significant force would be used to bring the situation under control and someone from the Committee should have been there to observe what was going on' (Shaw, 2004, p. 358).

One detainee testified at the inquiry that he was thrown to the ground, grabbed around the neck until he could not breathe, and had his head pulled back violently after officers in riot gear entered a cell and pressed the occupants against the wall with their shields. After the assault, the detainee claims: 'I was just left to lie on the ground in real pain. Eventually a doctor came to see me. He examined me but said he didn't think my neck was broken' (Shaw, 2004, p. 364). The Ombudsman found that this report was corroborated by a visitor, who saw the man's injuries, and another detainee, who saw the beginning of the incident and heard the rest. The Bishop of Bedford complained to the inquiry about the overuse of segregation, apparently at the behest of the police, when what was needed in his view was 'pastoral care and calming work' (Shaw, 2004, p. 362). In evidence presented to the inquiry, one detainee described his experience after the disturbance as follows:

> Some of the officers who were guarding us were extremely inti-midating. It felt as though they had decided that we were the trouble-makers and were trying to get their own back. I felt extremely confused and humiliated by the way in which we were treated. We had been involved in a very frightening incident and rather than being given any comfort and support we were treated as animals. (Shaw, 2004, p. 365)

Although the language of 'crime scene' was not used in the inquiry report, it seems that the primary concern of police was to find and secure the culprits – admittedly motivated at that time by the belief that people may have been killed. The Ombudsman levelled the fol-lowing criticism over the manner in which control was handed to police in the immediate aftermath of the disturbance, which also high-lights the dilemmas of shared responsibility arising from the contract-ing out of detention centre management:

> I am not clear that the decisions were lawful at all. Nor am I clear, more generally, under what powers the police were operating during this period ... I certainly do not agree with those who treated opera-tional decisions during this period simply as police matters, with which neither Group 4 nor IND could interfere. (Shaw, 2004, p. 370)

The hegemony of risk

The accounts presented so far point to many contradictions between the imperatives of pre-emption, control and protection; conflict over the attribution of responsibility to official actors, private contractors both licit (such as Group 4) and illicit (such as people smugglers), and to illegalized travellers themselves; and situations where illegalized travellers deliberately increase the risks faced by themselves and others out of desperation, fear and fury. In this section we ask three further questions about the ambiguous architecture of risk. First, can border surveillance perform the dual function of pre-emption and protection? Second, how do governments respond to interventions by third parties, and what do these responses tell us about the governmentalities of risk and rescue? And, finally, whose risks take precedence when the interests of border security and the safety of illegalized travellers come into open conflict?

Border surveillance as pre-emption or protection?

Unlike other catastrophic events in Australian waters, the sinking of an asylum seeker vessel code-named the SIEV 221 off Christmas Island in December 2010 occurred within a populated area. Images were transmitted almost contemporaneously to television screens across the mainland and beyond, showing asylum seekers reaching out their hands to others flailing desperately in the water, while island residents threw life jackets and anything they could find that would float from the cliff tops into the tumultuous seas. Although up to 50 people are believed to have perished, more than 40 were rescued. Many bodies were never recovered. Much was made of the heroism of the locals, some of whom had to be constrained to prevent them from entering the deadly waters themselves. Indeed, had they not thrown life jackets into the sea, it is certain that many more people would have died.

Christmas Island residents throw lifejackets from cliff tops into heavy seas as a boat carrying asylum seekers breaks up on the rocks below
© Ray Murray

One of the main questions to emerge from this tragedy concerned the failure of Australian coastal authorities to monitor the arrival of the boat and prevent its disastrous attempt at landing. In this public discourse, the surveillance function was aligned unambiguously with the protection of life. An internal review conducted by Customs and Border Protection concluded that no intelligence had been available to alert coastal patrols that the boat was on its way from Indonesia, and that patrol vessels deployed in other areas had converged on the scene to offer assistance as soon as they received emergency calls (Australian Customs and Border Protection Service, 2011). Perhaps in response to the public expectation that its surveillance role should preclude tragedies such as this, the official report included the following statement: 'Command and Control structure within BPC [Border Patrol Command] is structured to respond to security threats in Australia's maritime domain (including the detection and interception of SIEVs), not as an emergency search and rescue (SAR) operation' (Australian Customs and Border Protection Service, 2011, p. 3). Australian Prime Minister Julia Gillard also distanced herself from the surveillance-equals-protection equation by stressing the vastness of the area patrolled by Australia's overstretched coastal defences, reportedly making the astonishing claim that it covered 10 per cent of the earth's surface (Ferguson & Moor, 2010). At the time of writing, the Coronial Inquiry into the sinking had not yet reported. The head of Australia's Border Protection Command, Rear Admiral Tim Barrett, reiterated at the Coronial hearings that his organization was not responsible for preventing deaths at sea, and was tasked instead with maritime security and law enforcement (ABC News Online, 2011b). When asked by the Coroner which Commonwealth agency, if any, was responsible for preventing such tragedies, the Rear Admiral is said to have replied that he did not know.

Comments made by refugee advocate Ian Rintoul reveal the tensions between protection and pre-emption from a different angle. The crews and passengers on unauthorized boats, he said, were reluctant to contact authorities when in danger for fear of being towed back to Indonesia. According to this view, the risk that was foremost in the minds of asylum seekers was the risk of being prevented from entering Australia to make their asylum claims.

> I'm not blaming anyone – Customs for not intercepting this particular boat – but I do think the fact that there isn't a welcome refugee policy, that the Government has people smuggling laws in place makes it less

likely that people on boats are willing to contact Australian authorities and to rendezvous. (Ian Rintoul, quoted in Anderson, 2010)

Reports later emerged that passengers had tried to contact emergency services by mobile phone as their predicament worsened, but these calls were not understood. Within a few days of the tragedy Prime Minister Gillard announced that the laying of charges was imminent and reaffirmed the government's determination to 'smash the people-smuggling business model' (ABC News Online, 2010d). Indonesian authorities initially issued a statement describing the events as a tragedy not a crime, but later sent a police officer to join the investigation. The Opposition leader claimed the 'unspeakable horror' might have been avoided if a 'tougher regime' similar to the former Pacific Solution had been in place, repeating the Opposition's mantra that they had been successful when in office at 'turning back the boats' (ABC News Online, 2010e). This drew criticism from the Immigration Minister, who argued: 'As John Howard found out, people disable boats. He used to try to return them and he learnt that you couldn't do that because the boats were disabled' (Butterly & Probyn, 2009). Under the present government's partial dismantling of the Pacific Solution, boats are generally not simply 'turned back' or their occupants transported to Pacific Islands – they are interdicted and taken to Christmas Island. While interdicted asylum seekers still face indefinite detention and restricted access to legal and other assistance, at least they are held on Australian territory.[2] However, the translation of policy into practice is an inexact science; and what is salient is whatever people believe or understand they have been told, as the coronial inquiry surrounding the explosion on the SIEV 36 demonstrated. Following the shipwreck on Christmas Island, the Australian Lawyers Alliance called for an independent inquiry to determine beyond all doubt whether current interdiction policies mandate the 'shadowing' of vessels in order to drive them out of Australian waters (*Age*, 2010b).

It is not only in Australia that doubts have been raised about the capacity, and sometimes the willingness, of maritime surveillance patrols to rescue those in distress. Elsewhere, attempts by coastguard and naval vessels to effect rescues have sometimes led to collisions and unintentionally increased the numbers of deaths at sea (Kreickenbaum, 2004). Spijkerboer (2007, p. 132) notes that while the Global Approach to Migration adopted by the European Council in December 2005 is said to have the dual aims of saving lives at sea and tackling illegal immigration, 'the measures aimed at tackling illegal immigration greatly increase risks to migrants, including loss of life', while 'the policy outlines do not address how they will protect migrants from the risks they face'. The publicly available Frontex Work Program for 2011 sets out in detail the border protection priorities established for the agency by European Member States. It contains no mention of the word 'rescue'. Several instances of 'safety' appear, but they refer to the agency's new role in joint deportations, a role for which the agency admits it has little experience; and it is unclear precisely whose safety is being discussed (Council of the European Union, 2011). In a personal statement released on 11 June 2007, Frontex Executive Director Ilkka Laitinen – like his Australian counterpart in Customs and Border Protection quoted earlier – was anxious to disabuse EU citizens and Member States of any misconceptions about his organization's priorities. He lamented the notion that Member States 'want Frontex to become a search and rescue body', claiming this was 'out of the mandate not only of the agency but also the European Union' (Laitinen, 2007). By December 2009 the organization was announcing a seminar on 'the challenges of common interpretation of the International Law of the Sea', at which it was concluded that there was a need to agree common procedures for search and rescue (Frontex, 2009). The statement recognized a dazzling array of potentially competing demands, including those related to the preservation of life, refugee protection and the fight against organized crime.

Similar resistance occurs when governments attempt to transform rescue agencies into border enforcers. Former Italian Member of Parliament Tana de Zulueta has recalled how, in 2005, Italy commenced mass interdictions and summary returns of boats to Libya. She writes: 'Trained to rescue those in distress at sea, the Italian coastguards were shocked at first to learn that their orders had changed. On 7 May 2005, the crew of a patrol boat on duty between Lampedusa and Malta were told that the 227 men, women and children they had just pulled out of the sea were to be instantly deported back to Libya' (de Zulueta, 2009). Right-wing politicians are reported to have represented the rescue efforts of the Italian coastguard as assisting organized people-smuggling rackets (Fekete, 2009a). Questions about a new and unfamiliar interdiction role for the Australian Navy under Operation Relex were also raised by the Senate Inquiry into a Certain Maritime Incident, which examined the highly publicized 'children overboard' affair and the sinking of the SIEV X.

Where previously the Navy's role had been to escort unauthorized arrivals to an Australian port for reception and processing by relevant agencies, the new ADF [Australian Defence Force] role was to thwart their objective of reaching Australian territory. The new Australian response led to a corresponding change in the behaviour of the asylum seekers. From being cooperative and compliant, their behaviour changed to include threatened acts of violence, sabotage and self-harm, designed to counter the Navy's strategies. (Select Committee, 2002, Executive Summary, p. xxi)

The Committee commended the navy's ongoing commitment to perform rescues at sea, but queried the high level of political control over the deployment of the vessels, arguing that this was at odds with the practices established under the Safety of Life at Sea (SOLAS) Convention, in which decisions over life and death are clearly the responsibility of ships' captains rather than politicians or their advisers. In the case of the 'children overboard affair' the ship's commander had been ordered to tow the intercepted vessel out to sea. The crew then risked their lives to save all 223 people on board once the vessel got into difficulties. Trying to navigate this newly transformed matrix of risk and responsibility, the Australian Defence Force has been quoted as saying that it 'does not provide details on its procedures for apprehension of illegal vessels but remains a party to the Safety of Life at Sea Convention and the UN Convention Relating to the Protection [sic] of Refugees' (Toohey, 2009).[3]

In the US, the BSI, with its specialist BORSTAR rescue teams, works alongside regular Border Patrols under the umbrella of Customs and Border Protection. As reviewed earlier, statements issued by the organization link border control unquestioningly to the protection of human lives. Although US Border Patrol officials argue that the imperatives of enforcement and rescue are pursued with equal vigour, rescues can only be conducted where illegalized travellers are able to raise the alarm or seek help, or where people in distress are encountered in the course of enforcement efforts. A Border Patrol spokesperson interviewed about the BSI programme in Yuma County noted that '[a]n enforcement operation often turns into a rescue operation' (Gilbert, 2007), confirming enforcement as the agency's primary focus. Tragically, the BSI was unable to prevent the death in 2002 of 19 illegalized border crossers from Mexico, Honduras, El Salvador, Nicaragua and the Dominican Republic, who died from suffocation while concealed in a truck (Lozano, 2011). These deaths, which have been associated with the expansion of the people-smuggling trade, illustrate that the logic of evading border controls is inimical to the promotion of safety. The resolve to conduct rescues has also been called into question by University of California researchers, who claim that the Border Patrol refuses to send its agents into the All American Canal (a popular people-smuggling route) to rescue drowning immigrants because of the high levels of pollution (Hill & Kelada, 2010).

The contradictions between the pre-emption and protection roles of border agencies suggest that rescue efforts might be most effective when undertaken by independent parties. This leads us to consider what happens when third parties intervene to assist illegalized border crossers.

Criminalizing third-party rescue

In 2008, a Council of Europe resolution on border controls from the Committee on Migration, Refugees and Population expressed the concern that 'search and rescue obligations are not always being complied with, leading to increased risk to life and loss of life' (Committee on Migration, Refugees and Population, 2008). The statement expands on this point in a way that makes clear it is referring not only to rescue operations provided by governments, but also to those carried out by third parties:

> There are an increasing number of reports of ship's masters ignoring distress signals from vessels in trouble. A particularly regrettable incident occurred in May 2007 when survivors from a sunken boat clung to the nets of a fishing boat for several days while the ship's master refused to bring them on board and states argued over their respective responsibilities for rescue. Of further concern are allegations against the Maltese and Greek authorities that they have ignored distress calls and have at the same time pushed these boats away from their own shores or territorial waters. (Committee on Migration, Refugees and Population, 2008, p. 2)

The Committee called for compliance with international maritime obligations of search and rescue as well as supportive reception processes for asylum seekers and the closure of detention centres. In the view of this Committee, harsh border protection measures are antithetical to the safety of life at sea. This observation invites further questions about the specific factors that have led to this formerly unthinkable state of affairs. At least part of the answer lies in the way states have responded to third-party intervention in the dynamic of risk and rescue.

The Australian Government's refusal to allow the docking of the *MV Tampa* on Christmas Island in August 2001 was a defining moment in the evolution of Australian border control, and had repercussions around the world. The Norwegian merchant vessel, acting at the request of Australian maritime rescue authorities, had taken on board 430 asylum seekers when the vessel they had been travelling on broke down 80 nautical miles from Christmas Island. The subsequent events gained widespread media coverage and have been closely examined by numerous commentators (see Brennan, 2003; Magner, 2004; Morris, J., 2003; Mares, 2002; Marr & Wilkinson, 2003). Having originally set a course for the nearest port in Indonesia, the captain turned and headed for the Australian territory of Christmas Island following sustained protests from the asylum seekers. This put the *Tampa* on a collision course with the political will of a Prime Minister determined to personally decide who would set foot on Australian soil. As the humanitarian situation on board the stranded ship began to deteriorate, the response of the Australian Government was 'swift and decisive' (Howard, 2003). Forty-five armed Special Air Services (SAS) troops boarded the *Tampa*. Most of the rescuees were taken aboard the warship *Manoora* to the impoverished Pacific nation of Nauru to be detained (under whose authority is a matter of debate), while their claims for refugee status were considered under international (not Australian) procedures. According to Watson (2009), two factors enabled the Australian Government to take this extraordinary action. First, the *Tampa* was not an 'unseaworthy vessel'. Even Prime Minister Howard had declined to turn back vessels in immediate peril. Second, the actions of the rescued asylum seekers in forcing the ship to change course were used to justify the Prime Minister's announcement that the ship's captain had been operating 'under duress'. Watson recounts how talkback radio hosts described asylum seekers as 'hijackers' and 'pirates'. These terms were later applied by refugee supporters and human rights lawyers to the SAS troops who boarded the *Tampa* at the Prime Minister's direction. The failure of the rescued passengers to conform with the compliant behaviour expected of refugees enabled them to be portrayed as 'queue-jumping illegal immigrants who would intimidate their rescuers to get what they wanted' (Watson, 2009, p. 100). In the wake of the *Tampa* affair, the Norwegian Government is reported to have proposed the reform of maritime laws to strengthen the docking rights of ships' captains whose vessels rescue refugees at sea (ABC News Online, 2003). These proposals were actively opposed by the Australian and US governments.

Unlike the *Tampa*, which is a commercial shipping vessel, the *Cap Anamur* is a rescue vessel operated by a German NGO – the German Emergency Doctors Union. It was commissioned in 1979 to assist refugees fleeing Vietnam by boat. Since then, organizers claim to have rescued

10,375 people and treated 35,000 in a series of deployments in war zones (*Cap Anamur* website). In June 2004 the vessel rescued 37 sub-Saharan Africans from a sinking inflatable dinghy near the island of Lampedusa while it was returning from undertaking boat repairs in Malta. Whether or not the *Cap Anamur* was deliberately deployed to search and rescue in the region is a matter of dispute, both within and outside the organization. The *Cap Anamur* initially tried to deliver the rescued asylum seekers to Sicily, but was prevented from docking by Italian naval vessels and kept out at sea for several weeks. Permission to dock came only when the vessel issued an emergency call due to dwindling supplies, and announced that the rescuees were threatening to jump into the sea.

Although the *Cap Anamur* ultimately succeeded in docking at the port of its choice, the captain and other crew were arrested and prosecuted for facilitating illegal immigration. The eventual collapse of the prosecution was interpreted as a clarification that rescuing illegalized travellers at sea was not illegal. Yet the five years it took to reach this decision may well have contributed towards creating an environment of uncertainty which impacted on age-old maritime practices of rescue at sea (Pugh, 2004). According to one commentator, the prosecution was intended to send the message that 'the only permitted response is to sail right past their sinking boats' (Kreickenbaum, 2004). Moreover, while the fate of the *Cap Anamur* crew was being deliberated, this message was delivered in more decisive terms to less celebrated rescuers. A group of seven Tunisian fishermen were imprisoned for several weeks in 2007, after they landed on Lampedusa with 44 rescued travellers originating from the Horn of Africa. Fekete (2009a) reports that they were only released after 100 members of the European Parliament appealed on their behalf. These developments have led one UNHCR representative to describe the Mediterranean as a 'Wild West in which human life has lost its value and people in danger are left to fend for themselves' (Laura Boldrini, quoted in Fekete, 2009a, p. 96). Disputes over jurisdictional responsibilities for boats carrying rescuees have continued in Europe, and have also affected the operations of the EU's own border protection agency. In its 2008 programme of work, Frontex announced that Operation Nautilus had finally been given the go-ahead to patrol the central Mediterranean after being on hold due to 'differences of opinion' concerning the responsibility for migrants saved at sea (Frontex, 2008).

Attempts to restrict the assistance provided to illegalized travellers are not limited to the 'Wild West' zones of external frontiers. European governments have recently sought to criminalize those who assist illegalized migrants living in the community by providing medical or legal assistance, as well as intervening in life-threatening situations. Laws initially intended to target human traffickers are increasingly being deployed against people who provide humanitarian support or intervene in border enforcement processes (Fekete, 2009a). In May 2005, Italian anthropologist Franco La Cecla and two French nationals were charged with contravening security regulations for complaining about the violence inflicted by police on a Senegalese deportee, which the three complainants witnessed on a charter flight. The captain eventually ordered police to leave the plane, reportedly to the cheers of other passengers (Statewatch, 2005). A Statewatch article includes the following translated extract from a statement provided by La Cecla about his treatment following his arrest at Charles de Gaulle Airport:

> We were stripped of any right, we could not even telephone our embassies, or our parents; we were undressed, searched, warned that we would face some serious inconveniences and that we were not about to be released .... Worse still, we are guilty of having had some sensitivity, some pity, some human reactions, of having refused to accept the spectacle of someone else's suffering as 'normal'. (Statewatch, 2005)

Fekete (2009a) has documented numerous other examples of arrests, prosecutions and mistreatment of airline passengers who have intervened during forced deportations. Reports of prosecutions and threatened prosecutions are also emerging from the United Kingdom as residents seek to disrupt forced deportations from residential areas. A group of Glasgow grandmothers, sometimes referred to as the 'Glasgow girls', were said to be 'risking criminal charges' through their efforts to prevent the seizure of their neighbours in dawn raids (Gray, 2006). These women reportedly operate networks of surveillance and telephone tip-offs about the impending arrival of 'snatch squads'. Faced with teams of police and immigration officials, sometimes in full riot gear, they create physical barriers by linking arms and holding peaceful candle-light vigils. The women are described as forming part of a 'network of Scottish families harbouring asylum seekers'. At least one of them has been charged with obstructing the course of justice by refusing to allow immigration officials into her home (Gray, 2006). These charges were eventually dropped, apparently due to a failure by the Home Office to disclose to the defence the video they had taken of the dawn raid (Fekete, 2009a).

Community groups who provide water or other assistance to illegalized travellers crossing the US–Mexico borderlands also traverse a dangerous zone between humanitarian assistance and criminal prosecution. Motivated by a desire to assist and rescue, community groups began to operate proactively in the spaces not patrolled by the BSI. In 2000, the Humane Borders group started providing water in strategic locations, the Samaritans instigated day patrols to search for stranded border crossers soon after, while the No More Deaths coalition established a desert camp to enable them to search some of the more remote areas for people in distress (Cabrera, 2010). Other rescue groups include the Border Action Network, Border Links, Derechos Humanos and Healing our Borders (Guerette, 2007). Although they have argued that their actions fall within the law, Cabrera reports that No More Deaths and the Samaritans have been subject to surveillance and threats of arrest from the Border Patrol. Two volunteers from the No More Deaths camp were charged with conspiracy and aiding and abetting illegal entry into the US after they transported an injured border crosser to hospital (Guerette, 2007). In a seemingly recurring pattern, the charges were dropped, apparently for technical reasons (Cabrera, 2010).

Moreover, governments encounter points of resistance to their border protection projects not only from candle-burning grandmothers, water-carrying Samaritans and protesting airline passengers, but also from within their own ranks and from organizations that are recruited, with varying degrees of enthusiasm, into networks of border enforcement. Resistance emerges at the individual level when former security guards give evidence that implicates the conduct of their colleagues, or when female naval personnel appear to challenge an occupational culture that has become hostile to the wellbeing of asylum seekers. These sites of rupture are entirely consistent with contemporary modalities of government-at-a-distance, whereby governments increasingly rely on chains of responsibilized actors to enact their political will (Garland, 1997), and must therefore manage the risk of dissent arising from differences in individual values and conflicting institutional cultures.

Hierarchies of risk

The examples outlined above reveal that the logics of pre-emption and protection of illegalized border crossers are seriously at odds, and that third parties whose interests are wholly humanitarian are still required to demonstrate that they are not impeding the operation of border control. Where an enforcement mentality intersects with evidence about the risks faced by illegalized travellers claims, are often generated that stricter border enforcement is what is needed to save lives. Governments are not uniformly uncaring about the predicament of illegalized travellers, nor immune to criticism from domestic critics or the requirements of international human rights law. Responses are likely to vary according to political philosophies, perceptions of public sentiment and levels of individual empathy. The central questions around border protection and safety thus appear to be: who is being protected by border controls, and whose risks count the most? In this section we argue that assertions that border controls save lives are hegemonic because they misrepresent the degree of alignment between the interests of those who are excluded by border protection policies and the interests of those who are the beneficiaries of them.

Alongside the expressions of horror and sympathy following the Christmas Island shipwreck in 2010, government concerns over the maintenance of border control were consistently given priority over the needs of survivors. The extent of the tragedy was overwhelming: asylum seekers already detained on Christmas Island lost relatives, including spouses and small children, who were travelling to join them; at least three children on board the doomed vessel were orphaned; and grieving families, both in and out of detention, were distraught to find that – contrary to Muslim burial practices – bodies were not released to them until long after the deaths. One man who was already detained on Christmas Island lost seven members of his family. The sympathy engendered by the tragedy was also extended to the rescuers and other island residents, and the government announced it would fly in trauma counsellors to assist survivors and islanders. Meanwhile, apart from those who required hospitalization on the mainland, the government resolutely resisted calls for the survivors – who included a number of small children – to be moved out of mandatory detention on Christmas Island (Edwards, 2010). The message conveyed was that the rules were unbending. Those who had sought to breach Australia's borders – no matter how much they had suffered as a consequence – could not be seen to gain some advantage over other unlawful entrants, and certainly not over those asylum seekers who were waiting somewhere in the world, unseen by the Australian public, in a mythical refugee determination 'queue'.

The legacy of the longstanding rhetorical campaign against 'boat people' was also apparent. On the day on which most of the funerals were to be held in Sydney, a popular radio announcer ran an on-air competition in which listeners were invited to guess the number of asylum seekers, including babies, due to be buried that day (Background Briefing, 2011; Wilson, 2011). When it emerged that bereaved relatives detained on Christmas Island had been flown to Sydney at the taxpayers' expense to attend the funerals, the Opposition leader publicly criticized the decision. In a breathtaking display of the 'politics of envy', radio host and former adviser to the far-right One Nation Party, David Oldfield, told his audience: 'It really is a matter of one group who are not citizens, have not contributed and are not taxpayers of this country being treated to something the rest of us would never have had any chance for, isn't it?' (Background Briefing, 2011).

The 'treat' of being allowed to attend the funerals turned out not to be such a prize after all. Background Briefing reported 'an awful moment' at the televised funeral, when mourners refused to follow the instructions of Serco employees who manage the Christmas Island detention centre to return to the bus. The families protested that the funerals had not been conducted according to the Muslim tradition, as they had not been allowed access to the bodies because of 'health issues'. Worst of all, a nine-year-old Iranian boy who had been orphaned in the tragedy was to be removed from his brief stay with relatives in Sydney and returned with the other detainees to Christmas Island. Relatives claimed that this amounted to being 'returned to hell' and that the boy was already self-harming. The decision was reversed a few days later, but not until after the message had been sent that border control was to take precedence over the welfare of children. The Chairperson of the government's independent advisory council on the mental health of people in detention claimed that '[w]hat unfolded was a complex politics in which the actual needs of those children and other survivors, were really secondary considerations … it was a very clear determination on the part of government to return those children and survivors back to the island even if it meant that the following week they were shipped back again' (Background Briefing, 2011).

Relatives of those who died stated publicly that government policies were endangering the lives of people who would continue to come, despite all the risks, and urged the government to 'ease its immigration restrictions' (Edwards, 2010). However, one Christmas Island resident expressed the more commonly held view: 'I suppose you can only blame people that send them away in conditions that are in front of them. There's more that needs to be done about these smugglers' (ABC News Online, 2010c). Their assigned status as illegal entrants and their association with organized crime seems ultimately to have trumped any claims the survivors of the Christmas Island shipwreck may have had as traumatized victims in urgent need of care and protection. The government's line was that their needs as victims could only be met by means that did not dislodge the master status of 'unlawful non-citizen', and which operated within the framework of detention and control associated with that status. Intermittent reports of unrest among the survivors and other detainees at Christmas Island hastened the dissipation of human sympathy and refocused attention on the perceived risks to the Australian nation of unauthorized boat arrivals. As Pugh (2004, p. 55) has noted in relation to unauthorized boat arrivals more generally:

> In effect the issue is displayed as a threat to security rather than to people whose security is threatened (van Selm 2000: 15; Huysmans 1995). The 'risk' is inverted to represent a crisis or threat to wealthy societies that are thereby absolved not only from engaging in debates about the rationality of global economic policies but from too much contemplation about the hazards undertaken by boat people themselves.

The Christmas Island tragedy made the hidden processes of border control visible to the Australian public in a most confronting way. Yet the complex chain of events that led to the disaster – from the conflicts and insecurities from which these people were fleeing, to the barriers that prevented them from using safer modes of travel – have remained largely obscured beneath an ambiguous architecture of risk and responsibility in which what are essentially political risks to government, disguised as national security, remain paramount.

Quantifying risk

While we reject the notion that the costs and benefits of border control policies can be reduced to a set of numerical indices, it is nevertheless important to examine quantitatively the claims made by governments that border control saves lives. In this final section we examine the statistical relationships between illegalized border crossings and border-related fatalities in the context of both the BSI on the US–Mexico border and Frontex patrols in the Mediterranean. In discussing these statistics, we are mindful of all the shortcomings and pitfalls in the collection of statistics on border-related deaths discussed in Chapter 2. We note also that the number of illegalized border crossings cannot be directly measured. This, in fact, is one of the logical implications of unregulated travel. It is customary to substitute figures on apprehensions by border patrols as a proxy measure for the number of border crossings. However, this is problematic since it is bound to be influenced by levels of enforcement, by variability in the capacity of border crossers to evade detection at different times and locations, and by the different levels of risk associated with more and less detectible modes of border crossing.

Evaluating the Border Safety Initiative

A press release in July 2010 about the implementation of a BSI in the El Paso region of Texas notes that deaths due to border crossing in this sector dropped from 28 in the 2005 fiscal year to five in 2009. It is also claimed that the number of rescues dropped from 486 to 22 over the same period, possibly indicating a decrease in overall crossings (although other interpretations are possible). Border officials concluded that the decrease was due to the 'right mix in messaging, personnel, technology and infrastructure' (US Customs and Border Protection, 2010). Similar claims have been made in relation to other sections of the fortified border. However, these announcements are piecemeal, based on snapshots of recorded activity in local areas. They take no account of geographical displacement as border crossings, and deaths, are pushed to alternative places along the border. A systematic examination of the relationship between border enforcement and border deaths would require a comprehensive audit – providing a geographically complete and temporally dynamic picture of unfolding patterns of border crossings, border enforcement and deaths. It would also need to incorporate critical reflection on the shortcomings of and disputes over death counts and border enforcement statistics; multivariate techniques that take into account varying risk factors, differential levels of enforcement and the characteristics of border crossers; and acknowledgement of the difficulty of inferring causation even from these rigorous statistical analyses.

In 2005–06 the US GAO examined data collected by the BSI in the nine Border Patrol sectors along the US–Mexico border (GAO, 2006). An overall upward trend in officially recorded border-crossing deaths was noted, from 266 in 1998 when the BSI was implemented to 472 in 2005. The GAO researchers began by comparing data collected by the BSI with data from other sources. Despite finding different levels of undercounting in different Border Patrol sectors, all data sources confirmed the same broad trend: a decline in border crossing deaths from the late 1980s to the early 1990s, then a rapid rise through to 2005, with most of the increase concentrated in Tucson county. In order to evaluate the combined effects of increased border controls and increased

Table 7.1   Percentage change in entries, apprehensions and deaths across the US–Mexico border from 1998 to 2004

Statistical indicator	% change
Estimated undocumented entries	−9.5%
Apprehensions along south-western border	−24.9%
Deaths recorded by BSI	+29.1%

Source: GAO (2006), Appendix 1, Table 2

rescue efforts during this time period in terms of the risk of death, it is necessary to compare numbers of border deaths against some estimate of the levels of illegal border crossing over the same period. If the numbers of deaths rose alongside a major increase in border crossings, this would be a *prima facie* indication of a significant failure in deterrence, but would not suggest an increase in the objective risk of death. In this scenario, more travellers would be making illegalized crossings, but they would not, on average, be facing a greater likelihood of dying in the process.

In fact, the GAO concluded that the risk of death associated with attempting to cross the US–Mexico border illegally had increased substantially between 1998 and 2004 (see Table 7.1). Moreover, the statistical analysis confirmed that the greatest increase in risk was in the Tucson sector. In other sectors, apprehension rates and death rates were generally found to be positively correlated, but no such relationship was found in the Tucson sector, where the risk of death appeared to be independent of either enforcement activity or rates of border crossing. The GAO researchers inferred from this analysis that crossing the Arizona desert posed a particularly high objective risk of death and/or that apprehending migrants had become more difficult in Tucson than other sectors (GAO, 2006, p. 24). In fact, the particular pattern observed in Tucson – that apprehensions initially increased from 1998 to 2000, then declined until 2005, while deaths continued to rise steadily – is open to the interpretation that illegalized travellers, perhaps guided by facilitators, have continued to cross in significant numbers but have become more successful at evading detection. The GAO concluded that a full evaluation of the efforts of the BSI to prevent border-related deaths was inhibited due to inadequacies in the data and the difficulties of disentangling the effect of search and rescue efforts from the enforcement activities that constitute the Border Patrol's primary purpose. The GAO criticized the Border Patrol for its frequent assertions that the BSI had saved lives, noting its reliance on simple counts of migrant deaths that do not take into account the influence of 'other measurable factors'.

An independent evaluation of the impact of the BSI's life-saving efforts was subsequently conducted by Rob Guerette, and published with a series of commentary articles in *Criminology and Public Policy*. Guerette (2007) used multivariate and trend analysis techniques to assess the efficacy of various aspects of the BSI programme. He concluded that there had been no overall reduction in migrant deaths since the inception of the BSI, but that the BORSTAR search and rescue teams, and the Lateral Repatriation Program (LRP) that returns apprehended migrants to safer parts of the border during the hottest summer months, had saved lives. Specifically, Guerette calculated that the short-lived LRP had saved six lives. However, even when combined with the life-saving efforts of the BORSTAR teams, this was not enough to offset the overall increase in border-crossing deaths. In the face of political resolve to continue restrictive border security measures, Guerette recommended that expanded harm-reduction strategies incorporating situational crime-prevention and problem-solving policing techniques be implemented in the short term. Guerette's conclusion equates levels of undocumented border crossing with crime rates:

> Despite these positive effects, no overall decrease occurred in the number or rate of migrant deaths when examined on the aggregate level. In many ways, this finding is similar to results from evaluations of local crime prevention efforts. Although evaluations of many proactive policing and crime-prevention programs show discernible localized reductions, little evidence exists that they have contributed to overall declines in crime rates experienced across the country. (Guerette, 2007, p. 260)

While Guerette's recommendation that border authorities seek to form alliances with volunteer rescue groups rather than prosecute them is logical and humane, he fails to acknowledge the essential contradiction between the enforcement and rescue roles: '[W]hether lives were saved by volunteer groups or Border Patrol agents, they both have employed proactive life-saving measures. The end result then is the same: The development and refinement of proactive harm-reduction strategies can prevent deaths' (Guerette, 2007, p. 261). In his reply to Guerette, Welch (2007, p. 278) questioned the wisdom of drawing parallels between border control and crime prevention, arguing that 'the discussion on how to establish a secure and safe border clearly adopts a distinctive crime-control discourse, thereby taking our eye off the larger phenomenon of unwelcome migration'. In the same volume, Bejarano (2007) focuses her critique of Guerette's evaluation on his failure to note the disorientating and potentially dangerous impact of being deposited in unfamiliar terrain via the LRP, or the cultural clumsiness of the BSI's anti-border-crossing messages. Both commentators, in essence, find the statistical analysis useful, but call for a more socially and politically contextualized perspective informed by a deeper understanding of the dynamics of border crossing.

The Congressional Research Service has made a further contribution to the task of quantifying the risks of border crossing. Haddal (2010) calculated a standardized 'mortality rate per apprehension' figure for border-crossing deaths, which showed a significant and steady increase from 1.6 deaths for every 10,000 Border Patrol apprehensions in 1999, to 7.6 deaths per 10,000 apprehensions in the 2009 fiscal year. Notwithstanding the limitations of using apprehensions data as a proxy for levels of illegalized border crossing, this statistic provides a powerful and direct measure of risk, and shows that these risks are increasing. Haddal (2010, p. 27) concludes that, 'even as apparently fewer individuals have been entering the country illegally over the past few years, border crossing has become increasingly dangerous for those that do attempt to cross into the United States illegally'. Replication of this simple calculation of deaths per 10,000 apprehensions using both US and Mexican official data reported in Jimenez (2009) produced the figures shown in Figure 7.1, which confirm the continued upward trend and point to the consistent disparities in official data collected by the two governments.

The human costs of European border control

European researchers have also sought to quantify the risks of illegalized border crossing. In the absence of official European data on border-crossing deaths, Carling (2007) used data from the NGO UNITED 'list of deaths' to compare interceptions near the Canary Islands and Spanish mainland with migrant fatalities over the period 1994 to 2002. Carling found that the number of fatalities tracked fairly closely the number of interceptions. While this may indicate that the risk of mortality remained fairly constant during this period, this interpretation is complicated by the likelihood that a growing *proportion* of illegalized travellers were intercepted over this period as Spanish maritime patrols in the area increased. Using complex calculations and exploring a range of different hypothetical scenarios to fill gaps in actual data on travel patterns, Carling con-

Figure 7.1 Deaths per 10,000 apprehensions across US–Mexico border

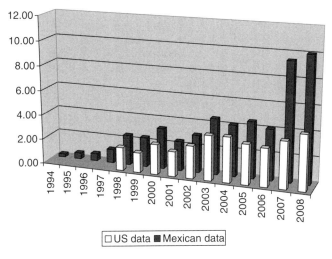

Data source: Jimenez (2009)

cluded that the mortality rate had fallen significantly. Increases in the absolute numbers of fatalities were due, in his view, to increases in attempted crossings. On this basis he proposed that there is a positive relationship between increased surveillance and improved safety, and endorsed an expansion of offshore patrols with improved search and rescue capabilities.

Carling's analysis was focused on only one section of the Mediter-ranean, and appears not to take into account the known geographical displacement effects associated with interdiction policies. The research on the US–Mexico border discussed above demonstrates the impor-tance of considering the operation of the border control system as a whole. Kiza constructed his own data set of border-related deaths across Europe by searching media reports published between 1999 and 2004 (Kiza, 2008). Because his intentions were to use the data for quantitative analysis, rather than as a basis for campaigning, Kiza adopted a narrower definition of border deaths than that used by UNITED, including only deaths that occurred while actively *en route* to the European Union. Even so, his collection of data produced com-parable or higher numbers than those on the UNITED list, suggesting a significant 'dark figure' of unrecorded deaths (see Table 7.2). Unlike Carling's analysis, which focused on a narrow geographical area, Kiza considered illegalized journeys into the EU via all entry points. His figures indicated a strong upward trend in border-crossing deaths from 1999 to 2004. As was the case with the statistical analyses of deaths along the US–Mexico border, Kiza noted that the risk of death was not evenly distributed, but was conditioned by geographical features, with sea crossings being by far the most dangerous. Considering only the data on sea crossings, Kiza found that the observed rise in deaths from 1999 to 2004 occurred despite a marked reduction over the same period in the number of interceptions by border patrols at sea, suggesting an overall increase in the riskiness of illegalized travel. Kiza therefore concluded 'that a moderate success in cutting off the routes established through time by undocumented migrants and their supporters has been paid [for] with a rising death toll' (2009, p. 9). In a more detailed analysis Kiza calculated a series of 'death quota' indices for the Italian, Spanish and Aegean maritime patrol areas, expressed as the number of deaths per 1000 migrants, which also confirmed a consistent upward trend. Taking 2003 as an indicative year, he calculated that 33 out of

Table 7.2   Estimates of European border-related deaths year by year from 1999 to 2010

Year	Total deaths recorded by Ernesto Kiza (during travel phase only)*	Total deaths recorded by UNITED (internal and external border) as of 20 January 2011 ○
1999	449	514
2000	693	687
2001	529	433
2002	913	800
2003	1259	1297
2004	930	1093
2005		814^
2006		2051
2007		1750
2008		1323
2009		1417
2010		208

Notes: ^According to Kiza (2009) the Guardia Civil estimated more than 1300 lives lost in that year *en route* to the Canary Islands alone, indicating significant undercounting
Sources: *Kiza, E. (2009) *The human costs of border control at the external EU borders between 1999 and 2004*
○ www.unitedagainstracism.org/pdfs/listofdeaths.pdf

every 1000 undocumented migrants died while trying to cross these maritime borders, figures which, if accurate, clearly dwarf the death rates per 100,000 interceptions calculated by Haddal in relation to the US–Mexico borderlands.

The pan-European border control agency Frontex was established in 2005. The effects of this increased patrol presence in the Mediterranean and at other European borders could therefore not be taken into account in Kiza's analysis of mortality risks. Frontex Director Ilkka Laitinen announced in 2007 that more than a thousand lives had been saved by Operation Hera III which diverted 1167 illegalized travellers back to their place of departure (Frontex, 2007). Such claims should be treated with caution for reasons identified by the US GAO in its assessment of the BSI. However, recent Frontex data on apprehensions, coupled with the striking drop in the number of deaths recorded by UNITED, does suggest that the steadily increasing risk of mortality observed from 1999 to 2004 was taking a different turn.

After reporting that irregular immigration had 'hit a new low' in the first quarter of 2010 (Frontex, 2010), the official report on Frontex operations released for the third quarter of 2010 (Frontex, 2011) notes an unexpected surge in apprehensions. While apprehensions appear to be significantly down at sea-crossing points, arrivals through Turkey into Greece have increased dramatically and now account for 80 per cent of all illegalized border crossings into Europe. At the same time, the UNITED list of deaths shown in Table 7.2, which include deaths at both the internal and external border, recorded the lowest number of border-related deaths for a decade, dropping suddenly from 1417 in 2009 to 208 in 2010. It is possible that diversion of illegalized travel away from risky sea voyages into land-based routes is shifting the matrix of risk experienced by illegalized travellers. As Kiza has demonstrated, sea voyages carry by far the highest statistical risk of death. However, there is a worrying possibility that deaths have been displaced to less easily monitored locations as greater numbers of illegalized travellers become stranded in North Africa or along the Sinai/Israel crossing, or are pushed into land routes even further north. Frontex reported in January 2011 that, following the implementation of Operation RABIT on the Greek–Turkish land border, apprehensions dropped from an average of 245 per day in October 2010 to 98 per day in January 2011 (Frontex, 2011). At the time of writing, the trends across this border are clearly volatile. The situation is further complicated by the uprisings across North Africa which are likely to have the dual effect of increasing dangerous sea crossings once again and placing bilateral border control agreements on hold. While an actual drop in border-related deaths would be a welcome development, there is reason to fear that intense surveillance across the entire southern border of Europe may have begun to push border-related deaths and harms still further out of sight, into areas where NGOs and researchers cannot measure their impacts.

Conclusion

Statistical analyses of the invariably flawed data that is available have generally failed to support assertions that stepping up border patrols at land or sea has a net life-saving effect, although the situation at the south-eastern perimeter of Europe is presently unclear. There have been genuine attempts across some border sites to expand the role of border control agents to include the protection of illegalized border crossers. However, in the end there is a dissonance between these two expectations which we believe can never be fully resolved. Our case studies have shown that when the logic of borders and the interests of illegalized border crossers come into conflict a space can be found to accommodate the humanitarian impulse to rescue, but the imperative to reinstate and maintain the performance of border protection soon re-emerges. While the vulnerability of illegalized border crossers may be acknowledged in these moments, their legitimate needs, agency and individual ambitions are largely subordinated to other agendas.

As noted in the opening quotation to this chapter, rescuing those in peril is a shared moral imperative, but it is also an official duty. However, the switch from border enforcer to rescuer is likely to be a difficult transition, for reasons to do with training, equipment and occupational culture. Even more important, perhaps, are the expectations of illegalized travellers themselves, who may perceive the risk of interception and return to be their greatest threat, and see this threat embodied in approaching border patrols. In the short term, rescue efforts by official agencies must of course continue, and be improved. At the same time governments should refrain from impeding individuals and groups who provide independent humanitarian assistance, whether through dehumanizing rhetoric that depicts illegalized travellers as unworthy of assistance, or by the direct threat of criminal sanction. However, private acts of heroism and human concern should not distract us from the more fundamental questions about the policy frameworks that ultimately shape and sustain a deadly matrix of risk.

Conclusion: Preventing Death by Sovereignty

No shift in the way we think can be more critical than this: we must put people at the centre of everything we do. No calling is more noble, and no responsibility greater, than that enabling men, women and children, in cities and villages around the world, to make their lives better. Only when that begins to happen will we know that globalization is indeed becoming inclusive, allowing everyone to share its opportunities. We must do more than talk about our future, however. We must start to create it, now.

> Statement by Kofi Annan in UN Millennium Report
> (UN, 2000, p. 7)

Your excellencies, EU members and leaders,
We have the great pleasure and confidence to write to you to discuss our suffering, the suffering of children and young people from Africa and the objective of our trip ... if you see that we sacrifice ourselves and risk our lives, it is because we suffer too much in Africa and we need you to fight against poverty and end the war in Africa. Nevertheless we want to study, and we ask you to help us study to become like you in Africa.

> Extract from a letter (translated from the French) found in the belongings of Yaguine Koita and Fodé Tounkara from Guinea, who died in the undercarriage of a plane travelling to Brussels in 1999, aged 15 and 14
> (Migreurop, 2009, p. 117)

Yaguine Koita and Fodé Tounkara did not have the opportunity to present their polite request to European leaders. Their terrible deaths illustrate in dramatic fashion the structural violence that prevents large populations from the Global South from 'realizing their actual potential'. The violence of borders is most immediately apparent in the boys' fatal choice of transportation. Borders, and the inequalities they help to sustain, are also implicated more broadly in the conflict and poverty Yaguine and Fodé were seeking to escape and their desperation to 'become like' Europeans. Crossing borders is not the only solution to urgent problems of human security. Other solutions, based on genuine projects of peacemaking and development,[1] or the regulation of global capital, would no doubt produce more widespread and sustainable results, and would probably be a preferred option for many. On the other hand, increases in social and economic opportunity have been found to enhance rather than curtail the desire to cross borders, which points to the role of individual agency and casts doubt on the efficacy (as well as the ethics) of using development as a tool of migration regulation. We contend that, in a globalizing age, disrupting the global hierarchy of mobility with the goal of making legal border crossing open to all who need it presents itself as a key imperative for a politics of global justice. This requires a fundamental shift from a state-centred to a human-centred analysis, which at present, we admit, is only dimly visible on the horizon.

We argued in Chapter 1 that border-related deaths have emerged as an outcome of changes in the distribution of risk and security in the context of globalization. In Chapters 2 and 3 we discussed the ideological processes that sustain and legitimize deadly border control practices by recasting border-related deaths as the product of risky personal choices, the unfortunate price to be paid to secure the nation, or as a fitting sanction for illegal actions. These represent, respectively, the rationales of risk, deterrence and punishment. As different as they may be in some respects, these rationales are all underpinned by either an active or an unreflective adherence to understandings of state sovereignty that were developed for an industrial age and are becoming increasingly dysfunctional (Dauvergne, 2008). We examined the human consequences of contemporary expressions of state sovereignty through border control in Chapters 4, 5 and 6, and identified the hegemony of risk and the limits of surveillance and rescue as life-saving measures in Chapter 7.

Problems of this scale and complexity are not readily reducible to any single explanatory framework, and such 'solutions' as can be found are likely to be drawn from a number of different sources. In searching for strategies to reduce the number of border-related deaths in the short term, we find some common ground with those who argue that constraints must be placed on the measures used by states to defend their borders against those who are not their citizens, by drawing on existing human rights frameworks. These approaches typically challenge the *means* by which states control their borders, while accepting their established right to do so. We contend that more sustainable and equitable solutions will require a recalibration of relations between individuals and states to provide a better fit with a globalizing world. This transformation will depend on radical new understandings of the limits of borders as sites of security production, and acceptance of the need to regulate global capital in the interests of human wellbeing. In the following sections we outline some critical frameworks for examining the harm of contemporary border controls, consider proposals for ameliorating the harmful effects of borders which do not fundamentally challenge current conceptions of state sovereignty, and then identify some emerging trends which may provide transformative pathways towards a less border-conscious future in which the benefits of security attach to people rather than territory.

Critiquing death by sovereignty

State crime and state harm perspectives

A state crime perspective uses the language and concepts of criminal law but subverts the usual relationship between states and legal sanctions by placing the analytical focus on the illegality of state behaviour. This provides a powerful foundation from which to critique harmful border control policies. Since harm can be either directly or indirectly inflicted, through acts of omission or commission, broadly conceived state crime frameworks are able to accommodate examples of structural violence as well as direct killings by state-sponsored agents. The terminology of 'state harm' broadens the framework further by dispensing with legalistic arguments about whether the nature or extent of the harm caused meets the criteria of 'crime' within existing frameworks of criminal law. Michalowski (2007, p. 73) argues that, '[w]hether or not [US border protection] policies violate domestic or international laws, they are as wrongful as state actions that are prohibited by law, and should be subject to the same national and international condemnation, as well as the same criminological scrutiny, as any other form of transnational crime'.

Since attaching a criminal label is essentially an act of censure, those applying a state crime or state harm perspective to the critique of border control have tended to emphasize the intentionality of border harms. For example, Michalowski asserts that '[t]he death, injury, and illness suffered by irregular migrants crossing the South-western US border-lands are *not* the unintended collateral damage of otherwise benign immigration policies. They are the *intentional* results of border militar-ization strategies designed to force migrants away from safer routes and toward more dangerous ones' (2007, p. 66, emphasis added). Grewcock's (2009) analysis of Australian border controls under the leadership of former Prime Minister John Howard similarly stresses the intentional infliction of harm through offshore interdiction and mandatory deten-tion. Indeed, these policies were pursued with such tenacity, despite the evidence of enormous suffering by the adults and children affected by them, that Grewcock characterizes them not only as 'border crimes' but also as denoting a 'war on illicit migrants' (Grewcock, 2009). The reported inclusion of 'sacks for transport of corpses' among budget items provided by the Italian Government to Libya to fund the expulsions of intercepted travellers (Trucco, 2005, cited in Baldwin-Edwards, 1997) aligns European policies as well with technologies of war, and demonstrates a conscious anticipation of their deadly consequences.

State crime frameworks make a valuable contribution to the arti-culation of the harmful, and sometimes fatal, consequences of border controls. Advocates of this approach may appeal to human rights norms contained within international human rights law (Cohen, 1993), and/or to judgements about the legitimacy of state-sponsored actions made by social audiences (Green & Ward, 2000), to provide a normative under-pinning to the labelling of state-sanctioned actions as state crime or harm.

Border iatrogenesis

The idea of 'policy iatrogenesis' provides another critical framework through which to analyse the harmful effects of border control policies (Bowling, 2010; Cohen, 1988). Put simply, iatrogenesis occurs where interventions that purport to ameliorate harms instead produce new ones. Cohen (1988) applied this idea to the transfer of criminal justice policies to countries of the Global South, and noted that traditional methods for dealing with social harms and illness were often displaced by inappropriate policies imported (and sometimes imposed) from the Global North. This has frequently created new harms and dependencies, which in turn required further interventions. Cohen's formulation encom-passes a variety of motives, ranging from situations in which 'surface intentions are genuinely benevolent', to actions cloaked in justificatory language that creates the 'pretence of good intentions'. This broadens the analytical framework beyond accounting for deliberately intended harm to also include the secondary effects of policies that engage state responsibility, but where the original intention to produce harm is less clear. Cohen dubs this grey area between deliberately inflicted harm and unintended consequences 'paradoxical counterproductivity'.

Weber and Grewcock (2011) have analysed the criminalization of people smuggling from this perspective, arguing that 'border iatrogenesis' can be seen in a spiral of harms, including border deaths, arising from counterproductive attempts to suppress people smuggling through prosecution and criminal sanctions. Border controls that cause deliberate harm to illegalized travellers themselves may fall readily within the purview of a state crime or state harm framework, as discussed above. However, it is less plausible to argue that it is the intention of those who devise border control policies to deliberately promote people smuggling.[2] Viewed from the most cynical perspective, some political and economic benefits to governments might be identified from the creation of people-smuggling markets; but these potential benefits are marginal at best, may accrue to third parties rather than governments, are difficult to calculate, and often carry their own risks.[3] Overall, it seems reasonable to conclude that the incursion of organized facilitators into the business of illegalized border crossing is disruptive, rather than supportive, of government projects to prevent border crossing through deterrence and interdiction. If governments of the Global North lack the will or vision to reduce the demand for people smugglers, we argue, it is not because people smuggling is seen to be of value in reducing border crossing, but because the logical alternative of allowing legal modes of mobility is seen as unconscionable or untenable. Paradoxically, this locks governments into adopting a cycle of countermeasures needed to tackle harms (to illegalized border crossers) and perceived harms (to domestic populations) that are largely of their own making.

The iatrogenesis framework supplements the legal or quasi-legal approach of state crime with a more sociological perspective. It is particularly suited to understanding systemically produced harms in which intentionality may be unclear, or unevenly distributed throughout harm-producing systems. The idea of 'paradoxical counterproductivity', while lacking the censorial power associated with the language of state crime, speaks directly to policymakers on their own terms by analysing policies in terms of their stated or imputed objectives. We contend that attention to the iatrogenic effects of border control policies does not displace state crime approaches. State crime approaches may be most salient in critiquing policies directed towards individual border crossers, which either intentionally or at least foreseeably cause them harm. Many examples of border practices that fit this criterion have been discussed in this book. Iatrogenic effects are most clearly discernible in the fuelling of people-smuggling enterprises which challenge the stated objectives of border controls, while justifying further crackdowns on both people smugglers and illegalized travellers (which may in turn be considered to constitute state crimes or harms). We feel there is a place for both these narratives in a comprehensive critique of the harm arising from border control policies. Moreover, there is a considerable area of overlap between the two frameworks – for example, where harmful consequences may have been intended (as part of a policy of deterrence) but then occur to an extent, or in a manner, that was unforeseen, which indicates *both* policy failure *and* the culpable infliction of harm.

Limiting deaths by sovereignty

Opening channels for legal entry

Even viewed from within a mainstream migration control perspective, a future of seemingly limitless demands for border enforcement is not an appealing prospect. As Zolberg (2006, p. 450) notes, '[t]he elimination of unauthorized immigration would require no less than the transformation of the United States and other affluent democracies into police states'. This has led many commentators to call for increased opportunities for legal border crossing. With respect to the US–Mexico border, proposed reforms emanating from a mainstream migration policy perspective have included the allocation of additional temporary work visas, with or without the regularization of illegal status (Anderson, 2010; Ewing, 2003; Cornelius, 2001; Massey, 2009), and the creation of a regional mobility zone across the territory covered by the NAFTA (Cabrera, 2010; Cornelius, 2001). In the European context, the notion of 'managed migration' has been championed (see Oelgemüller, 2010, for critical commentary), along with calls for renewed commitments to honour existing obligations towards refugees (Goodwin-Gill, 2008).

Whatever their merits, these approaches can only ever be partial and are still hostage to the needs of states. The creation of a zone of relatively free mobility for EU residents has increased the imperative to exclude those who do not belong, resulting in the fortification of the external EU border (Green & Grewcock, 2002). The European experience suggests that the creation of a zone of relatively free movement within the area covered by NAFTA would merely shift the 'migratory fault line' further south. Such an effect may already be occurring, as evidenced by the proposed fence along the Mexico–Guatemala border. Managed migration encourages 'cherry picking' of those skilled migrants most in demand in economies of the Global North, leaving others who are in desperate need of employment excluded from the possibility of accessing a work visa. Seeking asylum has proven to be a fragile source of protection within a system based on independent sovereign states, in which there is no direct obligation on states to admit asylum seekers. Zolberg (2006) argues that even a minimal observance of human rights within a migration control framework should entail the acceptance of all those who qualify under the current refugee definition and the expansion of the grounds for refugee status as befits a rapidly changing world.

Adopting crime prevention principles

In the absence of broader strategies to restrict the extent of illegalized border crossing, Guerette (2007) has suggested that criminological knowledge, particularly in relation to situational crime prevention and problem-oriented policing, could be applied to border control with the aim of reducing deaths in the short term. The objective would be to develop life-saving tactics that prevent illegalized border crossing, while seeking to minimize geographical displacement and other risk-increasing effects – much as one might seek to prevent speeding without merely shifting it to more dangerous stretches of road. Unlike state crime perspectives, Guerette takes the view that changes in border-crossing routes may have been expected as a response to enhancements in border control, but that increases in migrant deaths were not. In fairness to Guerette's position, he acknowledges that crime prevention measures are a short-term response intended to make illegalized crossings less dangerous, rather than an enduring solution. However, we agree with Welch that this approach perpetuates the framing of border policies within a crime control model, which has proven to be both limiting to policymakers and harmful to border crossers. A crime prevention approach leaves unexamined the underlying drivers of border crossing and fails to challenge the perception of those seeking to cross borders as a threat.

Situational crime prevention strategies operate largely within a risk reduction paradigm. Critics have often observed that policies based on risk avoidance embedded in neoliberal modes of governance can operate in ways that display an 'incredible myopia' with respect to power differentials and normative considerations (Coleman & Sim, 2005, p. 112), and thereby eclipse considerations of justice and human rights

(Hudson, 2003). At an individual level, risk frameworks deny the full implications of legal, social and moral personhood, and direct strategies of containment towards risk-producing groups who come to be viewed as perpetual suspects (Tsoukala, 2008). It is important to acknowledge that Guerette's approach does shift attention to the risks faced by illegalized travellers, potentially mitigating the 'myopia' of risk practitioners who are focused solely on state perspectives. However, by choosing to counter one risk mentality with another, the normative dimensions of border control are set aside.

We should clarify that we take no issue with the humanitarian efforts of groups who fill water tanks in the Arizona desert, give sustenance to destitute asylum seekers in the UK, throw life jackets into stormy seas off Australia's northern coastline, or provide a link to the outside world for individuals detained indefinitely in detention centres across the Global North. In fact we applaud these life-saving efforts, as each is designed to mitigate the risks faced by illegalized travellers. Involvement in such emergency humanitarian interventions does not preclude a political commitment to longer term and globally just solutions. Moreover, these rescue efforts differ significantly from crime prevention approaches in that they do not contribute to discourses of criminalization. On the contrary, they attest to our shared humanity.

Applying human rights standards

Appealing to human rights standards is one way to demarcate the legitimate limits of state actions that cause harm to illegalized border crossers, and to identify state obligations to protect them. To the extent that this can be translated into effective human rights enforcement, it offers one way of mitigating the harmful effects of border control policies. The most obvious application of human rights standards in relation to border control is to place limits on the *means* employed by states to defend their borders, since a general right for states to control borders underpins the system of international law in which human rights norms are currently embedded. Humanitarian organizations therefore routinely feel the need to acknowledge the state prerogative to control borders, even while strongly criticizing the manner in which they do so (see, for example, British Red Cross, 2010).

Many of the dilemmas and limitations associated with a human rights approach to border control are expressed in this extract from Eschbach et al. (1999, p. 452), which refers to the fortification of the

US–Mexico border, but is equally applicable to other sites along the global frontier:

> Ultimately, the most important questions may be ethical. How many migrants' deaths are acceptable to the United States in its quest to enforce its borders? Do the local successes of strict border enforcement justify the mortality bill? Is the United States showing the same respect and concern for the value of the life of undocumented migrants that it does for its own citizens? The equality of all human lives requires that each of these questions be carefully considered when setting border and immigration enforcement policies. Moral obligations to respect human life should not be conditional on accidents of birth and citizenship, but are universal imperatives.

Faced with the first question, it is tempting to respond by stating that no intended or even foreseeable increase in the risk of deaths from illegalized border crossing can be acceptable from a human rights perspective. This calculus is spelled out in more utilitarian terms by Spijkerboer (2007, p. 139) in arguing that '[i]ncreased human costs from intensifying border controls should factor into the debate about the future of European border control. What weight the human costs should have can only be determined when more information becomes available'. Aside from the problem of the incommensurability of the supposed costs and benefits of border controls, such a utilitarian equation is inherently unappealing from a human rights point of view. However, there is as yet no universally recognized right to cross borders which could be 'weighed' against the recognized right of states to control border crossing. Article 13 of the *Universal Declaration of Human Rights* guarantees only the right to move freely *within* state borders and the unconditional right to leave. The right to seek (but not necessarily obtain) asylum, and the associated prohibition against *refoulement* to danger, is one of the few recognized points of leverage; and this route is only available to a small proportion of those who cross borders illegally, and has failed in practice to protect many of those.

Individuals do have a well-recognized right to life. However, in reality, very few human rights protections are considered to be absolute, and the drafting of most substantive rights allows for considerations of collective security to trump individual rights. Etzioni (2010, p. 106) translates the universal right to life into a duty on states to provide 'conditions under which people can feel secure in their lives and in their homes and feel safe enough so they can freely use public spaces, can go to work, can let children go to school and can exercise their other rights, such as attending religious and political events – but not an environment in which they are risk-free'. On this definition, many of the restrictions described earlier that arise from the status of illegality can readily be seen to violate this basic right. In relation to the external border, Spijkerboer (2007, p. 138) argues that states should be held responsible for the 'foreseeable consequences' of border control policies and should therefore 'exercise their border controls in such a way that loss of lives is minimised'. Similarly, Grant (2011a, p. 69) argues that '[a]lthough states are entitled to control their borders, they are also under a duty to establish and take into account the foreseeable impact of frontier control on human lives and human rights'. At a minimum, it seems that human rights norms require that state agents must not directly imperil the lives of illegalized border crossers by using dangerous restraints and disproportionate levels of force during deportation; by capsizing their boats, whether deliberately or through lack of training or reckless indifference to their safety; by shooting them as they try to escape custody or protest their exclusion; by discouraging others from going to their rescue; or by deliberately withholding from them the means to sustain life. This list may seem disappointingly limited, given the wide-ranging examples of structural violence associated with border controls that have been considered in this book. However, it serves at least to shift attention away from the sovereign rights of states towards a debate about the existing rights that should be upheld by them in relation to individuals who are not their citizens.

Human rights protections for illegalized border crossers might be expanded beyond the circumstances of direct liability just described if responsibility could also be attributed for the unconscious, systemic harm arising from border controls. This is an ambitious undertaking since the law has difficulty incorporating even individual responsibility that operates beyond consciousness (Lacey, 2007). Indeed, Spijkerboer (2007) concludes that there does not seem to be a broad legal responsibility for border-related fatalities where those deaths arise from lawful measures to control borders. However, Lacey (2007) has argued in the context of criminal law that 'outcome responsibility' can be attributed where individuals play any part in 'risk creating activity', including through lawful acts. This provides some scope to establish a wider state responsibility for the risks associated with illegalized travel, although in what forum this could be argued is not clear.

Eschbach et al. also pose the question: 'Is the United States showing the same respect and concern for the value of the life of undocumented migrants that it does for its own citizens?' This same question could be asked in relation to other countries of the Global North. Border control brings into sharp relief the core contradiction within the international system of human rights law. What are commonly understood to be *human* rights are quickly revealed to be *citizens'* rights. So, for example, the British Home Secretary can feel fully justified in asserting that '[a]ccess to the benefits of UK residence and citizenship should be earned. It's not uncivilized to treat our own nationals differently from overseas citizens' (Home Office, 2007, p. 2). This view might find widespread acceptance in relation to access to everyday services and entitlements, but how does the calculus operate where it is the fundamental right to life that is in conflict with the accepted rights of states? Dauvergne concludes that border fatalities indicate a need for a 're-examination of whether we have the balance right between letting people in and keeping people out' (2008, p. 102). Eschbach et al. (1999) note that moral obligations to respect human life should not be conditional on accidents of birth and citizenship, but are universal imperatives. This seems to support a strong human rights position when it comes to border-related deaths. However, Nevins (2003) concluded after a review of the literature on US–Mexico border deaths that Eschbach, along with most other commentators on US border control, has operated within what he called a conservative human rights framework, which has consistently failed to challenge the fundamental right of states to exercise border controls. For Nevins, boundary policing as it now exists is violent precisely because 'it denies people the right to access the resources they need to realize [other] rights – rights contained within the Universal Declaration of Human Rights and other international covenants' (2008, p. 191).

Expanding existing human rights protections

A number of cracks are beginning to appear in the edifice of state sovereignty which could allow space for more substantial challenges to the border protection regimes operated by governments of the Global North. The Global Migration Group, which consists of 12 United Nations agencies, the World Bank and the International Organization for Migration – a group embedded firmly within the current international order – has recently issued the following statement:

> Too often, States have addressed irregular migration solely through the lens of sovereignty, border security or law enforcement, sometimes

driven by hostile domestic constituencies. Although States have legitimate interests in securing their borders and exercising immigration controls, such concerns cannot, and indeed, as a matter of international law do not, trump the obligations of the State to respect the internationally guaranteed rights of all persons, to protect those rights against abuses, and to fulfill the rights necessary for them to enjoy a life of dignity. (Global Migration Group, 2010)

In this regard, Grant (2011a, 2011b) notes a number of international human rights instruments that either implicitly acknowledge or openly avow the equal entitlements of legal and illegal migrants.[4] She also identifies many existing frameworks within international legal regimes which, while not directly preventing border-related deaths, could at least increase the accountability of states for what she calls 'the anonymous and "cosmopolitan" deaths which now take place during complex migration processes' (Grant, 2011a, p. 64). She argues that a duty on states to document deaths and a right for relatives to know about the fate of their loved ones could be derived from the existing right to family life. Indeed, Grant observes that the Commissioner for Human Rights within the Council of Europe has already called for such measures. Furthermore, she proposes that states should be required to evaluate the human impact of their border control policies, investigate and prosecute mistreatment and killings by smugglers and traffickers, and devise protocols for dealing with missing people – all of which could be achieved through international structures and protocols that are already applied in other contexts (Grant, 2011b).

At best, it seems that effective human rights protection might translate into requirements on states to avoid gross human rights abuses, which hold them accountable for the consequences of coercive actions that take place both within and beyond their borders, and which enforce Refugee Convention obligations for those who qualify. While this would be a major advance on the current situation of impunity, it would still not achieve the universalist standard of 'equality of all human lives' and remains a precarious basis from which to protect individuals whose border crossing has been labelled illegal. Khosravi (2010, pp. 126–7) has observed that '[c]onditional hospitality opens the gate only to those who "deserve" it, those who have passports, valid visas, adequate bank statements, or invitations ... What the stateless, asylum seekers, undocumented migrants face today is a hostile hospitality'. A more secure basis for ensuring protection for illegalized travellers would be to prohibit their illegalization in the first place. Yet this is fundamentally at odds with the precedence attached to state sovereignty in the international legal order. In the final section we identify signs of new developments in theory and practice which hold some promise for bridging the legal/illegal distinction, and transforming the existing human rights regime into 'genuinely *human* rights' that are 'accessible on the borders, [and] carried across borders' (Gready, 2004, p. 352).

Transforming sovereignty

Towards mobility rights?

Migration theorist Stephen Castles (2010, p. 1568) has proposed that the 'sedentary bias' that prevails within both the empirical world and migration theory should give way to the 'postulate that migration is a normal part of social relations'. He continues: 'If there is a normative goal, it should not be to reduce migration but to find ways in which it could take place under conditions of equality and respect for human rights' (Castles, 2010, p. 1569). While Castles rejects assertions that contemporary life is characterized by perpetual motion, he neverthe-less perceives the need for conceptual frameworks and forms of governance that better accommodate mobility. In an effort to shore up human rights protections against the harm of border controls, some commentators have advocated the recognition of an individual right to mobility (see, for example, Nevins, 2001; Juss, 2004). Juss bases his argument on the right to work and the frequent necessity in a globalizing world of crossing borders to find employment.

These emerging perspectives suggest a human-centred approach that recognizes that individuals should be accorded some space to solve their own security problems. Cross-border mobility may be one aspect of the solution – whether short-term, long-term or circular – and may result in the formation of transnational families and communities reliant on remittances, or may require the exercise of rights to family reunion. Ample precedent has already been established to support what we think of as 'fluid security', which follows the individual and is not limited to those occupying a particular territory.[5] Citizens of the stable and affluent states of the Global North already carry with them a bubble of security as they travel around the world – expecting rapid intervention by their own governments if they are threatened by natural disasters, armed conflict, personal victimization or entanglement with foreign legal systems. From a global justice perspective, the task is to extend similar protection to the citizens of less powerful nations. While sympathetic to the vision of universal mobility, Zolberg sees practical limits on its realization under present conditions of extreme global inequality, and proposes a compromise:

> To the extent that limits on admission prevail, priority must be given to those in greatest need, people who cannot survive in their country of origin because they are the target of persecution, because of life-threatening violence, or because there is no possible way of making a living. In this light, affluent democracies should forego mercantilist policies that deprive developing countries of precious manpower, but may promote the immigration of less skilled workers, so long as they are prepared to incorporate them. As for the control of unauthorized immigration, they must learn to live with imperfections, which are preferable to most of the draconian solutions being proposed. (2006, p. 457)

Whether the wholesale relaxation of border controls might usher in serious risks to both new arrivals and existing populations is a vexed question. It might be argued that previous experience has shown that opening borders creates an initial clamour to gain entry, but that these effects subside over time. The political reality is that any move towards relaxing state-operated border controls is likely to be graduated, should be accompanied by genuine efforts at promoting what Zolberg describes as 'bread and peace' initiatives to provide security solutions closer to home, and may take the form not simply of 'open borders' but borders that are regulated instead at a supranational level.

Human security and the right to have rights

There is an emerging constellation of ideas that seeks to transform the relationship between individuals and governments in a way that overcomes the current sources of governmental dysfunction that leave illegalized travellers and migrants relatively unprotected under the law. We will group these developments loosely under the still ill-defined concept of human security. We could equally refer to them as 'genuinely human rights' which are realizable in practice, and which guarantee the full range of citizenship and welfare rights irrespective of location and nationality. One potential advantage of using the language of human security is that it provides a counter-narrative to the primacy of national security and the widespread practice of seeking security for citizens through the exclusion of risky groups (Tsoukala, 2008). Our conception of human security acknowledges these social and legal shifts engendered by risk thinking, and seeks to wrest back the paradigm to argue for the primacy of individual security, and the ideal of equal security for all. This conception is both a legal and a politicized one, aimed at transcending the paternalism of some approaches to human rights, and the legal impasse that follows from reliance on guarantees of protection from nation-states.

Human security was understood by Arendt as 'an aspiration to be pursued through political action, rather than a right to be claimed' (Oman, 2010, p. 296). This political action needs, firstly, to address the limitations of state sovereignty in a globalizing world. A human security approach, which begins from the premise of universal human vulnerability and draws on established human rights principles, identifies the system of state sovereignty itself as the main barrier to preventing the structural violence associated with border controls. In a world where the fundamental rights of all human beings were recognized without distinction, the wellbeing of citizens could not be weighed more heavily in the balance than the lives of non-citizens. Alternative solutions to problems of human security would have to be found, rather than concentrating solely on keeping unwanted individuals out. In any case, Dauvergne (2008, p. 170) notes that borders are becoming less *able* to act as 'security screens' for populations, so that alternative modes of security production *need* to be found which succeed on a planetary level. Weber and Bowling (2008) have observed that English borders that were once heavily defended, such as parish boundaries, faded into obscurity once they were subsumed by larger ones which were better able to underwrite demands for individual and collective security in a new industrial order. The dynamics of globalization provide the conditions for a similar transformation to a differently bordered world.

As Arendt famously noted in relation to those denied the 'right to have rights': 'Their plight is not that they are not equal before the law, but that no law exists for them' (Arendt, 1968, pp. 295–6, cited in Oman, 2010, p. 281). According to Oman, Arendt saw the installation of states as the guarantor for human rights as an historical compromise for a system suited to an industrializing world. Ideally that role would have been performed by humanity itself, replacing the close social networks that had provided human security in the pre-industrial past.[6] Dauvergne (2008) points out that proposals for dealing with migration regulation in the global sphere were discussed in the early 20th century but were thwarted by state interests. This dependency on states has led to a situation in which international human rights norms are well developed but 'the political will to enforce the human rights necessary to protect human beings in "stateless" *or analogous circumstances* from extreme vulnerability has been slower to develop' (Oman, 2010, p. 290, emphasis added). We have argued throughout this book that attributions of illegality create conditions of 'extreme vulnerability' that are akin to the insecurity of formal statelessness and leave individuals unable to access many of the protections of the law.

One sign of the emergence of the political will to protect the citizens of other states can be seen in the doctrine of the 'responsibility to protect'. At present, this controversial principle is used primarily to justify military incursions across national borders aimed at protecting populations from threats posed by their own governments, although other forms of intervention are also possible (Barbour & Gorlick, 2008). However, a different view may still be taken towards those who, rather than being at risk within their country of origin, seek to provide their own security solutions by crossing the borders of other states. Barbour and Gorlick (2008) have addressed this dimension of the responsibility to protect, and concluded that the doctrine could support a more ready acceptance of refugees on what they call 'adequate terms'. Although the framework is still weak, Oman nevertheless detects a move towards person-centric rather than state-centric security in the assertion by the International Commission on Intervention and State Sovereignty that 'states are not only legally responsible for ensuring the human security of their own citizens but that they are also, in both a moral and legal sense, responsible for ensuring the human security of other states' citizens' (2010, p. 293).

These developments anticipate major changes to the accepted responsibilities of states, and the increasing importance of transnational normative frameworks and institutions. We argue that if individuals are to be secure from the threat of statelessness brought about by their formal exclusion from a particular polity, or from 'analogous circumstances' in which they are unable to access effective protection from either their own or some other state, then unconditional membership of a broader polity must be available to them, for which their humanity is the only criterion.

Towards the governance of people

The prospect, however distant, of a world system focused on the production of human security requires sweeping changes in the operation of law, economy and politics in the global arena. This final section identifies some nascent trends towards the development of new forms of global governance in each of these dimensions.

As Dauvergne (2008) observes, reliance on the present systems of law is a major limitation for the observance of human rights, particularly the rights of non-citizens. She cites as evidence the *International Convention on the Protection of the Rights of all Migrant Workers and Their Families*, which is avowedly state-centric and reads more like an agenda for the elimination of illegalized migration. Dauvergne (2008, p. 170) argues that 'the Convention stands as a marker of the difficulty of using law to remedy illegality. The law is deeply implicated in creating illegality. It is at the very edge of law's potential to imagine using law to create "not-law" – a space where people could not be made "illegal"'. Sovereignty is therefore part of the problem, not the solution:

> Strong commitment to national sovereignty is a barrier to addressing the myriad dilemmas of illegal migration. It prevents creativity in the political realm. But its power does not stop there. The sovereign state controlling its borders is such a powerful image that it prevents us from imagining a different way of organizing regulation of global migration .... New ideas are hard to come by in the realm of migration regulation, and sovereignty is why. (Dauvergne, 2008, p. 173)

Dauvergne therefore attributes considerable significance to legal developments that she interprets as signs that migration control is becoming 'unhinged' from sovereignty. A decentring of state sovereignty amounts to viewing sovereignty as 'belonging to individuals, not a pure creation of the state to bestow or withhold' (Dauvergne, 2008, p. 190). The examples she gives concern judicial activism in Australia aimed at providing administrative remedies for asylum seekers who are denied avenues of appeal, and legal challenges to immiseration policies pursued in the UK. Each example in which the will of the government does not prevail Dauvergne takes to be evidence of the precedence of the 'rule of law' over an absolute conception of sovereignty. This may be a difficult point for non-lawyers (such as ourselves) to appreciate. However, Dauvergne explains her excitement about these developments as follows: 'This speaks to understanding the rule of law in its robust sense, as embodying standards of treatment for those who come before it that are distinct from rights claims but that protect individual interests' (2008, p. 183). Following this logic, the problem which then arises is where to locate legitimacy for these human-centric practices, and how to reproduce them. Dauvergne notes that systems of human rights are legitimated by the voluntary commitment of states to honour them. In contrast, she looks for an underpinning for the 'rule of law' from within the 'ethical community', which she refers to as a 'community of law' that is unhinged from the nation itself and committed to the observance of universal legal protections.[7] As for the advantages of the 'rule of law' over state-based systems of human rights for achieving just approaches to migration, Dauvergne explains:

> Illegal migration, a creature of the law, is always and necessarily a creature of *domestic* law. International legal statements, by contrast, focus on rights to move rather than on restrictions. Rule of law that is not tied to a national frame offers the potential of a source of substantive protection, which has some degree of distance from the structure that creates, recreates, and endlessly reifies the problem of illegal migration. (2008, p. 183)

There is always the danger, of course, that unhinging sovereignty could create a concentration of more unaccountable power. However, Dauvergne notes that at present powerful nations can resist the influences of globalization, holding on to their sovereignty and deploying it virtually at will, while less powerful nations cannot. Mechanisms for democratic accountability at this level are therefore already needed to monitor this unchecked expansion of regulatory power. Although the decentring of sovereignty is fraught with dangers, and strains the limits of our imaginations, in Dauvergne's view it is the only way to progress beyond the current impasse.

Both the imperative to decentre sovereignty in the interests of human security, and the importance of ensuring the accountability of that decentred power, point to a need to create audiences who recognize border controls as harmful and illegitimate under conditions of globalization, and who support the ideal of universal protection under law. Many commentators see evidence for social transformations associated with globalization that support this essentially political project. For example, Oman (2010, p. 283) argues that:

> The development of transportation and communications technologies in the twentieth and twenty-first centuries have made it increasingly possible for us to enlarge our thinking in this way. As a result, the overlapping local communities in which each of us participates are beginning to comprise a community of humanity in fact.

A poster seen by one of us in King Street, Newtown – a socially progressive area of Sydney – following the suicide in Villawood Detention Centre of Ahmed Al Akabi, provides anecdotal support for this effect. It read: 'No death as a result of border protection brings us more freedom. People's desire to move will never be changed. Their struggle is also ours.'

In this conclusion, and arguably throughout this book, we have placed inadequate emphasis on the economic dimensions of illegalized border crossing. This no doubt reflects our own limitations as criminologists without a solid grounding in political economy. However, we have some sympathy for the view expressed by Michalowski (2007) that unauthorized border crossing can only be resolved by economic solutions. We also find ourselves in agreement with Castles (2010, p. 1578), who notes that current neoliberal structures such as the International Monetary Fund and the World Bank were not intended 'to protect weak economies or vulnerable social groups, but rather to ensure that all economies and societies were exposed to the cold winds of competition'. Just as Dauvergne has called for law to become 'unhinged from sovereignty', Castles (2010, p. 1577) argues that the global economy needs to be 're-embedded' in supranational social structures to counter the 'neo-liberal attempt to disembed economic globalisation from its societal context'. This combination of the unhinging of law, particularly migration law, from state sovereignty, and the re-embedding of economic relations within social structures, might be thought of as an antidote to Sassen's characterization of neoliberal globalization as the denationalizing of the economy alongside the renationalizing of sovereignty.

The advent of the structural changes contemplated in this section pose a myriad of questions about how an emerging form of global governance might function: what form it would take, how it would be held to account, how it would operate both locally and globally, how it could regulate and redistribute the benefits of global capital, and how it could guarantee basic rights to security for everyone. These are questions for which we have no answers. However, we agree that a fundamental challenge to current conceptions of state sovereignty appears to be the key to breaking the counterproductive and tragic cycle of border control, resistance and border-related deaths outlined in this book. Dauvergne (2008, p. 190) expresses well the uncertainty we feel about the possibility of such fundamental changes, while at the same time being certain that no other solution will be sustainable in a globalizing world:

The potential of thinking differently about illegal migration is breathtaking, even if its theoretical supports remain shaky. Nothing that we are currently doing about illegal migration holds much potential for serious change. A leap beyond what we can currently imagine is not only a risk worth taking, it is the only way forward from here.

Rethinking illegalized border crossing is indeed a breathtaking proposition. More audacious are the costs of current arrangements: the deaths of men, women and children documented in this book. The inhumanity of border-related deaths marks not only the border control approaches of the Global North, but also all of the lives that are bounded by those borders being protected. Audacity – political, legal and social – and all its associated uncertainty must be risked if we are confident that all human life is equal.

Appendix 1

Known Deaths Associated with Australian Border Controls from 2000 to 2010

Date	N Cases	Personal Details	Incident Details
21-Dec-2000	3	Unknown	Vessel (raft) codenamed 'Rosalie' crossing from Lagrange Island (Western Australia), victims died while searching for water
22-Dec-2000	1	Villiami Tanginoa, Tongan, male, 52	Died after plummeting from basketball pole at Maribyrnong Detention Centre, Melbourne after altercation with guards
24-Jan-2001	1	Hai Phuc Vo, Vietnamese, male	Died in Western General Hospital, Melbourne, after being transferred from Port Philip Prison
29-May-2001	1	Shahraz Kayani, Pakistani, male, 48	Set himself on fire outside Parliament House, Canberra, because family's application to migrate was denied
23-Jun-2001	1	Mohammed Saleh, Palestinian, male, 41	Died of medical condition in Hollywood Private Hospital, Perth after being transferred from Port Hedland Immigration Detention Centre
25-Jul-2001	1	Avion Gumede, South African, male, 30	Killed himself after arriving at Sydney Airport and being detained in Villawood Immigration Detention Centre, Sydney
01-Sep-2001	1	Ashmorey, Afghan, newborn baby	Died due to lack of medical care on board refugee vessel during Operation Relex interception at Ashmore Reef, off the coast of Western Australia; first interception post Tampa

Known Deaths Associated with Australian Border Controls from 2000 to 2010 – *continued*

Date	N Cases	Personal Details	Incident Details
06-Sep-2001	2	Said Sakhi, Afghan, male, 20, and Murtaza Roni, Afghan, male, infant	Drowned when refugee boat 'KM Harapan Jaya II' hit rocks off Indonesia en-route to Australia
26-Sep-2001	1	Puangthong Simaplee, Thai, female, 25	Trafficked into Australia for sex slavery age 12, heroin addiction, died of medical condition in Villawood detention centre, Sydney
19-Oct-2001	353	146 children, 142 women, 65 men, all Iraqi or Afghan	Drowned after refugee vessel codenamed 'SIEV X' sank off Indonesia, but in Australian aerial border protection surveillance zone
01-Nov-2001	1	Unknown	One or more asylum seekers feared drowned at Roti Island, Indonesia, after their boat en-route to Australia was forced back by Navy
08-Nov-2001	2	Nurjan Husseini, Afghan, female, 55, and Fatima Husseini, Afghan, female, 20	Passengers on refugee boat 'Sumber Lestari' drowned during Operation Relex off Christmas Island
13-Jan-2002	1	Thi Hang Ley, Vietnamese, female	Killed herself after being put in Villawood Immigration Detention Centre, Sydney, for overstaying visa. This was her 3rd suicide attempt
26-Aug-2002	1	Mohammed Sarwar, male	Died in Nauru Detention Centre
19-Jan-2003	1	Fatima Irfani, Afghan, female, 29	Died in Sir Charles Gairdner Hospital, Perth, of bleeding in her brain after transfer from Christmas Island
03-Feb-2003	1	Dr Habuibullah Wahedy, Afghan, male, 46	Killed himself at Murray Bridge, South Australia, after the Immigration Department said his TPV would soon expire and encouraged him to return to Afghanistan

Known Deaths Associated with Australian Border Controls from 2000 to 2010 – *continued*

Date	N Cases	Personal Details	Incident Details
19-Jun-2003	1	Quoc Kinh Phung, Vietnamese, male	Died in Western General Hospital, Melbourne, after being transferred from Maribyrnong Immigration Detention Centre, Melbourne
01-Jul-2004	1	Seong Ho Kang, Chinese, male	Run over by a taxi in Strathfield, Sydney, after being chased on foot by immigration enforcement officers
29-Aug-2004	1	Marc Lao Thao, French, male	Died in Villawood Immigration Detention Centre, Sydney
25-Mar-2005	1	Unknown, male	Died in Maribyrnong Immigration Detention Centre, Melbourne
20-Aug-2005	1	Mrs. Aziz Yaukob Agha, Syrian, female, 70	Died of medical condition at son's house in Melbourne, after refusal of visa extension and imminent deportation
09-Sep-2006	11	Unknown, Afghans, two females aged 6 and 9, and nine males	All eleven victims reportedly murdered in their homes in Afghanistan by locals calling them 'spies', after being deported as a group from Australia
11-Sep-2006	1	Wah Aun Chan, Malaysian, male, 27	Drowned in River Murray after running from police near Waikerie on the Sturt Highway, South Australia
13-Jan-2008	1	Mr. Fashovar, Iranian, male, 62	Died of a medical condition in Villawood Immigration Detention Centre, Sydney
16-Jun-2008	1	Mr. Zhang, Chinese, male	Committed suicide after being deported to China, feared persecution and torture in China
Unknown (reported 2008)	1	Mr. Cai, male	Died of medical condition in China after deportation from Villawood Immigration Detention Centre, Sydney
Unknown (reported 2008)	1	Mr. Mack, male, 76	Died in Villawood Immigration Detention Centre, Sydney, following surgery for a medical condition

Known Deaths Associated with Australian Border Controls from 2000 to 2010 – *continued*

Date	N Cases	Personal Details	Incident Details
16-Apr-2009	5	Mohammed Hassan Ayubi, 45, Muzafar Ali Sefarali, 45, Mohammed Amen Zamen, 38, Awar Nader, 50, and Baquer Husani, 26, all Afghan males	Died as a result of explosion on boat codenamed 'SIEV36' during Naval interception at Ashmore Reef
05-Oct-2009	105	Unknown, Afghan	Boat believed lost at sea en-route to Australia, no bodies ever found
30-Apr-2010	5	Unknown, Sri Lankan, males	Drowned after abandoning refugee vessel to seek help. Govt had prior knowledge of vessel being in the vicinity of Cocos Islands
07-Jun-2010	12	Thileep Kumar and Bahirathan, both Sri Lankan, and ten Afghans, all male	Drowned off the coast of Indonesia while changing from a large boat to a smaller boat – second attempt for Sri Lankans after previous interception
23-Aug-2010	1	Unknown, Afghan, male, 30	Died in Sir Charles Gairdner Hospital, Perth, Western Australia, of a medical condition after being found unconscious at the Curtin Immigration Detention Centre
20-Sep-2010	1	Josefa Rauluni, Fijian, male, 36	Jumped off a roof at Villawood Immigration Detention Centre, Sydney, hours before he was to be deported
13-Nov-2010	97	Afghan, Iraqi and Iranian asylum seekers, including children	Boat feared lost at sea *en route* from Indonesia. No direct confirmation of sinking, but relatives in Australia report no contact following embarkation on 13 November
16-Nov-2010	1	Ahmad al-Akabi, Iraqi, male, 40	Committed suicide at Villawood Immigration Detention Centre, Sydney, after refugee application was rejected twice
08-Dec-2010	1	David Saunders, British, male, 29	Committed suicide in Villawood Immigration Detention Centre, Sydney

Known Deaths Associated with Australian Border Controls from 2000 to 2010 – *continued*

Date	N Cases	Personal Details	Incident Details
15-Dec-2010	50	Eight children including infants, and estimated 42 adults, all either Iranian, Iraqi or Kurd	Drowned after refugee boat codenamed 'SIEV 221' crashed onto rocks on Christmas Island. 30 bodies recovered
18-Mar-11	1	Miqdad Hussain, Afghan man aged 20	Found dead in detention centre in Weipa, near Queensland by staff. Suspected suicide
27-Mar-11	1	Mohammad Asif Ata, Afghan man, aged 19	Found dead in detention centre in Curtin, Western Australia by other detainees. Suspected suicide
Total	673		

Notes

Chapter 1   Charting the Global Frontier

1   At the time of writing this agreement has become inoperative due to the Libyan civil war.

Chapter 2   Counting and Discounting Border Deaths

1   According to UNHCR figures, Australia hosted a mere 2350 asylum seekers at the end of 2009 compared with more than 48,000 in Greece, more than 60,000 in both Canada and the USA, and over 300,000 in South Africa (reported in Weber & Grewcock, 2011).
2   Available at http://www.unitedagainstracism.org/pdfs/listofdeaths.pdf
3   Testimonies available at http://sievx.com/articles/disaster/KeysarTradTranscript.html

Chapter 3   Accounting for Deaths at the Border

1   Available at http://www.revistafusion.com/2001/abril/entrev91.htm
2   Available at http://www.irr.org.uk/2003/july/ak000013.html
3   Identified people smuggler.
4   The text of these speeches is available on the SIEV X Memorial Project research website www.sievx.com.

Chapter 4   Structural Violence

1   In contrast to other analysts, Carling concludes that this shift was not associated with an increased risk of death. This claim will be examined in Chapter 7.
2   Data is taken from http://sievx.com/dbs/boats/ and boats in which the adult/child breakdown is not known have been excluded.
3   The time period covered by each average is not specified.
4   Available at http://www.humaneborders.org/news/documents/cumulative-map20002007.pdf
5   The problematic quality of initial asylum decisions has been the subject of ongoing criticism from lawyers and NGOs and variously attributed to direct political interference in the decision-making process, fast-track procedures, poor quality of information about countries of origin, a 'culture of disbelief' within the immigration bureaucracy, and incompetence – deliberate or unintended – among the junior bureaucrats who 'process' asylum claims. These bureaucrats are often accused of approaching their task as a process of compiling formulaic reasons for refusal, rather than as a serious duty to make well-informed, carefully considered and responsible decisions. These shortcomings create a heavy reliance on appeals.

Chapter 5   Suspicious Deaths

1 Full text of speech available at http://savageclown.wordpress.com/2010/11/17/
   jimmy-mubenga-indefinite-leave-to-remain/
2 In many jurisdictions, a legal distinction is made between deportations and
   removals – the former generally referring to the expulsion of an individual
   who has been lawfully present at some time, and the latter referring to individuals who have never been granted leave to remain. For ease of reference,
   the terms are used interchangeably in this chapter, with a preference for
   'deportation'.
3 In order to quantify the risks faced by any particular nationality during
   deportation, their level of representation among deported populations, and
   their representation among those subject to forced deportation, would need
   to be known. This would require comprehensive data on deportations, forced
   deportations and deaths arising from deportation, by nationality.
4 This seems to be an inadequate interpretation of 'systematic' in our view.
   If anything, abuses might be expected to involve a larger number of officers
   where abuse is systematic, and therefore considered to be the norm, rather than
   being concentrated among a few 'bad apples'.
5 UK Parliament website, http://www.parliament.uk/business/committees/com-
   mittees-a-z/commons-select/home-affairs-committee/news/101102-rules-
   governing-enforced-removals-from-the-uk/

Chapter 7   The Ambiguous Architecture of Risk

1 Available at http://www.parliament.uk/business/publications/business-papers/
   commons/early-day-motions/.
2 At the time of writing, the Australian Government has announced a controversial new policy of returning interdicted asylum seekers to Malaysia in the
   belief that this action will break the people smugglers' 'business model'. The
   policy, introduced in response to serious rioting on Christmas Island and at
   Villawood Immigration Detention Centre in Sydney, has been condemned
   by the UNHCR and ruled by the High Court to be without legal authority.
3 The relevant convention is actually the 1951 *UN Convention Relating to the
   Status of Refugees*.

Conclusion: Preventing Death by Sovereignty

1 We stress the word 'genuine' here, since 'development' projects driven by
   'managed migration' objectives are designed to meet the interests of donor
   countries, not necessarily the needs and desires of populations.
2 Note that in these two constructions, the *referent* in terms of harmful consequences of border policies is different: in the first case, the focus is directly
   on harm to individual border crossers, and in the second, on the creation of
   a criminal market (which may have further consequences in terms of harm
   to human beings).
3 Potential benefits might include the capacity of governments to use people
   smugglers as a political resource by offloading blame for border-related deaths

onto them; the growth and expansion of law enforcement industries, which may present a mixture of costs and benefits for government, depending on their level of privatization and other circumstances; and opportunities for government officials in countries of destination and transit to form symbiotic relationships with criminal groups.

4 For example, the *UN Convention Against Transnational Organised Crime* (UN Doc A/RES/55/25) and the UN Human Rights Commission Special Rapporteur Reports on the Human Rights of Migrants in 2004 (UN Doc A/59/377) and 2008 (UN Doc A/HRC/7/12).

5 We are grateful to our collaborators Claudia Tazreiter and Marie Segrave on the Australian Research Council project *Fluid Security in the Asia Pacific* for discussion of these ideas.

6 The considerable length of time separating the realization of even an imperfect system of human rights from the emergence of industrialization suggests that legal protections are slow to emerge in the wake of major structural change.

7 This resembles, in form at least, the appeal to the judgements of 'audiences' in Green and Ward's expanded conception of state crime (Green & Ward, 2000).

Bibliography

AAP (Australian Associated Press) (2011) 'Call for Malaysia to stop caning refugees', 11 March 2011, available at <http://www.news.com.au/breaking-news/call-for-malaysia-to-stop-caning-refugees/story-e6frfku0-1226019816348>.

Aas, K. (2007) *Globalization and Crime*, London, Sage.

Aas, K. (2011) '"Crimmigrant" bodies and bona fide travelers: Surveillance, citizenship and global governance', *Theoretical Criminology*, 15(3): 331–46.

ABC (2002) *Lateline*, Tony Jones interview with the Minister for Immigration, Phillip Ruddock, 6 June 2002, <http://www.abc.net.au/lateline/stories/s575825.htm>.

ABC News Online (2003) 'Norway plans maritime law changes after *Tampa* saga', ABC News Online, 29 April 2003, available at <http://www.abc.net.au/news/stories/2003/04/29/842107.htm>.

ABC News Online (2009) 'Defence to release boat blast footage', ABC News Online, 6 September 2009, available at <http://sievx.com/articles/psdp/2009/20090906-ABC.html>.

ABC News Online (2010a) 'Sabotage behind fatal asylum boat blast', ABC News Online, 17 March 2010, available at <http://www.abc.net.au/news/stories/2010/03/17/2848247.htm>.

ABC News Online (2010b) 'Australia "needs to deter" asylum seeker violence', ABC News Online, 19 March 2010, available at <http://www.abc.net.au/news/stories/2010/03/19/2850143.htm>.

ABC News Online (2010c) 'People "thrown through air" as boat smashed into rocks', ABC News Online, 16 December 2010, available at <http://www.abc.net.au/news/stories/2010/12/16/3094501.htm>.

ABC News Online (2010d) 'Shipwreck death toll could hit 50', ABC News Online, 20 December 2010, available at <http://www.abc.net.au/news/stories/2010/12/20/3097650.htm>.

ABC News Online (2010e) 'Calls for policy change in wake of shipwreck', ABC News Online, 19 December 2010, available at <http://www.abc.net.au/news/stories/2010/12/19/3097079.htm>.

ABC News Online (2011a) 'Castaway kids', ABC News Online, no date, available at <http://www.abc.net.au/news/events/castaway-kids>.

ABC News Online (2011b) 'Border chief defends shipwreck response', ABC News Online, 24 May 2011, available at <http://www.abc.net.au/news/stories/2011/05/24/3225583.htm>.

ACLU (American Civil Liberties Union) (2008) 'Fact sheet on U.S. "Constitution Free Zone"', 22 October 2008, ACLU, available at <http://www.aclu.org/print/technology-and-liberty/fact-sheet-us-constitution-free-zone>.

ACLUNC (American Civil Liberties Union of Northern California) (2011) *Costs and consequences: The high price of policing immigrant communities*, February 2011, ACLUNC, available from <http://www.aclunc.org/docs/criminal_justice/police_practices/ costs_and_consequences.pdf>.

Accurate Shooter (2010) 'US Border Patrol dominates national police shooting championship', accurateshooter.com, 24 September 2010, available at <http://bulletin.accurateshooter.com/2010/09/u-s-border-patrol-dominates-natl-police-shooting-championship/>.

AFP (Australian Federal Police) (2001) Media release on Operation Dogshark, 13 March 2001, available at <http://www.afp.gov.au/media-centre/news/afp/2001/March/operation-dogshark-cracks-international-people-smuggling-and-money-laundering-syndicate.aspx>.

Agamben, G. (1998) *Homo sacer: Sovereign power and bare life*, Stanford, Stanford University Press.

Agamben, G. (2005) *State of exception*, Chicago, University of Chicago Press.

Age (2010a) 'Almost 50 died in boat tragedy: PM', *The Age*, 21 December 2010, available at <http://www.theage.com.au/national/almost-50-died-in-boat-tragedy-pm-20101220-1937i.html?skin=text-only>.

Age (2010b) 'Boat inquiry needed, lawyers says', *The Age*, 16 December 2010, available at <http://news.theage.com.au/breaking-news-national/boat-inquiry-needed-lawyers-says-20101216-18z7x.html>.

AI (Amnesty International) (2009) *Immigration detention in the USA*, London, Amnesty International.

AI (2010) *Invisible victims: Migrants on the move in Mexico*, Index: AMR 41/014/2010, April 2010, London, Amnesty International.

Alberici, E. (2008) 'Recovered body parts "unlikely to be missing backpacker"', ABC News Online, 7 October 2008, available at <http://www.abc.net.au/news/stories/2008/10/07/2383617.htm>.

Allison, R. (2003a) 'Scandal of asylum riot', *The Guardian*, 16 August 2003, available at <http://www.guardian.co.uk/uk/2003/aug/16/immigrationandpublicservices.immigration1>.

Allison, R. (2003b) 'Judge slates Group 4 in Yarl's Wood riots', *The Guardian*, 16 August 2003, available at <http://www.guardian.co.uk/uk/2003/aug/05/immigration.immigrationandpublicservices>.

Anderson, B. (2010) 'Blame game begins after asylum boat tragedy', ABC News Online, 15 December 2010, available at <http://www.abc.net.au/news/stories/2010/12/15/3094221.htm>.

Anderson, B. & Parks, B. (2008) 'Symposium on border crossing deaths: Introduction', *Journal of Forensic Psychology*, 53(1): 6–7.

Anderson, S. (2010) *Death at the border*, NFAP Policy Brief, May 2010, National Foundation for American Policy, available at <http://carnegie.org/fileadmin/Media/Publications/NFAP_Policy_Brief_Death_at_Border.pdf>.

Andreas, P. (2001) *Border games*, London, Cornell University Press.

Andreas, P. (2010) 'The politics of illicit flows and measuring policy effectiveness', in P. Andreas and K. Greenhill (eds), *Sex, drugs and body counts*, New York, Cornell University Press.

Andreas, P. & Greenhill, K. (2010) 'Introduction: The politics of numbers', in P. Andreas and K. Greenhill (eds), *Sex, drugs and body counts*, New York, Cornell University Press.

Andreas, P. & Nadelmann, E. (2006) *Policing the globe: Criminalization and crime control in international relations*, Oxford, Oxford University Press.

Annas, G. (1995) 'Hunger strikes', *British Medical Journal*, 311: 1114.

AOL News (2011) 'Slain girl pleaded for her life, mom testifies at militia leader's trial', AOL News, 26 January 2011, available at <http://www.aolnews.com/2011/01/26/shawna-forde-trial-victims-mom-says-brisenia-flores-pleaded-fo/>.

Archibold, R. (2006) 'Risky measures by smugglers increase toll on immigrants', *The New York Times*, 9 August 2006, available at <http://www.nytimes.com/2006/08/09/us/09crash.html?_r=1>.

Arendt, H. (1968) *The origins of totalitarianism*, San Diego, Harcourt.

Arizona Daily Star (2010) <http://azstarnet.com/>.

Associated Press (2011) 'Family of Mexican teen killed by border agent sues U.S.', Associated Press, 17 January 2011, available at <http://www.msnbc.msn.com/id/41125520/ns/world_news-americas/#>.

Athwal, H. (2003) 'Yarl's Wood trial: A miscarriage of justice?', Institute of Race Relations, London, 3 September 2003, available at <http://www.irr.org.uk/2003/september/ha000005.html>.

Athwal, H. (2010) *Driven to desperate measures: 2006–2010*, Institute of Race Relations, London, available from <http://www.irr.org.uk/pdf2/DtDM_2006_ 2010.pdf>.

Athwal, H. & Bourne, J. (2007) 'Driven to despair: Asylum deaths in the UK', *Race and Class*, 48(4): 106–14.

Australian Customs and Border Protection Service (2011) SIEV 221 Internal Review, Commonwealth of Australia, Canberra, available at <http://www.customs.gov.au/webdata/resources/files/110124CustomsInternalReview.pdf>.

Australian Human Rights Commission (2011) Immigration detention at Villawood: Summary of observations from visit to immigration detention facilities at Villawood, Australian Human Rights Commission, <http://www.humanrights.gov.au/human_rights/immigration/idc2011_villawood.pdf>.

Background Briefing (2011) 'The boy on Christmas Island', 13 March 2011, ABC Radio National, transcript available at <http://www.abc.net.au/rn/backgroundbriefing/stories/2011/3158004.htm>.

Baldwin-Edwards, M. (1997) 'The emerging European immigration regime: Some reflections on implications for Southern Europe', *Journal of Common Market Studies*, 35(4): 497–519.

Banham, C. (2004) 'New boat arrival tests migration zone', *Sydney Morning Herald*, 5 March 2004, available at <http://www.smh.com>.

Barbour, B. & Gorlick, B. (2008) 'Embracing the "responsibility to protect": A repertoire of measures including asylum for potential victims', *International Journal of Refugee Law*, 20(4): 533–66.

Bauman, Z. (1998) *Globalization*, Cambridge, Polity Press.

Bauman, Z. (2002) *Society under siege*, Cambridge, Polity Press.

Bauman, Z. (2004) *Wasted lives: Modernity and its outcasts*, Cambridge, Polity Press.

BBC News (1999) 'Joy Gardner's family sues police', BBC News online, 15 February 1999, available at <http://news.bbc.co.uk/2/hi/uk_news/279922.stm>.

BBC News (2003) 'Chinese human smugglers jailed', 27 June 2003, BBC News online, available at <http://news.bbc.co.uk/2/hi/europe/3024866.stm>.

BBC News (2010) 'Murdered bodies found in Mexico "were migrants"', 25 August 2010, BBC News online, available at <http://www.bbc.co.uk/news/world-latin-america-11090563>.

BBC News (2011) 'Migrants end Greek hunger strike after government offer', BBC News online, 9 March 2011, available at <http://www.bbc.co.uk/news/world-europe-12694104>.

Bejarano, C. (2007) 'Senseless deaths and holding the line', *Criminology and Public Policy*, 6(2): 267–74.

Benito, G. (2003) 'Nothing is true, nor is it a lie', Statewatch Online News, 21 July 2003, available at <http://www.statewatch.org/news/2003/jul/21spain.htm>.

Blanchard, E., Clochard, O. & Rodier, C. (2008) 'Compter Les Morts' [Counting the Dead], *Plein Droit*, 77, June 2008, La Revue du GISTI, Paris.

Bloch, A. & Schuster, L. (2005) 'At the extremes of exclusion: Deportation, detention and dispersal', *Ethnic and Racial Studies*, 28(3): 491–512.

Boehm, D. (2011) 'US–Mexico mixed migration in an age of deportation: An inquiry into the transnational circulation of violence', *Refugee Survey Quarterly*, 30(1): 1–21.

Border Network for Human Rights (2006) 'Behind every abuse is a community'. US/Mexico Border report to the United Nations Human Rights Committee Regarding the United States' Compliance with the International Covenant on Civil and Political Rights, June 2006, Border Network for Human Rights, El Paso, available at <http://www.borderaction.org/PDFs/BNHR_Report_to_HRC.pdf>.

Border Safety Initiative (2005) Border Safety Initiative (Information Sheet), available at https://www.hsdl.org/?view&did=457099.

Bosworth, M. & Guild, M. (2008) 'Governing through migration control: Security and citizenship in Britain', *British Journal of Criminology*, 48: 703–19.

Bowcott, O. (2010) 'European court demands halt to forcible return of Iraqi asylum seekers', *The Guardian* online, 5 November 2010, available at <http://www.guardian.co.uk/uk/2010/nov/05/strasbourg-forcible-returns-iraqi-asylum>.

Bowcott, O. (2011) 'Deportation flights to Iraq resume despite UN warning', *The Guardian* online, 9 March 2011, available at <http://www.guardian.co.uk/uk/2011/mar/09/deportation-flights-iraq-resume>.

Bowen, C. (2008) 'New directions in detention: Restoring integrity to Australia's immigration system', Ministerial speech delivered at Australian National University, Canberra, 29 July 2008, available at <http://www.minister.immi.gov.au/media/speeches/2008/ce080729.htm>.

Bowling, B. (2010) 'Transnational criminology and the globalization of harm production', in C. Hoyle and M. Bosworth (eds), *What is criminology?*, Oxford, Oxford University Press.

Brennan, F. (2003) *Tampering with asylum: A universal humanitarian problem*, St Lucia, University of Queensland Press.

British Red Cross (2010) *Not gone, but forgotten: The urgent need for a more humane asylum system*, June 2010, London, British Red Cross.

Brotherton, D. (2008) 'Exiling New Yorkers', in D. Brotherton and P. Kretsedemas (eds), *Keeping out the other: A critical introduction to immigration enforcement today*, New York, Columbia University Press.

Brown, M. (2010) 'People smuggling task force shares rare insight', 8 June 2010, ABC News Online, available at <http://www.abc.net.au/news/stories/2010/06/08/2921993.htm>.

Brown, R. (1991) 'Vigilante policing', in C. Klockars and S. Mastrofski (eds), *Thinking about police: Contemporary readings*, New York, McGraw Hill.

Burnside, J. (2003) *From nothing to zero: Letters from refugees in Australia's detention centres*, Melbourne, Lonely Planet Publications.

Butler, J. (2004) *Precarious life: The powers of mourning and violence?* London, New York, Verso.

Butler, J. (2010) *Frames of war: When is life grievable?* London, New York, Verso.

Butterly, N. & Probyn, A. (2009) 'Rescued Sri Lankans sabotaged boat', *The West Australian*, 22 October 2009, available at <http://au.news.yahoo.com/thewest/ a/-/mp/6371562/rescued-sri-lankans-sabotaged-boat/1/oldest/>.

Cabrera, L. (2009) 'An archeology of borders: Qualitative political theory as a tool in addressing moral distance', *Journal of Global Ethics*, 5(2): 109–23.

Cabrera, L. (2010) 'Underground railroads: Citizen entitlements and unauthorised mobility in the antebellum period and today', *Journal of Global Ethics*, 6(3): 223–38.

Campaign for Justice in the Yarl's Wood Trial (2003) 'Yarl's Wood re-opens: The disgrace continues', 15 September 2003, available at <http://www.labournet.net/events/0309/Yarlsdis.html>.

Campbell, D. (2007) 'Geopolitics and visuality: Sighting the Darfur conflict', *Political Geography*, May 2007, 26(4): 357–82.

Cap Anamur website <http://www.cap-anamur.org/eng>.

Carling, J. (2007) 'Migration control and migrant fatalities at the Spanish–African borders', *International Migration Review*, 41(2): 316–43.

Carpenter, J. (2006) 'The gender of control', in S. Pickering and L. Weber (eds), *Borders, mobility and technologies of control*, Amsterdam, Springer.

Castañeda, H. (2009) 'Illegality as a risk factor: A survey of unauthorized migrant patients in a Berlin clinic', *Social Science and Medicine*, 68: 1552–60.

Castles, S. (2010) 'Understanding global migration: A social transformation perspective', *Journal of Ethnic and Migration Studies*, 36(10): 1565–86.

Caulfield, S. & Wonders, N. (1993) 'Personal and political: Violence against women and the role of the state', in K. Tunnell (ed.), *Political crime in contemporary America: A critical approach*, New York, Garland.

Cavanagh, G. (2010) *Inquest into the death of Mohammed Hassan Ayubi, Muzafar Ali Sefarali, Mohammed Amen Zamen, Awar Nadar, Baquer Husani* [2010] NTMC 014, 17 March 2010, Northern Territory Coroner.

Cevallos, D. (2005) 'Challenges 2005–2006: US builds up its fences against migration', 12 December 2005, IPS News, available at <http://ipsnews.net/ news.asp?idnews=31559>.

Cevallos, D. (2008) 'Mexico – Kidnapped migrant women: Out of sight, out of mind', 14 November 2008, available at <http://ipsnews.net/news.asp?idnews= 44706>.

Chavez, L. (2007) 'The condition of illegality', *International Migration*, 45(3): 192–6.

Chin, K. (1999) *Smuggled Chinese: Clandestine immigration to the United States*, Philadelphia, Temple University Press.

Christian, K. (2009) 'Sabotage unlikely cause of boat explosion: Refugee advocate', 17 April 2009, available at <http://www.news.com.au/breaking-news/sabotage-unlikely-cause-of-boat-explosion-refugee-advocate/story-e6frfku 0-1225715395149>.

Coalición de Derechos Humanos (2007) 'Arizona recovered remains', 23 January 2007, available at <http://www.derechoshumanosaz.net/index.php?option= com_content&task=view&id=20&Itemid=34>.

Coffey, G., Kaplan, I., Sampson, R. & Tucci, M. (2010) 'The meaning and mental health consequences of long-term immigration detention for people seeking asylum', *Social Science and Medicine*, 70: 2070–9.

Cohen, J. (2008) 'Safe in our hands?: A study of suicide and self-harm in asylum seekers', *Journal of Forensic and Legal Medicine*, 15: 235–44.

Cohen, S. (1988) 'Western crime models in the Third World: Benign or malignant', in *Against Criminology*, New Brunswick, New Jersey.

Cohen, S. (1993) 'Human rights and crimes of the State: The culture of denial', *Australian and New Zealand Journal of Criminology*, 26: 97–115.

Cohen, S. (2001) *States of denial: Knowing about atrocities and suffering*, Cambridge, Polity Press.

Coleman, R. & Sim, J. (2005) 'Contemporary statecraft and the "punitive obsession": A critique of the new penology', in J. Pratt, D. Brown, M. Brown, S. Hallsworth and W. Morrison (eds), *The new punitiveness: Trends, theories, perspectives*, Uffculme, Devon, Willan Publishing.

Collyer, M. (2006) 'States of insecurity: Consequences of Saharan transit migration', Centre on Migration, Policy and Society, working paper no. 31, 1–32.

Collyer, M. (2010) 'Stranded migrants and the fragmented journey', *Journal of Refugee Studies*, 23(3): 273–93.

Committee on Migration, Refugees and Population (2008) Europe's boat people: Mixed migration flows by sea into southern Europe, Parliamentary Assembly Resolution 1637(2008), Council of Europe, available at <http://assembly.coe.int/main.asp?Link=/documents/adoptedtext/ta08/eres1637.htm>.

Cornelius, W. (2001) 'Death at the border: Efficacy and unintended consequences of US immigration control policy', *Population and Development Review*, 27(4): 661–85.

Cornelius, W. (2005) 'Controlling "unwanted" immigration: Lessons from the United States, 1993–2004', *Journal of Ethnic and Migration Studies*, 31(4): 775–94.

Council of Europe (2011) 'Greece: Council of Europe urges Greece to improve detention conditions', 18 March 2011, Brussels, available at <http://www.detention-in-europe.org/index.php?option=com_content&view=article&id=296:greece-cpt-sees-no-improvement-in-migration-detention&catid=3:newsflash>.

Council of the European Union (2011) Frontex Programme of Work 2011, Report 5691/11 FRONT 4 COMIX 43, 25 January 2011, Council of the European Union, Brussels, available at <http://www.frontex.europa.eu/work_programme>.

Courts Administration Authority South Australia, South Australian Coroners Court information sheet, available at <http://www.courts.sa.gov.au/courts/coroner/information.html>.

Coutin, S. (2005) 'Contesting criminality: Illegal immigration and the spatialization of legality', *Theoretical Criminology*, 9(1): 5–33.

CPT (European Committee for the Prevention of Torture and Inhuman or Degrading Treatment of Punishment) (2003) 13th General Report on the CPT's activities covering the period 1 January 2002 to 31 July 2003, CM(2003)90, 10 September 2003, available at <https://wcd.coe.int/wcd/ViewDoc.jsp?id=65161>.

CPT (2011) Public statement concerning Greece, CPT/Inf (2011) 10, 15 March 2011, Strasbourg, available at <http://www.statewatch.org/news/2011/mar/coe-greece-statement-mar-11.pdf>.

Customs Today (2004) 'Border Safety Initiative: A multi-faceted approach to enhancing border safety', June 2004, Customs and Border Protection Today, available at <http://www.cbp.gov/xp/CustomsToday/2004/June/bsi_falfurrias.xml>.

Daley, S. (2011) 'Greece tries to shut a back door to Europe', *The New York Times*, 31 January 2011, available at <http://www.nytimes.com/2011/02/01/world/europe/01greece.html>.

Dauvergne, C. (2004) 'Migration and the rule of law in global terms', *The Modern Law Review*, 67(4): 588–615.

Dauvergne, C. (2008) *Making people illegal: What globalization means for migration and law*, New York, Cambridge University Press.

De Genova, N. (2002) 'Migrant "illegality" and deportability in everyday life', *Annual Review of Anthropology*, 31: 419–47.

De Giorgi, A. (2010) 'Immigration control, post-Fordism, and less eligibility: A materialist critique of the criminalisation of immigrants across Europe', *Punishment & Society*, 12(2): 147–67.

Department of Homeland Security (2005) *Fact Sheet: Arizona Border Control Initiative – Phase II*, 30 March 2005, archived material available at <http://www.dhs.gov/xnews/releases/press_release_0646.shtm>.

de Zulueta, T. (2009) 'A cruel end for Italy's asylum-seekers', *The Guardian* online, 16 May 2009, available at <http://www.guardian.co.uk/commentisfree/2009/may/16/italy-asylum-seekers-berlusconi>.

DIMIA (Department of Immigration, Multicultural and Indigenous Affairs) (2000) *Protecting the border*, available at <http://www.immi.gov.au/illegals/border2000/border09.htm> accessed 9 February 2004.

DIMIA (2004) *Managing the border: Immigration compliance*, Canberra, Department of Immigration, Multicultural and Indigenous Affairs.

Dodd, M. (2009) 'Officers used feet to repel refugees', *The Australian*, 7 September 2009, available at <http://sievx.com/articles/psdp/2009/20090907MarkDodd.html>.

Donnan, H. & Wilson, T. (1999) *Borders: Frontiers of identity, nation and state*, Oxford, Berg Publishers.

Douzinas, C. (2002) 'Postmodern just wars: Kosovo, Afghanistan and the new world order', in J. Strawson (ed.), *Law after Ground Zero*, London, Cavendish.

Eastley, T. (2010) Transcript of radio interview on the ABC Radio National, AM program, ABC, 20 December 2010, available at <http://www.abc.net.au/am/content/2010/s3097261.htm>.

Economist (2010) 'People smuggling: No safe passage – add drugs gangs to the long list of dangers facing migrants', *The Economist*, 9 September 2010, available at <http://www.economist.com/node/16994348>.

ECRE (European Council on Refugees and Exiles) (2011) *ECRE Weekly Bulletin*, 21 January 2011, European Council on Refugees and Exiles, available at <http://www.ecre.org/files/ECRE_Weekly_Bulletin_21_January_2011.pdf>.

Edwards, M. (2010) 'Families reveal torment after boat disaster', ABC News Online, 18 December 2010, available at <http://www.abc.net.au/news/stories/2010/12/18/3096660.htm>.

ERA (European Race Audit) (2010) 'Accelerated removals: A study of the human cost of EU deportation policies, 2009–2010', Briefing paper No. 4, October 2010, London, Institute of Race Relations.

Eschbach, K., Hagan, J. & Rodriguez, N. (1999) 'Death at the border', *The International Migration Review*, 33(2): 430–54.

Etzioni, A. (2010) 'Life: The most basic right', *Journal of Human Rights*, 9(1): 100–10.

Ewing, W. (2003) 'A moratorium on common sense: Immigration accord on hold while failed border enforcement policies continue', Immigration Policy Centre Policy Brief, May 2003, available at <http://www.imigrationpolicy.org>.

Fan, M. (2008) 'When deterrence and death mitigation fall short: Fantasy and fetishes as gap fillers in border regulation', *Law and Society Review*, 42(4): 701–34.

Faulkner, J. (2002) Senate estimates, Senate Hansard, 23 September 2002, ADJOURNMENT: Immigration: Border Protection.

Fekete, L. (2003) 'Death at the border: Who is to blame?' *European Race Bulletin*, Institute of Race Relations, 44: 1–12.

Fekete, L. (2005) *The deportation machine: Europe, asylum and human rights*, London, Institute of Race Relations.

Fekete, L. (2009a) 'Europe: Crimes of solidarity', *Race and Class*, 50: 83–96.

Fekete, L. (2009b) 'Europe's shame: A report on 105 deaths linked to racism or government migration and asylum policies', *European Race Bulletin*, 66, Winter 2009, London, Institute of Race Relations.

Ferguson, J. & Moor, K. (2010) 'Police close in on man who organized Christmas Island death boat', news.com.au, available at <http://www.news.com.au/national/police-close-on-man-who-organised-christmas-island-death-boat/story-e6frfkvr-1225973023705>.

FIAC (Florida Immigrant Advocacy Center) (2009) Dying for Decent Care: Bad medicine in Immigration Custody, February 2009, Florida Immigrant Advocacy Center, Miami, available at <http://www.fiacfla.org/reports/DyingForDecent-Care. pdf>.

Friedrichs, D. (1995) 'State crime or governmental crime: Making sense of the conceptual confusion', in J. Ross (ed.), *Controlling state crime: An introduction*, New Brunswick, Transaction Publishers.

Frontex (2007) 'Hera III operation', Media Release, 13 April 2007, available at <http://www.frontex.europa.eu/newsroom/news_releases/art21.html>.

Frontex (2008) 'Go ahead for Nautilus 2008', Media Release, 7 May 2008, available at <http://www.frontex.europa.eu/newsroom/news_releases/art36.html>.

Frontex (2009) 'International law of the sea: Seminar organized by Frontex', Media Release, 10 December 2009, available at <http://www.frontex.europa.eu/newsroom/news_releases/art73.html>.

Frontex (2010) 'Irregular immigration hits new low in first quarter 2010, facilitator detections up 13%', Media Release, 7 July 2010, available at <http://www.frontex.europa.eu/newsroom/news_releases/art68.html>.

Frontex (2011) FRAN Quarterly Q03 2010, 'Situation at the external borders', 16 January 2011, available at <http://www.frontex.europa.eu/situation_at_the_external_border/art22.html>.

GAO (Government Audit Office) (2006) 'Illegal immigration: Border crossing deaths have doubled since 1995; Border Patrol's efforts to prevent deaths have not been fully evaluated', GAO-06-770, August 2006, United States Government Accountability Office.

García de Olalla, P. et al. (2003) 'Tuberculosis screening among immigrants holding a hunger strike in churches', *International Journal of Tuberculosis and Lung Disease*, 7(12): S412–16.

Garland, D. (1997) '"Governmentality" and the problem of crime: Foucault, criminology, sociology', *Theoretical Criminology*, 1(2): 173–214.

Gavrilis, G. (2008) *The dynamics of interstate boundaries*, Cambridge, Cambridge University Press.

Gilbert, J. (2007) 'Border Patrol announces safety initiative', 27 April 2007, YumaSun.com, available at <http://www.yumasun.com/news/border-33652-yuma-calhoon.html>.

Gillard, J. (2010) Speech by Prime Minister Julia Gillard, press conference 17 December 2010, available at <http://www.pm.gov.au/press-office/press-conference-sydney>.

Global Migration Group (2010) Statement of the Global Migration Group on the Human Rights of Migrants in Irregular Situation, adopted by the Global Migration Group in Geneva 20 September 2010, available at <http://www.global-migrationgroup.org/pdf/GMG%20Joint%20Statement%20Adopted%2030%20Sept%202010.pdf>.

Goodwin-Gill, G. (2008) 'The politics of refugee protection', *Refugee Survey Quarterly*, 27(1): 8–23.

Grant, S. (2011a) 'Migration and frontier deaths: A right to identity?', in M. Dembour and T. Kelly (eds), *Are human rights for migrants? Critical reflections on the status of irregular migrants in Europe and the United States*, London, Routledge.

Grant, S. (2011b) 'Recording and identifying European frontier deaths', *European Journal of Migration and Law*, 13: 135–56.

Granville-Chapman, C., Smith, E. & Moloney, B. (2004) *Harm on removal: Excessive force against failed asylum seekers*, London, Medical Foundation for the Care of Victims of Torture.

Gray, L. (2006) 'Grandmothers who tend their flock of asylum seekers against dawn raids', *The Scotsman*, 26 December 2006, available at <http://thescots-man.scotsman.com/education/Grandmothers-who-tend-their-flock.2837918.jp>.

Gready, P. (2004) 'Conceptualising globalisation and human rights: Boomerangs and borders', *International Journal of Human Rights*, 8: 345–54.

Green, P. (2006) 'State crime beyond borders: Europe and the outsourcing of irregular migration control', in S. Pickering and L. Weber (eds), *Borders, mobility and technologies of control*, Dordrecht, Springer.

Green, P. & Grewcock, M. (2002) 'The war against illegal immigration: State crime and the construction of European identity', *Current Issues in Criminal Justice*, 14: 1.

Green, P. & Ward, T. (2000) 'State crime, human rights, and the limits of criminology', *Social Justice*, 27(1): 101–15.

Green, P. & Ward, T. (2004) *State crime: Governments, violence and corruption*, London, Pluto Press.

Grewcock, M. (2003) 'Irregular migration, identity and the state: The challenge for criminology', *Current Issues in Criminal Justice*, 15(2): 114–35.

Grewcock, M. (2009) *Border crimes: Australia's war on illicit migrants*, Sydney, Institute of Criminology Press.

Grewcock, M. (2010) 'The great escape: Refugees, detention and resistance', UNSWLRS 8, http://www.austlii.edu.au/au/journals/UNSWLRS/2010/8.html.

Guerette, R. (2007) 'Immigration policy, border security, and migrant deaths', *Criminology and Public Policy*, 6(2): 245–66.

Guerette, R. & Clarke, R. V. (2005) 'Border enforcement: Organized crime and deaths of smuggled migrants on the United States–Mexico border', *European Journal on Criminal Policy and Research*, 11: 159–74.

Haddal, C. (2010) *Border security: The role of the U.S. Border Patrol*, 11 August 2010, Congressional Research Service, available from <http://www.crs.gov>.

Hardie, A. (2002) 'Tough response to asylum riot', 26 February 2002, *The Scotsman*, Edinburgh, available at <http://news.scotsman.com/news/Tough-response-to-asylum-riot.2305673.jp>.

Harrell-Bond, B. (1985) 'Humanitarianism in a straight jacket', *Afr Aff (Lond)* (1985) 84(334): 3–14.

Hiemstra, N. (2010) 'Immigrant "illegality" as a neoliberal governmentality in Leadville, Colorado', *Antipode*, 42(1): 74–102.

Hill, L. & Kelada, A. (2010) 'The US–Mexico border, San Diego and imperial counties: Changes to policy and structure, with concomitant trends in injury and death rates', 20 October 2010, *SciTopics* available at <http://www.scitopics.com/The_US_Mexico_Border_San_Diego_and_Imperial_Counties_Changes_to_policy_and structure_with_concomitant_trends_in_injury_and_death_rates.html>.

Hillier, T. (2011) 'Songs for the world's wronged', *The Australian*, 17 February 2011.

HMIP (HM Inspectorate of Prisons) (2006) *Inquiry into the quality of healthcare at Yarl's Wood immigration removal centre*, 20–24 February 2004, London, HM Inspectorate of Prisons.

HMIP (2009) *Short thematic report by HM Inspectorate of Prisons: Detainee escorts and removals – A thematic review*, August 2009, available at <www.justice.gov.uk/inspectorates/hmi-prisons/docs/detainee_escorts_and_removals_2009_rps.pdf>.

HMIP (2010) *Report on an unannounced full follow-up inspection of Yarl's Wood Immigration Removal Centre*, 9–13 November 2009, Her Majesty's Chief Inspector of Prisons, <http://www.justice.gov.uk/inspectorates/hmi-prisons/docs/Yarls_Wood_2009_rps.pdf>.

Home Affairs Committee (2003) *Asylum removals*, Fourth Report of Session 2002–03, HC654, House of Commons, London.

Home Office (2007) *Enforcing the rules: A strategy to ensure and enforce compliance with our immigration laws*, London, Home Office, March 2007.

Howard, J. (2003) 'To deter and deny: Australia and the interdiction of asylum seekers', *Refuge*, 21(4): 35–50.

HRC (Human Rights Commissioner) (2001) *A report on visits to immigration detention facilities by the Human Rights Commissioner 2001*, Human Rights and Equal Opportunities Commission, Sydney, available at <http://www.hreoc.gov.au/human_rights/immigration/idc2001.html>.

HREOC (Human Rights and Equal Opportunity Commission) (2004) *A Last Resort? National Inquiry into Children in Immigration Detention*, April 2004, Human Rights and Equal Opportunities Commission, Sydney, available at <http://www.hreoc.gov.au/human_rights/children_detention_report/index.html>.

Hudson, B. (2003) *Justice in the risk society*, London, Sage.

Hutchinson, T. & Martin, F. (2004) 'Australia's human rights obligations relating to the mental health of refugee children in detention', *International Journal of Law and Psychiatry*, 27: 529–47.

Hutton, M. (2002) *We need to know their names*, available at <http://www.sievx.com/archives/2002_10-11/20021031.shtml>.

Huysmans, J. (1995) 'Migrants as a security problem: Dangers of "securitizing" societal issues', in R. Miles and D. Thränhardt (eds), *Migration and European integration*, London, Pinter.

Inquest (2011) 'Briefing on the death of Jimmy Mubenga', April 2011, London, available at <http://www.inquest.org.uk/pdf/briefings/INQUEST_parliamentary_inquiry_call_Jimmy_Mubenga_briefing.pdf>.

IRR (Institute of Race Relations) (2003) 'The other asylum statistics', 29 July 2003, available at <http://www.irr.org.uk/2003/july/ak000013.html>.

IRR (2006) *Driven to desperate measures*, London, Institute of Race Relations, available from <http://www.irr.org.uk/pdf/Driventodesperatemeasures.pdf>.

Jacobsen, D. (1996) *Rights across borders: Immigration and the decline of citizenship*, Baltimore, John Hopkins University Press.

Jamieson, R. & McEvoy, K. (2005) 'State crime by proxy and juridical othering', *British Journal of Criminology*, 45: 504–27.

Jimenez, M. (2009) *Humanitarian crisis: Migrant deaths at the US–Mexico border*, American Civil Liberties Council of San Diego and Imperial Counties, Mexico's National Commission of Human Rights.

Juss, S. (2004) 'Free movement and the world order', *International Journal of Refugee Law*, 289–335.

Kauzlarich, D., Mullins, C. & Matthews, R. (2003) 'A complicity continuum of state crime', *Contemporary Justice Review*, 6(3): 241–54.

Keller, A., Rosenfeld, B., Trinh-Shevrin, C., Meserve, C., Sachs, E., Leviss, J., Singer, E., Smith, H., Wilkinson, J., Kim, G., Allden, K. & Ford, D. (2003) 'Mental health of detained asylum seekers', *The Lancet*, 362(9397): 1721–3.

Kelman, H. & Hamilton, V. (1989) *Crimes of obedience: Toward a social psychology of authority and obedience*, London, Yale University Press.

Kevin, T. (2004) *A Certain Maritime Incident and the sinking of the SIEV X*, Melbourne, Scribe Publications.

Khalili, L. (2005) 'Places of memory and mourning: Palestinian commemoration in the refugee camps of Lebanon', *Comparative Studies of South Asia, Africa and the Middle East*, 25(1): 31–45.

Khosravi, S. (2010) *'Illegal' traveller: An auto-ethnography of borders*, Basingstoke, Palgrave Macmillan.

Kirby, T. (1993) 'Doubts delay inquiry into Joy Gardner's death', 12 December 1993, *The Independent* on Sunday, available at <http://www.independent.co.uk/news/doubts-delay-inquiry-into-joy-gardners-death-1466994.html>.

Kiza, E. (2008) *Tödliche Grenzen: Die Fatalen Auswirkungen Europäischer Zuwanderungspolitik* [Deadly borders: The fatal consequences of European migration policies], Münster, Lit Verlag.

Kiza, E. (2009) *The human costs of border control at the external EU borders between 1999 and 2004*, paper prepared for the workshop 'The Human Costs of Border Control in the Context of EU Maritime Migration Systems', 25–27 October 2009, Amsterdam, available at <http://www.rechten.vu.nl/nl/Images/Kiza%20-The%20Human%20Costs%20of%20Border%20Control%20at%20the%20EU%20Borders%20._tcm22-112314.pdf>.

Kleinig, J. (1996) *The ethics of policing*, Cambridge, Cambridge University Press.

Krasmann, S. (2007) 'The enemy on the border: Critique of a programme in favour of a preventive state', *Punishment and Society*, 9(3): 301–18.

Kreickenbaum, M. (2004) 'European governments make an example of *Cap Anamur* refugees', World Socialist Web Site, 22 July 2004, available at <http://www.wsws.org/articles/2004/jul2004/anam-j22.shtml>.

Kretsedemas, P. & Brotherton, D. (2008) 'Open markets, militarized borders', in D. Brotherton and P. Kretsedemas (eds), *Keeping out the other: A critical introduction to immigration enforcement today*, New York, Columbia University Press.

Lacey, N. (2007) 'Denial and responsibility', in D. Downes, P. Rock, C. Chinkin and C. Gearty (eds), *Crime, social control and human rights: From moral panics to states of denial, essays in honour of Stanley Cohen*, Uffculme, Willan Publishing.

Laitinen, I. (2007) 'Frontex: facts and myths', Media Release, 11 June 2007, available at <http://www.frontex.europa.eu/newsroom/news_releases/art26.html>.

Lancet (2008) 'Migrant health: What are doctors' leaders doing?', Editorial, *The Lancet*, 371(9608), 19–25 January 2008, p. 371.

Levi, P. (1995) *If this is a man and the truce*, London, Abacus Books.

Lewis, P. (2010) 'Jimmy Mubenga death: Witness accounts', 15 October 2010, *The Guardian* online, available at <http://www.guardian.co.uk/uk/2010/oct/15/ jimmy-mubenga-death-witness-accounts>.

Lewis, P. & Taylor, M. (2010) 'G4S loses UK deportations contract', *The Guardian* online, 29 October 2011, available at <http://www.guardian.co.uk/uk/2010/oct/ 29/g4s-deportations-contract-reliance>.

Lewis, P. & Taylor, M. (2011) 'Jimmy Mubenga: Security firm G4S may face charges over death', *The Guardian* online, 16 March 2011, available at <http://www. guardian.co.uk/uk/2011/mar/16/mubenga-g4s-face-charges-death>.

Lewis, P., Taylor, M. & Bowcott, O. (2010) 'Chaos over restraint rules for deportees', *The Guardian* online, 27 October 2010, available at http://www.guardian.co.uk/ uk/2010/oct/27/deportation-restraint-rules-chaos.

Lozano, J. (2011) '19 illegal immigrants "suffocated" in truck', *The Australian*, 25 January 2011, available at <http://www.theaustralian.com.au/news/breaking-news/illegal-immigrants-suffocated-in-truck/story-fn3dxity-1225994011352>.

Lyneham, M., Larsen, J. & Beacroft, L. (2010) *AIC deaths in custody report 2010*, Deaths in custody in Australia: National Deaths in Custody Program 2008, Monitoring Report No. 10, Canberra: Australian Institute of Criminology.

Maccanico, Y. (2006) 'EU/Africa: Carnage continues as EU border moves south', Statewatch News online, available at <http://www.statewatch.org/news/2006/ sep/Immigration-analysis.pdf>.

Macpherson, W. (1999) *The Stephen Lawrence Inquiry Report*, Report of an Inquiry by Sir William Macpherson of Cluny, CM 4262-1, London, Home Office.

Magner, T. (2004) 'A less than "Pacific" solution for asylum seekers in Australia', *International Journal of Refugee Law*, 16(1): 53–90.

Maley, P. (2009) 'Opposition quick to blame Kevin Rudd for loss of life', *The Australian*, 17 April 2009, available at <http://www.theaustralian.com.au/ news/opposition-quick-to-blame-rudd/story-e6frg6no-1225699718728>.

Maley, P. & Lower, G. (2009) 'Sabotage craft, asylum seekers told: Philip Ruddock', *The Australian*, 17 April 2009 available at <http://www.theaustralian.com.au/ news/sabotage-craft-asylum-seekers-told/story-e6frg6no-1225699718557>.

Maley, P. & Toohey, P. (2009) 'Deaths raise boatpeople stakes as political war of words rages', *The Australian*, 17 April 2009, available at <http://www.the australian.com.au/national-affairs/defence/deaths-raise-boatpeople-stakes-as-political-war-of-words-rages/story-e6frg8yx-1225699718112>.

Malkki, L. (1996) 'Speechless emissaries: Refugees, humanitarianism, and dehistoric-ization', *Cultural Anthropology*, August, 11(3): 377–404.

Malloch, M. & Stanley, E. (2005) 'The detention of asylum seekers in the UK: Representing risk, managing the dangerous', *Punishment and Society*, 7(1): 53–71.

Manne, R. (2003) 'The road to *Tampa*', in L. Jayasuriya, D. Walker and J. Gothard (eds), *Legacies of White Australia: Race, culture and nation*, Perth, University of Western Australia Press.

Mansouri, F. & Cauchi, S. (2007) 'A psychological perspective on Australia's asylum policies', *International Migration*, 45(1): 123–49.

Mares, P. (2002) *Borderline: Australia's response to refugees and asylum seekers in the wake of the Tampa*, Sydney, UNSW Press.

Mares, S. & Jureidini, J. (2004) 'Psychiatric assessment of children and families in immigration detention – clinical, administrative and ethical issues', *Australian and New Zealand Journal of Public Health*, 28(6): 520–6.

Marosi, R. (2008) 'Agent cleared in 2005 border shooting', 16 February 2008, *Los Angeles Times*, available at <http://articles.latimes.com/print/2008/feb/16/local/me-shoot16>.

Marr, D. & Wilkinson, M. (2003) *Dark victory*, Sydney, Allen & Unwin.

Massey, D. (2009) Testimony of Douglas S. Massey before the Senate Judiciary Committee, 20 May 2009, available at <http://judiciary.senate.gov/hearings/testimony.cfm?id=3859&wit_id=7939> accessed 10 February 2011.

McDowell, M. & Wonders, N. (2009/2010) 'Keeping migrants in their place: Technologies of control and racialized public space in Arizona', *Social Justice*, 36(2): 54–72.

McGirk, J. (2000) 'UN envoy is sent to investigate Rio Grande shootings by posses of vigilante ranchers', 24 May 2000, *The Independent*, UK, available at <http:// www.independent.co.uk/news/world/americas/un-envoy-is-sent-to-investigate-rio-grande-shootings-by-posses-of-vigilante-ranchers-716094.html>.

McLoughlin, P. & Warin, M. (2008) 'Corrosive places, inhuman spaces: Mental health in Australian immigration detention', *Health & Place*, 14: 254–64.

Media Monitors (2010) 2010 Election Debate: Tony Burke MP, Minister for Sustainable Population vs Scott Morrison MP, Shadow Minister for Immigration & Citizenship, 5 August 2010, National Press Club Address (transcription obtained from Media Monitors).

Meneses, G. (2003) 'Human rights and undocumented migration along the Mexican–US border', *UCLA Law Review*, 267–81.

Michalowski, R. (2007) 'Border militarization and migrant suffering: A case of transnational social injury', *Social Justice*, 34(2): 62–76.

Migrants Rights Watch (2011) website <http://migrantsrightswatch.org/news/2011/03/statement-by-the-300-migrant-hunger-strikers/272903>.

Migreurop (2009) Atlas des Migrants en Europe: Géographie critique des politiques migratoires (Atlas of Migrants in Europe: Critical geography of migratory politics), Paris, Armand Colin.

Milmo, D. (2010) 'Jimmy Mubenga: Questions raised over flight guidelines for deportations', *The Guardian* online, 15 October 2010, available at <http://www.guardian.co.uk/uk/2010/oct/15/jimmy-mubenga-questions-guidelines-deportations>.

Mitchell, C. (1994) 'U.S. policy towards Haitian boat people, 1972–93', *The Annals of the American Academy*, 534: 69–80.

Morris, J. (2003) 'The spaces in between: American and Australian interdiction policies and their implications for the refugee protection regime', *Refuge*, 21(4): 51–62.

Morris, S. (2003) 'Asylum seekers "were locked in during fire"', *The Guardian* online, 23 July 2003, available at <http://www.guardian.co.uk/uk/2003/jul/23/immigration.immigrationandpublicservices>.

Morvern, A. (2010) 'Brutal deportations must stop', *The Guardian* online, 15 October 2010, available at <http://www.guardian.co.uk/commentisfree/2010/oct/15/deportation-jimmy-mubenga-borders>.

Motomura, H. (1993) 'Haitian asylum seekers: Interdiction and immigrants' rights', *Cornell International Law Journal*, 26: 698–717.

Mountz, A. (2010) *Seeking asylum: Human smuggling and bureaucracy at the border*, Minneapolis, University of Minnesota Press.

NAO (National Audit Office) (2005) *Returning failed asylum seekers*, Report by the Comptroller and Auditor General, HC 76 Session 2005–2006, 14 July 2005, London, National Audit Office.

Napolitano, J. (2010) 'How the DREAM Act would bolster our Homeland Security', 14 December 2010, The White House Blog available at <http://www.whitehouse.gov/blog/2010/12/14/how-dream-act-would-bolster-our-homeland-security> accessed 1 March 2011.

Nevins, J. (2001) 'Searching for security: Boundary and immigration enforcement in an age of intensifying globalization', *Social Justice*, 28(2): 132–48.

Nevins, J. (2002) *Operation Gatekeeper: The rise of the 'illegal alien' and the making of the US–Mexico boundary*, New York, Routledge.

Nevins, J. (2003) 'Thinking out of bounds: A critical analysis of academic and human rights writing on migrant deaths in the US Mexico Border region', *Migraciones Internacionales*, 2(2): 171–90.

Nevins, J. (2008) *Dying to live: A story of U.S. immigration in an age of global apartheid*, San Francisco, City Lights.

Nevins, J. (2010) *Operation Gatekeeper and beyond*, 2nd edition, New York, Routledge.

New York Times (2010) 'Massacre in Tamaulipas', *The New York Times*, Editorial, 29 August 2010, available at <http://www.nytimes.com/2010/08/30/opinion/30mon3.html>.

Nicholls, G. (2007) *Deported: A history of forced departures from Australia*, Sydney, UNSW Press.

Núñez, G. & Heyman, J. (2007) 'Entrapment processes and immigrant communities in a time of heightened border vigilance', *Human Organisation*, 66(4): 354–65.

O'Loan, N. (2010) *Report to the United Kingdom Border Agency on 'Outsourcing Abuse'*, March 2010, available at <http://www.medicaljustice.org.uk/images/stories/reports/reportonoutsourcingabuse.pdf>.

Oelgemöller, C. (2010) '"Transit" and "suspension": Migration management or the metamorphosis of asylum-seekers into "illegal" immigrants', *Journal of Ethnic and Migration Studies*, 37(3): 407–24.

Oman, N. (2010) 'Hannah Arendt's "right to have rights": A philosophical context for human security', *Journal of Human Rights*, 9(3): 279–302.

Opotow, S. (1990) 'Moral exclusion and injustice: An introduction', *Journal of Social Issues*, 46(1): 1–20.

Perera, S. (2002) 'A line in the sea', *Race & Class*, 44(2): 23–39.

Perera, S. (2006) '"They give evidence": Bodies, borders and the disappeared', *Social Identities*, 12(6): 637–56.

Phillips, J. & Spinks, H. (2011) *Boat arrivals in Australia since 1976*, Parliamentary Library Background Note, updated 11 February 2011, available at <http:// www.aph.gov.au/library/pubs/bn/sp/BoatArrivals.htm>, accessed 4 April 2011.

PHR (Physicians for Human Rights) (2003) *From persecution to prison: The health consequences of detention for asylum seekers*, Physicians for Human Rights and the Bellevue/NYU Program for Survivors of Torture.

Pickering, S. (2001) 'Common sense and original deviancy: News discourses and asylum seekers in Australia', *Journal of Refugee Studies*, 14(2): 169–86.

Pickering, S. (2004) 'The production of sovereignty and the rise of transversal policing: People-smuggling and federal policing', *Australian and New Zealand Journal of Criminology*, 37(3): 362–79.

Pickering, S. (2005) *Refugees and state crime*, Sydney, Federation Press.

Pickering, S. (2010) *Women, borders and violence*, New York, Springer.

Pickering, S. & Weber, L. (eds) (2006) *Borders, mobility and technologies of control*, Dordrecht, Springer.

Pourgirides, C., Sashidharan, S. & Bracken, P. (1996) *A second exile: The mental health implications of detention of asylum seekers in the United Kingdom*, University of Birmingham/The Barrow Cadbury Trust.

PPO (Police and Prisons Ombudsman for England and Wales) (2004) *Investigation into allegations of racism, abuse and violence at Yarl's Wood Removal Centre*, A Report by the Prisons and Probation Ombudsman for England and Wales, available at <http://www.ppo.gov.uk/docs/special-yarls-wood-abuse-03.pdf>.

Pratt, A. (2005) *Securing borders: Detention and deportation in Canada*, Vancouver, UBC Press.

Provine, D. M. & Sanchez, G. (2011, forthcoming) 'Suspecting immigrants: Exploring links between racialized anxieties and expanded police powers in Arizona', forthcoming in *Policing and Society*, special issue on Stop and Search in Global Context, edited by Leanne Weber and Benjamin Bowling.

Pugh, M. (2004) 'Drowning not waving: Boat people and humanitarianism at sea', *Journal of Refugee Studies*, 17(1): 50–69.

Refugee Council of Australia (2009) 'Refugee Council calls for rational public debate in wake of asylum seeker boat tragedy', Media Release, 17 April 2009, available at <http://www.refugeecouncil.org.au/docs/releases/2009/090417_Boat_tragedy.pdf>.

Refugee Survival Trust/British Red Cross (2009) *Destitution and the asylum system: 21 days later*, January 2009, Refugee Survival Trust, Edinburgh, British Red Cross, Glasgow.

Reyes, B., Johnson, H. & Van Swearingen, R. (2002) *Holding the line? The effect of recent border build-up on unauthorized immigration*, California, Public Policy Institute of California.

Roberts, D. (2008) *Human insecurity*, London, Zed Books.

Rochdale Observer (2006) 'Asylum rejection led to suicide', 23 December 2006, available at <http://menmedia.co.uk/rochdaleobserver/news/s/521570_asylum_rejection_led_to_suicide>.

Rodgers, E. (2009) 'Smith waits for evidence after sabotage claim', ABC News Online, 22 October 2009, available at <www.abc.net.au/stories/2009/10/22/2720846.htm>.

Rodier, C. (2006) 'Illegal emigration: A notion than should be banished', *Liberation*, 13 June 2006.

Rose, N. (1999) *Powers of freedom: Reframing political thought*, Cambridge, Cambridge University Press.

Rose, N. (2000) 'Government and control', *British Journal of Criminology* (Special Issue on Criminology and Social Theory), 40(2): 321–39.

Rubio-Goldsmith, R., McCormick, M., Martinez, D. & Duarte, I. (2006) *The 'Funnel Effect' and recovered bodies of unauthorized migrants processed by the PIMA county office of the medical examiner, 1990–2005*, Binational Migration Institute, Arizona.

Rubio-Goldsmith, R., McCormick, M., Martinez, D. & Duarte, I. (2007) 'A humanitarian crisis at the border: New estimates of deaths among unauthorized immigrants', Policy Brief, February 2007, Immigration Policy Centre, Washington DC, available at <http://www.immigrationpolicy.org/sites/default/files/docs/Crisis%20 at%20the%20Border.pdf>.

Russell, M. (2003) 'Detainee's death draws criticism', *The Age*, 29 November 2003, <http://www.theage.com.au/articles/2003/11/28/1069825988712.html>.

Sassen, S. (1996) *Sovereignty in an age of globalisation*, New York, Columbia University Press.

Schrover, M., van der Leun, J., Lucassen, L. & Quispel, C. (2008) 'Illegal migration: How gender makes a difference', IMISCOE Policy Brief No. 10, August 2008, European Network of Excellence on International Migration, Integration and Social Cohesion.

Schuster, L. (2005) 'The continuing mobility of migrants in Italy: Shifting between places and statuses', *Journal of Ethnic and Migration Studies*, 31(4): 757–74.

Schwendinger, H. & Schwendinger, J. (1975) 'Defenders of order or guardians of human rights', in U. Taylor, I. Walton and J. Young (eds), *Critical criminology*, London, Kegan Paul.

Scott-Bray, R. (2006) 'Fugitive performances of death and injury', *Law Text Culture*, 10: 41–71.

Select Committee (2002) *Inquiry into a Certain Maritime Incident: Report of the Select Committee for an Inquiry into a Certain Maritime Incident*, 23 October 2002, the Australian Senate, Canberra, available at <http://www.aph.gov.au/senate/ committee/maritime_incident_ctte/index.htm>.

Shaw, S. (2004) *Report of the Inquiry into the disturbance and fire at Yarl's Wood Removal Centre*, October 2004, Prisons and Probation Ombudsman for England and Wales, London, available at <http://www.ppo.gov.uk/docs/special-yarls-wood- fire-02.pdf>.

Shearing, C. & Johnston, L. (2005) 'Justice in the risk society', *Australian and New Zealand Journal of Criminology*, 38(1): 25–38.

Sheptycki, J. (1998) 'The global cops cometh: Reflections on transnational- ization, knowledge work and policing subculture', *The British Journal of Sociology*, 49(1): 57–74.

Silove, D., Austin, P. & Steel, Z. (2007) 'No refuge from terror: The impact of detention on the mental health of trauma-affected refugees seeking asylum in Australia', *Transcultural Psychiatry*, 44: 359–93.

Silove, D., Steel, Z. & Mollica, R. (2001) 'Detention of asylum seekers: Assault on health, human rights and social development', *The Lancet*, 357: 1436–7.

Silove, D., Steel, Z. & Watters, C. (2006) 'Policies of deterrence and the mental health of asylum seekers', *Journal of the American Medical Association*, 284(5): 604–11.

Smith, M. (1999) *Foley: The spy who saved 10,000 Jews*, London, Hodder and Stoughton.

Sontag, S. (2003) *Regarding the pain of others*, Picador.

Spijkerboer, T. (2007) 'The human costs of border control', *European Journal of Migration and Law*, 9: 127–39.

Stanhope, J. (2006) Speaking notes for the opening of SIEV X National Memo- rial Remembrance temporary installation, 15 October 2006, Weston Park, Yarralumla.

Statewatch (2001) 'Questions ask whether the death of 58 Chinese immigrants was a "controlled delivery"', *Statewatch Bulletin*, 11(2), available from <www. statewatch.org/news/2001/jun/06deaths.htm>.

Statewatch (2005) 'France: Passengers to face trial for preventing a violent deport-ation', Statewatch News Online, 12 February 2005, available at <http://www.statewatch.org/news/2005/feb/12france-deportation.htm>.

Steel, Z. (2003) *The politics of exclusion and denial: The mental health costs of Australia's refugee policy*, 38th Congress of Royal Australian and New Zealand College of Psychiatrists, Hobart.

Steel, Z., Momartin, S., Bateman, C., Hafshejani, A. & Silove, D. (2004) 'Psychiatric status of asylum seeker families held for a protracted period in a remote deten-tion centre in Australia', *Australian and New Zealand Journal of Public Health*, 28(6): 527–36.

Steel, Z., Silove, D., Brooks, R., Momartin, S., Alzuhairi, B. & Susljik, I. (2004) 'Impact of immigration detention and temporary protection on mental health of refugees', *British Journal of Psychiatry*, 188: 58–64.

Steinhauer, J. (2009) 'Scouts train to fight terrorists, and more', *The New York Times*, available at <http://www.nytimes.com/2009/05/14/us/14explorers.html>.

Stop Prisoner Rape (2004) 'No refuge here: A first look at sexual abuse in immi-gration detention', Stop Prisoner Rape, Los Angeles <www.spr.org>.

Sultan, A. & O'Sullivan, K. (2001) 'Psychological disturbances in asylum seekers held in long term detention: A participant observer account', *The Medical Journal of Australia*, 175: 593–6.

Sydney Morning Herald (2010) Mexico urges US probe of border deaths, 11 June 2010, *SMH* online, available at <http://news.smh.com.au/breaking-news-world/mexico-urges-us-probe-of-border-deaths-20100611-y0yc.html>.

Taylor, S. (2008) 'Offshore barriers to asylum seeker movement: The exercise of power without responsibility?', in J. McAdam (ed.), *Forced migration, human rights and security*, pp. 93–127, Oxford, Hart Publishing, available at SSRN: <http://ssrn.com/abstract=1725554>.

Ting, I. (2010) 'Immigration detention: 27 dead and (not) counting', *Crikey*, 24 September 2010, available at <http://www.crikey.com.au/2010/09/24/immi-gration-detention-27-dead-and-not-counting>.

Toohey, P. (2009) 'Secret footage of refugee rescue struggle', *The Australian*, 5 September 2009, available at <http://sievx.com/articles/psdp/2009/2009-0905PaulToohey.html>.

Torode, J. (1993) 'When deportation means death: Joy Gardner died after police raided her home – John Torode sifts fact from prejudice', *The Independent*, 3 August 1993, available at <http://www.independent.co.uk/opinion/when-deportation-means-death-joy-gardner-died-after-police-raided-her-home-john-torode-sifts-fact-from-prejudice-1458919.html>.

Transatlantic Trends (2008) 'Transatlantic Trends Immigration: Key Findings 2008', Published by the German Marshall Fund of the United States, Bradley Foundation, Compagnia di San Paolo, Barrow Cadbury Trust.

Tsoukala, A. (2008) *Security, risk and human rights: A vanishing relationship*, Brussels, Centre for European Policy Studies.

UKBA (UK Border Agency) (2011a) <http://www.ukba.homeoffice.gov.uk/>, accessed 4 April 2011.

UKBA (2011b) Detention Centre Rule 35 Audit, 4 February 2011, UK Border Agency, London, available at <www.ukba.homeoffice.gov.au/sitecontent/documents/aboutus/reports/detention-centre-rule-35-audit/det-centre-rule-35-audit?view=Binary>.

UNITED (United Against Racism and Fascism) (2007) 'The fatal realities of Fortress Europe', <http://www.unitedagainstracism.org/pages/info14.htm>, accessed 15 March 2007.

UNITED (2008) 'The fatal realities of Fortress Europe', available at <www.unite-dagainstracism.org/pages/campfatalrealities.htm>, accessed 16 April 2008.

United Nations (2000) *We the peoples: The United Nations in the 21st century*, New York, UNDP, available at <http://www.un.org/millennium/sg/report/>.

United Nations Commission on Human Rights (2004), *Report on the Human Rights of Migrants*, Submitted by the Special Rapporteur of the Commission on Human Rights, 22 September 2004, UN DOC A/59/377.

US Customs and Border Protection (2004) 'U.S. Customs and Border Protection announces Border Safety Initiative aimed at preventing migrant deaths', Media Release, 6 May 2004, US Customs and Border Protection, available at <http://www.cbp.gov/xp/cgov/newsroom/news_releases/archives/2004_press_releases/052004/05062004.xml>.

US Customs and Border Protection (2008) Securing America's Borders: CBP 2008 Fiscal Year in Review, 11 May 2008, available at <http://www.cbp.gov/xp/cgov/newsroom/highlights/08year_review.xml>.

US Customs and Border Protection (2010) 'El Paso, Texas Border Patrol kicks off safety initiative', Media Release, 15 July 2010, available at <http://www.customs.gov/xp/cgov/newsroom/news_releases/archives/2010_news_releases/july_2010/07162010_3.xml>.

Van Selm, J. (ed.) (2000) *Kosovo's refugees in the European Union*, London, Pinter.

Walsh, J. (2008) 'Community, surveillance and border control: The case of the Minuteman Project', *Law & Deviance*, 10: 11–34.

Walsh, J. (2010) 'From border control to border care: The political and ethical potential of surveillance', *Surveillance and Society*, 8(2): 113–30.

Ware, S. (2008) 'Anti-memorials and the art of forgetting: Critical reflections on a memorial design practice', *Public History Review*, 1: 61–76.

Watson, S. (2009) *The securitization of humanitarian migration: Digging moats and sinking boats*, Abingdon, Oxford, Routledge.

Webber, F. (1996) *Crimes of arrival: Immigrants and asylum-seekers in the new Europe*, Statewatch.

Webber, F. (2004) 'The war on migration', in P. Hillyard, C. Pantazis, S. Tombs and D. Gordon (eds), *Beyond criminology: Taking harm seriously*, London, Pluto Press.

Weber, L. (2002) 'The detention of asylum seekers: 20 reasons why criminologists should care', *Current Issues in Criminal Justice* (Special Issue on Refugees and Criminology), 14 (1 July 2002).

Weber, L. (2005) 'The detention of asylum seekers as a crime of obedience', *Critical Criminology*, 13(1): 89–109.

Weber, L. (2006) 'The shifting frontiers of migration control', in S. Pickering and L. Weber (eds), *Borders, mobility and technologies of control*, Amsterdam, Springer.

Weber, L. (2007) 'Policing the virtual border: Punitive pre-emption in Australian offshore migration controls', *Social Justice*, Special Issue on Transnational Criminology, 34(2).

Weber, L. (2011) '"It sounds like they shouldn't be here": Immigration checks on the streets of Sydney', forthcoming in *Policing and Society*, Special Issue 'Stop and Search in Global Context' (Leanne Weber and Ben Bowling, eds).

Weber, L. (2012) 'Policing a world in motion', in S. Pickering and J. McCulloch (eds), *Borders and transnational crime: Pre-crime, mobility and serious harm in an age of globalization*, London, Palgrave.

Weber, L. & Bowling, B. (2004) 'Policing migration: A framework for investigating the regulation of global mobility', *Policing and Society*, 14(3): 195–212.

Weber, L. & Bowling, B. (2008) 'Valiant beggars and global vagabonds: Select, eject, immobilise', *Theoretical Criminology*, Special Issue on *Globalization, Ethnicity and Racism*, 12(3): 355–75.

Weber, L. & Gelsthorpe, L. (2000) *Deciding to detain: How decisions to detain asylum seekers are made at ports of entry*, Cambridge, Institute of Criminology, University of Cambridge.

Weber, L. & Grewcock, M. (2011) 'Criminalising people smuggling: Preventing or globalizing harm?', in F. Allum and S. Gilmour (eds), *The Routledge handbook of transnational organized crime*.

Welch, M. (2007) 'Deadly consequences: Crime-control discourse and unwelcome migrants', *Criminology and Public Policy*, 6(2): 275–82.

Welch, M. & Schuster, L. (2005) 'Detention of asylum seekers in the US, UK, France, Germany and Italy: A critical view of the globalizing culture of control', *Criminal Justice*, 5(4): 331–55.

Wilkie, A. (2003) 'People-smuggling: National myths and realities', speech delivered at Charles Darwin Symposium on Irregular Migration, Darwin 30 September 2003, available at <http://safecom.org.au/wilkie.htm>, accessed 28 June 2010.

Willen, S. (2007) 'Exploring "illegal" and "irregular" migrants' lived experiences of law and state power', *International Migration*, 45(3): 2–7.

Wilson, J. (2011) 'A grim anniversary', ON-Line Opinion, 24 February 2011, available at <www.onlineopinion.com.au/print.asp?article=11665>.

Wistrich, H., Arnold, F. & Ginn, E. (2008) *Outsourcing abuse: The use and misuse of state-sanctioned force during the detention and removal of asylum seekers*, July 2008, Birnberg Peirce & Partners, Medical Justice, National Coalition of Anti-Deportation Campaigns, London, available at <http://www.medicaljustice.org.uk/images/stories/reports/outsourcing%20abuse.pdf>.

Women's Refugee Commission (2010) *Migrant women and children at risk in custody in Arizona*, New York, Women's Refugee Commission.

Wonders, N. (2006) 'Global flows, semi-permeable borders and new channels of inequality', in S. Pickering and L. Weber (eds), *Borders, mobility and technologies of control*, pp. 63–86, Amsterdam, Springer.

Young, A. (1996) *Imagining crime*, London, Sage.

Youssef, S. (2011) 'Yarl's Wood: A case study. Immigration prisons: Brutal, unlawful & profitable', March 2011, London, Corporate Watch.

Zolberg, A. (2006) *A nation by design: Immigration policy in the fashioning of America*, New York/Cambridge, Russell Sage Foundation/Harvard University Press.

Index